NATIONAL LIBRARY OF AUSTRALIA CATALOGUING-IN-PUBLICATION DATA

Book Title: Bazza's beaut book of gut-busting great grub for bachelors, blondes, bimbos and blokes with half a brain

Book Subtitle: Cookbook and Recipes for World Food

Book Author: Barry Bakes

ISBN 978-0-9872728-1-2

COPYRIGHT NOTICE

Copyright © 2013 Barry Bakes.

This work is copyright. Apart from any use permitted under the Copyright Act 1968, no part of this work may be reproduced by any process without the prior written permission of the author.

This simply means—Don't steal 'em without askin' me first.

Publisher Details: The publisher of this book is People Maintenance.

Contact details for permissions and all other inquiries can be found at www.peoplemaintenance.com

---

To:

Message:

From:

Barry Bakes

'The writer writes in order to teach himself, to understand himself, to satisfy himself; the publishing of his ideas, though it brings gratification, is a curious anticlimax.'
— Alfred Kazin

BOOK DISCLAIMER

I've had a go at making this recipe book as easy to use and as simple to follow as possible. I've given it my best shot, so please consider this recipe collection to be my suggestions or opinions, and see how well you fare (no pun intended).

I give a complete list of ingredients where necessary; but in many cases the simpler recipes are 'short and sweet', with rough quantities given as it goes along. In these cases, it probably doesn't matter too much whether there is a little bit more or less of a particular ingredient. Use your noggin, and add what you think looks about right.

If it doesn't taste quite how you expected it to, don't worry about it too much. It'll probably taste a little different the next time you cook it anyway. In my opinion, it only needs to be exactly the same every time if people are paying you to cook it for them!

I want you to know too, that if anybody gets crook from trying these recipes, I don't accept any blame at all. Maybe you've used old ingredients, put the wrong things in, or you just plain did it badly. Or, maybe you and your helpers didn't wash your hands like your mothers taught you to do. Even so, I certainly hope you don't get crook. I had a dud oyster myself once, and I know how bad it can get! I was pretty green around the gills, and was driving the porcelain bus for quite a while I can tell you. And I certainly hope that the thought of what can go wrong doesn't put you off trying out new things. You've just got to have a crack at it.

By the way, cooking is a whole lot of fun, especially with a glass of red wine near your drinking hand. It is great stress relief too (remember, 'desserts' is 'stressed' spelled backwards), and it gives you a warm, fuzzy feeling when it all turns out really well. Also, it does wonders for your self-esteem when people tell you three times how good the meal that you prepared really was (I personally insist on at least three times).

Oh, and another thing. I don't want any mug trying to sue me over a recipe that they think is theirs. Likely it wasn't theirs in the first place, even if it looks a bit similar. It, or a version of it, was probably borrowed in some form at least three times before that. A lot of recipes are derived from classic old recipes that nobody owns any more, others are family hand-me-down recipes that have developed over generations, some are reverse-engineered from something that somebody once ate, and yet others are contributed by acquaintances who obtained them from who-knows-where (thank you, by the way, to the people who contributed some of their ideas to this book). And that's how it is with this book of my retro, received, rejigged and reinvented recipes.

It's sad; but while some recipes are genuinely new, a lot of recipes these days seem to be just some joker's idea of how to fill up a book with something that just looks new. Reading those becomes very tedious. There's none of those recipes in this recipe book. These recipes are a genuine attempt to make cooking as simple and enjoyable as possible, especially for you folks who are starting out from scratch. So, if you want to be much more than just an ordinary bait-layer, have a go at some of these beauties.

Anyway, I'm pretty sure you won't find any other recipe book written in quite the same copyright way as mine. Have fun. Life is for the living! Bon appétit!

CONTENTS

- NATIONAL LIBRARY OF AUSTRALIA CATALOGUING-IN-PUBLICATION DATA 1
- COPYRIGHT NOTICE 1
- BOOK DISCLAIMER 2
- **CONTENTS** 3
- **ALL THE BASICS** 6
  - HOW TO FIND WHAT YOU WANT 6
  - ABOUT THE RECIPES 6
  - BARBECUES 6
  - ONE POT MEALS 6
  - FRESHNESS OF FOOD 7
  - USING QUALITY SALT 7
  - COOKING METHODS EXPLAINED 8
- **APPETIZERS, ANTIPASTI, HORS D'OEUVRES, TAPAS, PINTXOS AND MEZE** 9
  - HOT PLATES 9
  - BREADS 11
  - TOOTHPICK TEMPTERS 13
  - PASTRIES 14
  - DELECTABLE DIPS 15
  - PÂTÉ 17
  - SIZZLING SKEWERS 19
  - MARVELLOUS MARINADES 19
  - USING OLIVE OIL 19
- **BEEF AND VEAL** 21
  - ABOUT GOOD BEEF STEAK 21
  - HOW TO COOK GOOD BEEF STEAK 22
  - THE SCIENCE OF BROWNING MEAT 23
  - THICKENING MEAT DISHES 23
  - BUTTER TOPPINGS FOR BEEF 23
  - PRIME BEEF STEAK 25
  - ROAST BEEF 28
  - BRAISED BEEF 32
  - OTHER BEEF RECIPES 40
  - CLASSIC VEAL RECIPES 42
  - BRAISED VEAL DISHES 44
- **BREADS** 47
  - INFORMATION ABOUT FLOUR 47
  - THE SCIENCE OF BAKING POWDER 48
- **CAKES, SLICES AND BISCUITS** 53
  - CAKE INGREDIENTS 53
  - TRUE SPONGE CAKE 53
  - ANGEL FOOD CAKE 54
  - GÉNOISE SPONGE CAKE 55
  - CHIFFON CAKE 56
  - BUTTER CAKE 57
  - OTHER CAKES 58
  - MUFFINS 63
  - SLICES 65
  - BISCUITS 69
- **CHICKEN** 72
  - ROAST CHICKEN 72
  - BRAISED CHICKEN THIGH FILLETS 73
  - CHICKEN BREAST FILLETS 81

MARINATED CHICKEN DRUMSTICKS	88
CURRIES	**89**
INFO ON SPICES	89
BEEF CURRY	90
LAMB CURRY	93
PORK CURRY	95
CHICKEN CURRY	96
SEAFOOD CURRY	99
VEGETABLE CURRY	100
DUCK	**101**
ROAST DUCK	101
EGGS	**102**
BASIC EGGS	102
FRITTATA	103
OTHER EGG RECIPES	104
FAST FOOD	**107**
A WORD ABOUT FAST FOOD	107
BONZER TAKE-AWAY-FOOD-SHOP TUCKER	107
PIES, PASTIES AND SAUSAGE ROLLS	109
BURGERS	112
PIZZA AND FOCACCIA	113
MEXICAN FOOD	115
FISH AND SEAFOOD	**116**
FOR A SEAFOOD BANQUET	116
FISH STEAKS AND FILLETS	117
MARINATED RAW FISH	123
OTHER FISH RECIPES	124
PRAWNS	125
OYSTERS	127
SCALLOPS	128
LOBSTER	129
LANGOUSTINES	132
CALAMARI	133
ABALONE	134
OCTOPUS	135
LAMB	**136**
ROAST LAMB	136
BRAISED LAMB	139
LAMB STEW	143
LAMB CHOPS AND FILLETS	144
MINCED LAMB	145
OTHER LAMB DISHES	147
NOODLES	**148**
INFO ABOUT NOODLES	148
PASTA	**150**
INFO ABOUT PASTA	150
PASTA COOKING TIPS	150
ABOUT CURED MEATS	150
TRADITIONAL PASTA RECIPES	151
PORK	**162**
ROAST PORK	162
BRAISED PORK	166
PORK STEW	168
PORK MINCE	169
RICE	**171**

SALADS **174**
    BEEF SALAD 174
    LAMB SALAD 176
    CHICKEN SALAD 177
    SEAFOOD SALAD 179
    VEGETABLE SALAD 180

SAUCES AND DRESSINGS **183**
    CLASSIC SAUCES 183
    ROUX 184
    STOCK 184
    EMULSIFIED SAUCES 187
    DRESSINGS 190

SOUPS **191**
    BEEF SOUP 191
    LAMB SOUP 192
    CHICKEN SOUP 193
    HAM SOUP 195
    FISH AND SEAFOOD SOUP 196
    SEAFOOD BISQUE 199
    VEGETABLE SOUP 200

STIR-FRIES **203**
    BEEF 203
    LAMB 205
    PORK 206
    CHICKEN 208
    PRAWNS 211

SWEETS AND DESSERTS **212**
    SWEET CLASSICS 212
    CUSTARDS 214
    BAKED CHEESECAKE 224
    NO-BAKE CHEESECAKE 225
    PIES 227
    MOUSSE 229
    CRÊPES 230
    TRADITIONAL PUDDINGS 231
    SELF-SAUCING PUDDING 235

VEGETABLES **237**
    MIXED VEGETABLE DISHES 237
    POTATOES AND SWEET POTATOES 239
    ONIONS LEEKS AND GARLIC 242
    MUSHROOMS AND ASPARAGUS 243
    CARROTS AND PARSNIPS 244
    PUMPKIN ZUCCHINI AND SQUASH 245
    BEANS AND PEAS 246
    SPINACH AND SILVER BEET 247
    CABBAGE TURNIP AND SWEDE 248
    BROCCOLI CAULIFLOWER AND BRUSSELS SPROUTS 249
    EGGPLANT AND ARTICHOKE 250
    TOMATOES CAPSICUMS AND CHILLIES 251

APPENDIX 1 – MEASURES AND CONVERSIONS **254**
APPENDIX 2 – GUIDE TO HERBS AND SPICES **255**
APPENDIX 3 – AN AUSSIE SLANG REFERENCE **258**

ALL THE BASICS

HOW TO FIND WHAT YOU WANT

I have tried to make these recipes easy to find, because there are hundreds of them. So I have categorised them simply by their main ingredient, or by their basic description, in bold type. Simply go to the Table of Contents and find the main section that you want, and then the sub-section that will help you to narrow down your search.

ABOUT THE RECIPES

All of the recipes here are made using basic techniques, basic equipment, and healthy, easily-acquired ingredients. Even many classic recipes are found here, with methods simplified, some recipe items substituted, and preparation times down to a minimum. I have included 'Fast Food' in its own section, because it is something that many people are familiar with, and a good starting point. Many people these days seem to just scoot down to the junk food outlets to buy their dinner, being unable to cook even the simplest of dishes using basic ingredients. But it is not difficult or expensive to cook real food! So get a life, and get cooking! Life is too short to eat bad food!

BARBECUES

Barbecues are not in a separate section, because there are recipes in many sections that can be easily adapted for the barbecue. Look for this icon.
Incidentally, the word 'barbecue' can refer to the party you have, the outside implement that you cook the food on, the act of cooking, or the food itself.

| BARBECUE FRIENDLY |

The word 'barbecue' seems to originate either from the Spanish 'barbecoa', which is a raised cooking platform, or from the French of the Florida settlers, 'de barbe en queue', meaning 'from beard to tail'. This latter description probably more closely describes a full spit roast!

ONE POT MEALS

The idea of one-pot meals is that you have a selection of meals that will take much of the mental anguish out of dinner preparation. You can launch straight into it without chewing it over for too long (pardon the pun). Look for this icon.
These dishes require the use of normal ingredients that you probably have on hand, or that will require minimal advance shopping, and will often provide some leftovers that are ideal for lunch the following day.

| ONE POT MEAL |

Designed for two to four servings, they have the following advantages:
- they require minimum preparation and clean-up time, often using just one pot
- they use a variety of healthy ingredients including vegetables, herbs and spices
- they ensure quantity control of ingredients, and good portion control
- they belong to a variety of national cuisines, cooking methods and techniques

FRESHNESS OF FOOD

Expiration dates are not some marketing ploy to get you to throw away good food so that you'll spend more on groceries. Please consult your calendar.

Fresh food tastes better, is more nutritious, and if you can buy it when it is in season, all the better. It really makes a difference to your cooking efforts.

Some foods, especially fruit and vegetables, are better purchased when labelled as 'organic', meaning that they have not been filled up with pesticides and such. These will include fruits like apples, pears, peaches, nectarines, tomatoes, and strawberries, and vegetables such as carrots, celery, capsicums, and lettuce. These products are usually treated with loads of pesticides. If you don't buy organic, wash them well.

Sesame seeds and Poppy seeds are the only acceptable 'spots' that should be evident on a loaf of bread, or when you open a jar of something found at the back of the fridge.

Any canned goods in the pantry that have become the size or shape of a small pumpkin should be disposed of very carefully and very quickly.

Milk has gone off when it looks like yogurt. Yogurt has gone off when it looks like cottage cheese. Cottage cheese has gone off when it looks like cheddar cheese. Cheddar cheese has gone off when it looks like blue cheese. Blue cheese is in a sense already off, so that one could be a little more difficult to identify.

Most foods should not be harder than your teeth. And flour or cereals of any sort are well past edible standard if they wriggle at all.

Any vegetable that you can tie knots in is not as fresh as required, and any vegetable that has liquefied, or that you cannot remove from the bottom of the vegetable compartment is of no further use to you. It's off; like a bucket of prawns in the sun.

Frozen foods that have become an integral part of any defrosting problem must go.

Potatoes are unusable if they have roots, branches, or dense, leafy undergrowth.

Onions are no good if…; well, you will really know about it if an onion has gone off.

If stray dogs are gathering, check out the meat compartment in your fridge.

The good news is that salt will probably never actually go off. On that topic…

USING QUALITY SALT

Salt is really an edible rock, essential to the diet. Get yourself some quality sea dust. Let's shake on that. Here are some types of highly-acclaimed additive-free sea salt:
- Australian Lake Salt–organic surface salt skimmed from Lake Deborah (WA)
- English Maldon Sea Salt–pyramid crystals of natural salt containing minerals
- Sicilian Ittica D'Or– unwashed and unrefined with high magnesium and potassium
- French Fleur de Sel–organic hand collected salt from the surface of salt pans
- Celtic Sea Salt–unrefined salt collected from various world coastal regions
- Welsh Anglesey Halen Mon–pure white organic salt with trace minerals
- Cyprus Flake Salt–natural pyramid shaped crystals
- Australian Murray River Pink Flake Salt–from Murray-Darling Basin groundwater
- American Sonoma Sea Salt–pure from solar evaporated Pacific Ocean water
- Himalayan Pink Salt–high mineral content salt from deep deposits
- New Zealand Marlborough Flaky Sea Salt–naturally produced from sea water

COOKING METHODS EXPLAINED

Stewing

A 'stew' is usually cooked on the stovetop without any browning of the meat first. Examples of this are the old French 'Pot au Feu', Pot on the Fire. The English have the Lancashire Hotpot, or Liverpool Scouse, from the Norwegian lapskaus or 'stew'. There is Welsh Cawl, and of course the world-famous Irish Stew. In the USA there is Mulligan Stew, and Brunswick Stew, often cooked with rabbit, and Burgoo, a term which has come to mean a dish cooked using almost anything that moves.

Braising

The term 'braising' usually refers to browning and cooking the meat in a suitable dish on the stovetop, or browning it on the stovetop, adding other ingredients, and then slipping it straight into the oven to finish. A 'casserole' recipe uses the braising method. As well as being the food inside, it also refers to the covered dish, which provides even heat and helps to prevent food from sticking to the bottom of the dish. I have come to rely on a large stainless steel 'casserole' dish with a heavy base and lid for this purpose. Similar recipes are cooked in a 'tajine' in Morocco, a cast-iron 'camp-oven' in Australia, and a cast-iron three-legged Dutch 'potjie' (pron. poy-kee) in Holland or South Africa. Cooking in a slow-cooker is also considered to be a method of braising.

Grilling or Broiling (USA)

This refers to cooking under direct heat, as for the grilling section in the top of the oven of many domestic stoves.

Char Grilling

Similar to grilling, but the heat source is underneath, as for barbecuing over an open cast-iron griddle. The basic cooking is done by conduction of hot air. The occasional flaming of the flat contributes a little to the unique smoky flavour of a char grill.

Pan Frying

Pan frying is carried out in a heavy frying pan, usually with a minimum of oil. Sometimes a grill-pan or griddle-pan with raised ridges might be used to put grill marks on the food and drain the fat, but this is not grilling, as the heat is conducted through the pan.

Deep Frying

I'll give you the good oil (pardon the pun) on this one! This method uses a large quantity of very hot oil; therefore, it can be quite dangerous. It is also considered to be very unhealthy by many experts due to the creation of trans-fats. The oil also needs to be changed more frequently than is economical. Pressure cookers that can deep fry foods at very high temperatures are often used in commercial kitchens, to compound the problem. I prefer, for health and safety reasons, to avoid using deep frying altogether.

Microwaving

I prefer to use microwaving only for the occasional warming or reheating task.

APPETIZERS, ANTIPASTI, HORS D'OEUVRES, TAPAS, PINTXOS AND MEZE

The name 'Appetizers' covers many national variations of the idea of small dishes served as a snack or a preliminary dish to whet the appetite. The Italian equivalent is 'Antipasti'. The French call them 'Hors d'oeuvres', meaning 'apart from the main work'. The Spanish equivalent is 'Tapas', meaning 'to cover', and are small tasty food dishes that were originally placed over the top of your drink to keep out the dust and flies. The Basque equivalent is 'Pintxos', meaning 'to prick'. 'Meze' are a range of small snack dishes from Turkey, Greece and the Middle East, and includes many tasty dips eaten with bread. Here is a selection of what I consider to be the best and tastiest. You might consider serving up several of these dishes as the main fare for a Tapas Party. Otherwise, be careful not to ruin your appetite with too many tasty appetizers.

HOT PLATES

'Patatas Bravas' (Spain) - Brave Potatoes

Boil 1Kg of peeled and cubed potatoes in salted water for 5 minutes. Dry the potatoes, and fry them in oil until golden. Meanwhile, fry an onion, and one clove of chopped garlic, and one finely chopped red chilli, in olive oil until lightly browned, and add 1 cup quality tomato sauce (Italian passata or similar) to cook for a couple of minutes. Serve the potatoes over the tomato sauce on a plate, and top with some finely chopped parsley.

Salt and Pepper Calamari (Italy)

Cut squid hoods lengthways into about ten strips after scoring the inside of the tube in a crosshatch pattern. Toss them in a mixture of plain flour, salt, and black pepper in a plastic bag. Cook for a few minutes in a pan in a shallow layer of hot light olive oil, until tender and slightly browned, turning to cook each side. You will find that they will curl up as they cook, for a nice presentation. This should only take about 1 minute per side.

'Gambas al Ajillo' (Spain) - Garlic Prawns

Fry 500gms peeled green prawns (raw) in hot olive oil along with 1 red chilli, very finely chopped, until they just start to turn pink. Add 1tspn crushed garlic to fry for one minute more, along with a squeeze of lemon juice. Top with some chopped parsley for colour and flavour. Serve with fresh crusty bread and cold beer. These are mighty good!

Pan-Fried Peppers with Capers (Italy)

Pan-fry strips of red capsicums (bell peppers) in oil in a pan. When the skins begin to scorch at the edges, add 2 cloves crushed garlic and 1Tbsp capers for 30 seconds. Add a little balsamic vinegar and salt to sizzle for a minute. Serve with fresh crusty bread.

'Caponnata' (Italy)

Fry cubed eggplant, then celery, then capers. Add pitted olives, chopped tomatoes and a little red wine vinegar. Remove from the heat and stir in lemon juice, parsley, salt and pepper. Serve with fresh bread.

'Peperonata' (Italy)

Fry chopped onions and garlic in oil. Add chopped capsicum, zucchini, eggplant, tomatoes, oregano, salt and freshly ground black pepper. When browned a little, add a splash of white wine vinegar. When the liquid has evaporated, serve with fresh bread.

Chillies with Kalamata Olives (Greece)

Pan fry some sliced red and yellow chillies in some olive oil and add some pitted kalamata olives and sliced garlic for a couple of minutes more. Add a dash of white wine vinegar, and serve it hot in a dish with fresh bread when it looks ready.

Harissa Olives (Tunisia)

Simply serve warm some pitted kalamata olives in a bowl coated with some Harissa chilli paste. In a mortar and pestle, crush 6 deseeded and chopped long red chillies, 2 cloves garlic, and 1tsp sea salt in 1Tbsp good quality extra virgin olive oil. Add 1tsp caraway seeds, 1tsp cumin seeds, and 1tsp coriander seeds that have been lightly toasted in a dry hot frying pan, and grind to a smooth paste. Provide toothpicks to self-serve.

Breaded Chillies (Spain)

Slice open the side of twenty red and green chillies and carefully remove the seeds and membranes. Pack the chillies with vintage cheese and dip them in egg and breadcrumbs. Refrigerate for about an hour. Fry in a little olive oil, drain on kitchen paper, and serve.

Scallops with Chorizo (Spain)

Line two muffin trays (about 12 total serves) with some flour tortillas and bake them for 5 minutes in the oven. Then fill them with a mixture that is made by frying some scallops in oil in a frying pan for a couple of minutes only before removing them. Then fry some sliced chorizo and remove it. Then fry some finely chopped onion and garlic, add some tomato puree, salt and pepper, and chopped oregano.
Put some sauce, then chorizo, then scallops in the tortilla bases and serve them.

Corn Fritters (International)

Whisk 2 eggs with ½ cup milk and stir it into a mixture of 1 cup S. R. Flour, a drained 400gm can corn kernels, 1 chopped green shallot, 1Tbsp finely chopped parsley, 1tsp ground coriander, 1tsp sea salt and 1tsp white pepper. Fry spoonfuls of the mixture in some butter or oil for 3 minutes each side until golden brown. Serve with some chutney or pickles.

BREADS

'Ħobż biż-Żejt' (Malta) - Bread with Oil

Malta produces some of the best sourdough bread in the world, made using traditional methods to secret recipes. Many people believe in the superior health benefits of good sourdough bread (you knead to be serious about this; it is a loaf or death situation!). The simplest possible version of this dish is to dip pieces of bread in some warmed high-quality extra virgin olive oil. Don't underrate this Maltese staple; it is magnificent! Some good balsamic vinegar or some truffle oil can also be added to the dipping oil. The more up-market, and a superbly delicious version of this dish, is to spread some tomato paste thinly over slices of sourdough bread. Sprinkle over some capers and some finely chopped parsley, and top this with some anchovy fillets, sea salt and black pepper, and lastly a drizzle of some high-quality extra virgin olive oil (EVOO).

Garlic Bread (France)

You wouldn't believe that ordinary bread could be so tasty! It is usually made using a baguette which is partially sliced through, and spread inside with a minced garlic and butter mixture which will soak into the loaf while keeping it in one piece. Roll it in a foil package and heat it in the oven for about fifteen minutes.
You can make Anchovy Bread in the same way, just with the addition of some finely chopped anchovies. This is absolutely magical—if you like anchovies; and I surely do!

Creamed Eggs and Caviar (France)

These are delicious! Boil four eggs for five minutes and set aside to cool a little. Peel the eggs and mash them. Mix in half a cup of whole egg mayonnaise, salt and pepper, and about 1tsp finely chopped chives. Spoon the mixture onto slices of baguette, toast, dry biscuits, or squares of flour tortilla, and top with a little spoonful of black caviar, which is available in small jars from the supermarket.

Salmon Toast

Make a mixture using a small tin canned red salmon, a finely chopped onion, 1 finely chopped dill cucumber, 1Tbsp horseradish cream, 2tsp capers, and a little curry powder. Roll up the mixture in fresh bread slices, cut them in half, and secure them with toothpicks. Spray the tops with olive oil and bake for 15 minutes on an oven tray.

Angels on Horseback

These are a type of finger food called canapés, from the French word for 'couch', in that the food on the bread often looks like people sitting on a couch.
Wrap some quarter rashers of lightly fried streaky bacon around some freshly opened and washed oysters. Place two wrapped oysters on each slice of some buttered white bread toast that has had the crusts removed. Cook (broil) them under a hot grill for about 5 minutes until the bacon starts to sizzle.

'Crostini' with Parmesan cheese (Italy)

Bake some small slices of Italian bread in the oven with some Parmesan cheese on top.
As a savoury topping, heat some anchovies in a pan in butter along with chopped black olives, a chopped green shallot, and some capers.
Alternatively, put on top some freshly cooked and peeled king prawns sprinkled with sea salt and freshly ground black pepper.

'Crostini' with Zucchini and Tomatoes (Italy)

Halve some zucchinis lengthways and fry them in oil till browned both sides.
Add some halved cherry tomatoes to fry a little along with them. Serve the zucchini slices on toasted Italian bread (or half pieces of toast) with a cherry tomato on top, and a toothpick to hold it together. Sprinkle with sea salt and black pepper.

'Bruschetta' (Italy)

Lightly toast some sliced Italian bread and top with a mixture of extra virgin olive oil, freshly chopped garlic, freshly chopped basil, finely chopped ripe, red tomatoes, sea salt and freshly ground black pepper.

Baguette with Camembert and Ham (France)

Slice a quality wheel of camembert or brie, and place the slices on pieces of baguette bread (or stick loaf). Top with chopped sun-dried tomatoes, capers, sea salt and freshly ground black pepper. Grill (broil) them for a few minutes until the cheese begins to melt. Lay on the top some strips of Bayonne ham (or some other high quality cured ham such as Parma, Serrano or Iberian ham), and serve.
Or, you could put some smoked salmon on top.

> **Safety Tip**
> Don't overindulge on cheese;
> I did, and now I camembert it!

'Pissaladière' (France) – salted fish

Cut two sheets of puff pastry into two, and fold the edges up to make some tarts.
Make a mixture for the topping by caramelising some chopped onions in oil in a frypan along with a pinch of sugar, then adding some chopped garlic.
Spread the mixture over the tarts, sprinkle over some sea salt flakes and cracked black pepper, and some fresh thyme, and then put some anchovy fillets in a criss-cross pattern across the top with halved and pitted black olives between them.
Bake them in the oven for about 20 minutes at 180^0C before serving.

Prawn Toast (China)

Process in a food processor some peeled green prawns, a chopped spring onion, 1tsp minced ginger, 1tsp minced garlic, 1tsp soy sauce, 1tsp sesame oil, an egg, salt and pepper. Spread the mixture thinly on fresh bread, sprinkle some sesame seeds on top, and shallow fry in peanut oil until golden brown. Cut into wedges and serve.

TOOTHPICK TEMPTERS

Olive 'Polpette' (Italy)

Get some green olives stuffed with anchovies or feta cheese from the deli and push them into some small balls of pork and veal mince to which you have added an egg, some dried thyme, some chopped parsley, salt and pepper. Dip them in plain flour, then beaten egg, and breadcrumbs, and fry them in some extra virgin olive oil until golden all over.

Goanna Balls with Chilli Sauce (Australia)

Make some meat balls by rolling up into round portions about 3cm in diameter, about 500gm finely minced steak, 2 eggs, 2Tbsp breadcrumbs, 1Tbsp plain flour, 1tsp dried mixed herbs, 1tsp sea salt and 1tsp ground black pepper. Fry them in oil until cooked, and serve them on toothpicks with some Special chilli sauce on the side (see Sauces).

Spicy Chicken Balls in Yoghurt (Australia)

Chop up some chicken thigh fillets in bite size pieces and roll them in a mixture of ½ cup of plain yoghurt and ½ tsp each of ground cumin, ground coriander, ground cloves, ground nutmeg, ground turmeric, dried chilli, ground black pepper and sea salt. Put them on a tray and bake them in the oven at 180^0C for about 20 minutes until cooked through.

Potato and Cheese Balls (Australia)

Mix mashed potatoes with an egg, a little milk, some finely chopped onion, salt and pepper. Coat balls of the mixture in some breadcrumbs and grated parmesan cheese. Fry them in some light olive oil all over in a frying pan and serve them on a plate.

'Falafel' (Israel) - Chick Pea Balls

Drain a can of chick peas, and blend them with a chopped onion, a garlic clove, an egg, some minced chilli, ground cumin, ground coriander, chopped parsley, salt and pepper. Form the mixture into small balls, and dip them in egg and then seasoned flour. Chill for an hour or so and then fry them in oil. Serve them on toothpicks.

Fried Chorizo (Spain) and Fried Haloumi Cheese (Greece)

Slice a chorizo sausage fairly thinly and slice some haloumi cheese into cubes.
Fry them both in a little olive oil in a frypan and serve them on a plate on toothpicks stuck through one of each of these to use as a handle, along with some lemon wedges.

Atlantic Salmon with smoked paprika (Spain)

Cut some boneless Atlantic salmon fillets into cubes and dust them with a mixture of plain flour, smoked paprika, salt and pepper, by putting it all in a plastic bag and giving it a shake. Lightly fry the cubes in some light olive oil all over and serve them on toothpicks.

PASTRIES

Savoury 'Vol-au-Vents' (France)

Vol-au-Vent means 'windblown' in French.
Sauté some finely chopped onion, garlic and bacon in a little butter. Add some chopped champignons, chopped chives and salt and pepper to cook a little. Add some light sour cream to heat through and spoon into ready made vol-au-vent cases that have been heated in the oven for a few minutes.
Alternative fillings might be:
Chopped ham and asparagus added to a basic white onion sauce (See Sauces).
Some canned smoked oysters added to a basic white onion sauce (See Sauces).
A mixture of canned red salmon, horseradish cream and capers, heated through.

Samosas (India)

Fry some chopped onion and garlic in a little oil until lightly browned. Add some lamb mince to brown a little. Add a little grated ginger, a finely chopped chilli, a finely diced potato, a finely diced carrot, a finely diced spinach leaf or other green vegetable, 1tsp garam masala or other spice blend, salt and pepper, and about ½ cup lemon juice. Using filo pastry, brush two sheets at a time with a little melted butter and with one sheet on top of the other, cut them into three strips which can be folded over and rolled into triangles with some filling in each. Bake them on a tray 10 minutes or so until cooked.

Spinach Triangles (Greece)

Lightly cook and chop some spinach. Mix in some finely chopped onion, toasted pine nuts, feta cheese, ground cumin, ground coriander, salt and pepper. Roll up portions of the mixture in filo pastry into triangles and place on a lightly oiled tray. Spray a little oil on top and bake for about 15 minutes.

Savoury Cheese Twists

Thaw a couple of sheets of frozen puff pastry, brush them with some beaten egg, and sprinkle over some grated parmesan cheese. Slice into 2cm strips and twist them from the ends to make twisted strips and bake them in the oven for about 15 minutes.

Savoury Roll-ups

Thaw a couple of sheets of frozen puff pastry, and spread a thin layer of cream cheese on top, then a thin layer of pesto, or some olive tapenade. Sprinkle with a little grated parmesan cheese. Slice into 1cm strips and roll them up flat. Place them on their ends on a baking tray and bake them for about 15 minutes.

Safety Tip
Be careful of all of these very tasty little treats;
because overweight can very quickly snack up on you.

DELECTABLE DIPS

'Tapenade' (France) – Olive, Anchovy and Caper Dip

The word 'tapenade' is from the French word 'tapenas' meaning 'capers'.
Blend some pitted kalamata olives and some anchovy fillets with about 2Tbsp capers, a little extra virgin olive oil, a squeeze of lemon juice and some freshly ground black pepper. You can add a dash of brandy if you wish. Serve with some fresh crusty bread.

'Tzatziki' (Greece) - Yoghurt Dip

Mix together some plain Greek-style yoghurt, a finely chopped Lebanese cucumber, 1tsp crushed garlic, chopped dill, chopped parsley, a little olive oil, a little white wine vinegar, sea salt and freshly ground black pepper.

'Guacamole' (Mexico) - Avocado Dip

Blend together a chopped avocado, the juice of one lemon, half a chopped red onion, a chopped garlic clove, 1 whole jalapeño chilli, a dash of Worcestershire sauce, sea salt and freshly ground black pepper.

'Baba Ghanoush' (Turkey) - Roasted Eggplant Dip

Brush whole eggplants with olive oil and bake in the oven until cooked through and the skin blisters. Also put some cloves of garlic in the dish while roasting. Scoop out the flesh, add the squeezed roasted garlic puree, ½tsp ground cumin, lemon juice, salt and pepper and mash to a puree. Serve with fresh Turkish bread.

'Skordalia' (Greece) - Garlic Dip

Soak white bread slices in some milk and add a chopped clove of garlic. Blend in ½ cup of olive oil, the juice of one lemon, salt and pepper to get a paste of dip consistency. Chopped capers and mashed potato can also be added if you wish.

'Hommus' (Lebanon) - Chickpea Dip

To a can of drained chickpeas add the juice of one lemon, ¾ cup tahini (sesame paste, available in jars), one clove of crushed garlic, a dash of ground cumin, salt and pepper, and some extra virgin olive oil. Blend the mixture till smooth. Serve with some fresh sourdough bread.

'Taramasalata' (Greece) - Smoked Cod's Roe Dip

This is the tasty pink dip you've seen. Scrape the centre from a smoked cod's roe into a bowl, add four slices of bread that have been soaked in water and squeezed out, the juice of one lemon, a chopped red onion, some sea salt and freshly ground black pepper. Process the mixture. Gradually pour in some extra virgin olive oil, a little at a time until smooth. Chill. Garnish with some chopped parsley and some pitted kalamata olives.

Hot Chilli Dip (Italy)

Fry chopped onions and garlic in olive oil. Then add 2 chopped red capsicums (red bell peppers) to fry for 5 minutes. Add 2 cans chopped tomatoes and about 8 chopped hot red chillies, or as many as you can tolerate. Add salt and pepper, and simmer for about 20 minutes. Serve hot or warm with fresh Italian bread and very cold Italian beer.

'Dukkah' (Egypt) - pron. 'doo-ka' meaning 'to pound'

Toast the following ingredients for a couple of minutes in a hot, dry frying pan until fragrant (using no oil), and then blend or pound them together.
½ cup sesame seeds
½ cup hazelnuts
½ cup almonds
1Tbsp cumin seed
1Tbsp coriander seed
1Tbsp cardamom seed
2tsp sea salt
2tsp black pepper
Dip pieces of Turkish bread in some warmed extra virgin olive oil, and then the Dukkah.

Vegetable Dip (France)

Boil some cauliflower florets for 3 minutes. Then blend it with a roasted red capsicum, a little chopped basil, a little chilli, a couple of pitted green olives, a little white wine vinegar, 1tsp sea salt and 1tsp white pepper. Serve with crudités (French for raw vegetables) of sliced carrot, beans, celery and broccoli.

Broad Bean Dip (Greece)

Process a drained can of broad beans with some extra virgin olive oil, the juice of one lemon, 2 cloves crushed garlic, a pinch of mixed herbs, some mint, some crumbled fetta cheese, 1tsp sea salt and 1tsp white pepper.

'Bagna Cauda' (Italy) - wet dip

This is from the Piedmont area of Italy, and is sort of like a fondue for anchovy lovers. Serve it as a dip with finely sliced vegetables and slices of fresh sourdough bread.
Fry 3 cloves chopped garlic lightly in ½ cup extra virgin olive oil. Add 8 chopped anchovy fillets, 25gm butter, 10 chopped capers, the juice of 1 lemon and a little zest, 1tsp good quality sea salt and 1tsp white pepper. Stir until it is smooth over low heat.

Beetroot Dip

Blend together a can of cooked baby beetroot, ½ cup Greek-style natural yoghurt, 1tsp ground cumin, 1tsp sugar, 1tsp sea salt and 1tsp freshly ground black pepper.
Serve with savoury dry biscuits or slices of fresh bread.

PÂTÉ

Red Wine, Mushroom and Peppercorn Pâté (France)

Fry a chopped brown onion, 2 rashers chopped bacon, and a clove of garlic in oil and remove from the pan. Then fry some brown mushrooms and remove. Fry some washed and finely chopped chicken livers. When cooked, add the onion mixture and mushrooms, along with some green peppercorns, a splash of red wine and some fresh or dry mixed herbs. Cook a little longer. Blend into a smooth paste. When the mixture has cooled a little, put the mixture into some ramekins, pour over a thin layer of melted butter to seal them, and refrigerate. Serve this cold with toast, fresh bread, or dry biscuits. You can freeze some till later if you wish.

Pâté with Anchovies and Capers (France)

Wash and clean up some chicken livers. Fry them in some olive oil with some sage leaves. When they have changed colour and are cooked, chop them up a bit, add some salt and pepper, anchovies and capers and enough red wine to allow them to simmer a little. Process until smooth and serve with toast or fresh bread and butter, accompanied by some lightly fried champignons and fresh cherry tomatoes.

Chick Pea Pâté (Middle-East)

De-bitter some eggplant by sprinkling it with salt and weighting it down to allow the juices to run. Rinse it and pat it dry. Fry a chopped onion with a clove of garlic, and then the chopped eggplant in oil. Add a can of cooked and drained chickpeas, a small can of kidney beans, some chopped chives, salt and pepper, to heat through. Blend the mixture and serve on hot toast with tomato slices.

Fish Pâté

Simmer some boneless white fish fillets with chopped onions, white wine, chicken booster, lemon juice, lemon rind and butter. When the fish is very tender, blend it with a little cream. Serve it cold with toast.

Prawn Pâté aka Cold Potted Prawns

Melt 100gm butter in a large frypan, and add 1 clove chopped or minced garlic, ½tsp dried chilli flakes, ½ chopped green shallot, some sea salt and pepper, and about 200gm small (great for this dish) peeled green prawns (frozen prawns are OK, thawed).
Cook over medium heat for about 3 minutes or so until the prawns are just starting to turn opaque.
Remove the prawns and divide them between 6 small ramekins. Pour the flavoured butter through a strainer over the top of the prawns.
Refrigerate them until the mixture is solid. Serve this with squares of toast, chopped parsley and some lemon wedges.

Pork, Lamb and Chicken Pâté en Terrine (France)

Pâté en terrine means that it was originally a 'pie made in an earthenware mould'.

It began with the idea of cooking cheap off-cuts of various meats with fat and seasonings for a high-energy meal, and the lard provided a protective layer for storage.

The secret to this dish is the cooking in a water bath, or 'bain-marie'. This provides low, even heat without browning, resulting in the cooking of the proteins and the mingling of the flavours and juices, producing a delicious clear jelly at the end.

This is the ultimate picnic food when partnered with maybe a chilled pinot gris white wine, and is very impressive visually. It can also be served as a dip with fresh bread.

Ingredients

1 onion, diced
2 green shallots, finely chopped
2 Tbsp butter
500gm diced pork, or pork mince
200gm lambs fry, diced
100gm chicken livers, diced
2 rashers bacon, rind removed, diced
2 eggs
1 cup breadcrumbs
2 cloves garlic, crushed
1/3 cup cream
3 Tbsp cognac or brandy
herbs and spices as listed
6 rashers bacon, whole, rind removed

Herbs and Spices

1tsp fresh thyme, chopped
1tsp fresh sage, chopped
1tsp fresh marjoram or oregano, chopped
1tsp fresh parsley, chopped
$\frac{1}{2}$tsp ground nutmeg
$\frac{1}{2}$tsp sea salt
$\frac{1}{2}$tsp freshly ground black pepper
3 bay leaves

Method

Cook the onion and shallots in butter in a pan and let them cool for a while.

Mix together the pork, lamb, chicken, and diced bacon.

Stir in the eggs, breadcrumbs, garlic, cream, cognac, herbs and spices. Stir in the cooked shallots and onion mixture.

Grease with butter a terrine or glass casserole dish that has a lid. Place the bay leaves across the bottom of the dish for flavour and decoration. Line the terrine with the bacon rashers. Press the mixture down well, fold over the bacon, and put the lid on.

Stand the terrine in a bath of water to 5cm below the rim. Cook in a 120^0C oven for 2-3 hours, till the juice runs clear when pierced.

When it is cooled, remove the lid, put some foil on the top, and weight it down (a house brick covered in foil will do the trick), to remove air pockets. Wait till it is cooled, though, or all the fat and juices will be forced out, making it dry.

Refrigerate overnight before serving it upside down with pickled cucumbers and capers, and fresh crusty bread (French baguettes are perfect).

SIZZLING SKEWERS

Skewers are a great appetiser, can form part of an interesting selection of small dishes, or they can be a meal in themselves. They provide a very relaxed means of enjoying good food and good company around the barby.

Known as 'sate' in Malaysia, Thailand, Brunei, Singapore, Indonesia and the Netherlands (Indonesia is a former Dutch colony), they are called 'shish kebab' in Turkey, the word 'sis', meaning sword, and 'kebab', meaning roasted meat. In the Caucasus they are called 'shashlik'. The Chinese equivalent is 'chuanr', and in Japan it is 'yakitori'. In south Africa, the same thing is known in Afrikaans as 'sosatie', from 'sate' and 'saus'.

Assembly involves threading marinated meat and vegetables onto bamboo skewers that have been soaked in water to prevent them from burning. You can thread the meat onto the skewers before marinating it, or you can skewer it later, but it's a bit messier that way. Also, you can alternate pieces of meat with chopped onion, celery, mushrooms, capsicum or cherry tomatoes for variety. On the following pages are some good ways of marinating various types of meat skewers. They are easy to make and very tasty.

As you cook, you can brush or baste the meat with some of the marinade if you wish, but for reasons of good food hygiene make sure to cook the food well after basting it, if you are using the same marinades that contained the raw ingredients. Following are some of the best marinade combinations.

Serve the skewers with additional sauces, plain yoghurt, or even a nice mango puree.

MARVELLOUS MARINADES

Marinades usually combine an acid to tenderise the meat, an oil, and herbs and spices.

Light meats marinate more quickly, and room temperature marinating is quicker than in the fridge.

It is better not to use salt in marinades as it can toughen the meat by drawing out moisture. It is easy to add salt to the skewers later.

BARBECUE FRIENDLY

If you're in a hurry to get a barby ready, you could use a commercially prepared marinade from the supermarket, such as hoi sin, teriyaki, black bean, chilli, or satay.

If you have the time, do it yourself; because if you are using good quality ingredients, you'll get a better result for less money, and learn something into the bargain.

These marinades are also great for steaks or fillets of these meats that can be cooked on a barbecue hotplate, in a frying pan, or in the oven.

USING OLIVE OIL

Many of these recipes specify using good quality extra virgin (first press) olive oil. The pulp of many fruits is mostly water, but with olives it is oil. Oil is the primary reason for the growing of so many olive trees, and it is extremely good for you.
There are many high quality extra virgin olive oils available.
Do yourself a favour and buy only very fresh, good quality oil.

Beef Skewers – using cubed rump, round or scotch fillet

French Wine and Garlic	Red wine, crushed garlic, olive oil, soy sauce, honey, minced chilli, minced ginger, mixed herbs, and ground black pepper
Belgian Beer and Mustard	Beer, Dijon mustard, olive oil, lemon juice, crushed garlic, mixed herbs, and ground black pepper
Chinese Sesame Soy	Sherry, soy sauce, honey, olive oil, garlic, grated ginger, ground black pepper, and a little sesame oil

Lamb Skewers – using cubed lamb rump, leg or shoulder

Greek Lemon and Herb	Lemon juice, olive oil, ground coriander, chopped rosemary, chopped oregano, crushed garlic, and ground black pepper.
Moroccan Harissa	White wine, olive oil, ground cumin, ground coriander, crushed garlic, minced chilli, and ground black pepper.
Indian Spice and Yoghurt	Yoghurt, ground cumin, ground coriander, turmeric, ground nutmeg, cinnamon, minced chilli, and ground black pepper.

Pork Skewers – using cubed pork leg or loin

Creole Chilli and Sage	Orange juice, minced chilli, grated ginger, crushed garlic, olive oil, sage, ground coriander, and ground black pepper.
English Apricot Ginger	Apple cider vinegar, apricot jam, olive oil, minced ginger, ground black pepper, and a little mixed spice.
Moroccan Chermoula	Lemon juice, olive oil, ground cumin, ground coriander, chopped parsley, smoked paprika, and ground black pepper.

Chicken Skewers – using cubed chicken breast or thigh

Thai Honey and Soy	White wine, honey, soy sauce, olive oil, grated ginger, crushed garlic, ground coriander and ground black pepper.
Indian Lemon Tikka	Lemon juice, yoghurt, ground cumin, ground coriander, crushed garlic, ground chilli, and ground black pepper.
Japanese Yakitori	Rice wine, olive oil, crushed garlic, minced chilli, ground ginger, soy sauce, and ground black pepper.

Prawn Skewers – using peeled green prawns

Italian Lemon Chilli	Lemon juice, olive oil, honey, minced chilli, crushed garlic, thyme leaves, and ground black pepper.
Portuguese Piri Piri	White wine, olive oil, ground chilli, crushed garlic, ground pimento, lemon juice and zest, fresh coriander (cilantro)
Spanish Chilli Garlic	White wine, olive oil, ground chilli, crushed garlic, smoked paprika, rosemary, and ground black pepper.

BEEF AND VEAL

ABOUT GOOD BEEF STEAK

Before we start on this major topic, a little bit of thought needs to be given to the quality of the meat that you use for a barbecue or for steak meals.

There is a great deal of difference between a good piece of steak and a little more ordinary piece of steak that you might buy, say, from a supermarket. This relates to the breed of the animal, where and how it was grown, what it was fed, at what age it was killed, how it was killed, how long it was aged for, and at what temperature it was aged. Talk to a good butcher about these things if you are serious about enjoying a good steak, or a good piece of lamb for that matter.

What I mean is this; you can't chase an animal around the yard six times when it is about to be slaughtered, especially when it knows its mates have copped it, and expect to end up with a nice, tender piece of meat. Not going to happen.

The bottom line is that you get what you pay for. When you consider that a 500Kg yearling beef animal will have a carcass of about 250Kg, and of that, you might end up with about 170Kg of meat, including about 17Kg of prime cuts of steak. So, in short, expect to pay a bit of money for a good piece of steak.

There are varying opinions and preferences about the types of beef available and the best cuts. Some like grain fed beef while others prefer grass fed. Some heavily marbled types of beef are also now bred for consumption.

In my humble opinion, for what it's worth; cows are meant to roam free and eat grass.

Also, a lot of prime beef is now sold in sealed vacuum packs, and there are arguments for and against that practice as well.

To enjoy a really good steak you will want to buy one of the following top cuts:

- Scotch fillet (rib-eye) which comes from the big muscle on either side of the spine behind the shoulder, and can be bought on or off the bone. The on-the-bone cut is the one used for the very handsome standing beef rib roast.
- Eye Fillet (tenderloin, or undercut)
- Porterhouse (sirloin, strip loin, entrecote, or New York cut)
- T-Bone (which is a cross section of the vertebrae and has both the tenderloin on the inside and the sirloin on the outside)
- Rump (from the hind quarters, or butt)

Here is a small observation of mine though, learned from experience (and experience is something you get just after you need it). If you are buying from a cheaper meat outlet and you need the meal to be a good one, it is best to buy eye fillet steak, as it is usually the tenderest cut of meat, and this will give you the best chance of it being a winner. It is also lean, and can dry out in cooking, so think about using a nice sauce with it, or a cooking method to complement it.

HOW TO COOK GOOD BEEF STEAK

The difficulty in cooking steak perfectly can be understood from the following details. The surface of the meat needs to reach in excess of $120^\circ C$ for the Maillard (browning) reaction to begin, while the internal temperature cannot exceed $55^\circ C$ for a steak cooked to medium doneness.

The internal temperature of the meat and the approximate cooking time are:

Rare	Medium-rare	Medium	Medium-well	Well done
$35^\circ C$	$45^\circ C$	$55^\circ C$	$65^\circ C$	$75^\circ C$
Very soft	Soft	Springy	Firm	Very firm
6 minutes	8 minutes	10 minutes	12 minutes	14 minutes

Some try to get the right result by using steaks of about 1cm thickness, and cooking them quickly. Others recommend cooking the steak to one stage below what is desired, then resting it for about 15 minutes, and finally cooking it to required doneness. However, most chefs will recommend a steak of about 3cm thickness to retain juices and flavour, and cooking them to no more than medium. This means that you need to be able to get some serious heat into the meat, so that the outside and inside are both right. This comes down to good technique and good equipment. If you don't have enough heat, the meat will start to stew and toughen. So, things like starting out with the meat at room temperature are very important to getting a good result. Also, turn the steak once only. And, don't put everything on at once; put the pieces of meat on first that need the longest cooking time. That way you won't lose too much heat at any one time.

Get your cooking surface as hot as possible before starting, and then get ready to stand back from the smoke and spitting fat. You are looking for a nice brown crust. By the way, don't expect a clean kitchen afterward. There is a lot to be said for cooking steaks on an outdoor barbecue.

Another important thing is to handle the meat carefully. Use tongs to turn and test the meat; not a fork or a knife, as the essential juices will escape and toughen the meat.

A simple method that I have found that works pretty well is to buy a cheap, heavy cast iron frying pan, and use it over a very hot barbecue or the large gas wok burner that is on the side of many gas barbecues. Then, a 3cm thick steak cooked to medium doneness should take about 5 minutes per side, as shown in the table.

To summarise—use seriously good meat and seriously good heat!

The Hand Method

To test how well the meat is cooked, touch your thumb to each finger, and with the index finger of your other hand, press the fleshy area between your thumb and wrist. This will give an approximate indication of what the meat should feel like when pressed.

- Rare   Thumb to index finger
- Medium Rare   Thumb to middle finger
- Medium   Thumb to ring finger
- Medium to Well Done   Thumb to little finger

THE SCIENCE OF BROWNING MEAT

Browning of meat and onions in oil is an important part of the process in many braised meat dishes, and adds greatly to the flavour. This is because oil boils at over 154^0C, producing sugars in the meat as the proteins break down, and this provides the flavour. This is called the 'Maillard reaction', after the Frenchman who discovered it in 1912.

Food cooked in water does not provide the same result, as it will never exceed the boiling point of water which boils at 100^0C. It will never brown. Comprendo?

Browning meat at a high temperature will help to prevent moisture loss from the meat too, as it has already started to cook. Do it in small batches, otherwise the steam will make the meat damp, and it will stew, and this will interfere with the browning process.

THICKENING MEAT DISHES

When flour is used with meat, usually to thicken the dish, it is added early in the cooking; otherwise a floury flavour will result. Sometimes flour is added to the pan after browning the meat so that it can cook in the juices, sometimes the meat is rolled in seasoned flour, and sometimes a paste of flour and butter, called a 'beurre manié' is added a little later in the cooking process. The idea here is that the butter coats the flour, and when it is added to the hot dish the butter melts and releases the flour, thickening it without forming any lumps.

A quick thickening method is to add to the dish a little cornflour mixed in water.

If you don't want to use flour, for some dishes you can simply let the dish simmer with the lid off for a while, so that the amount of liquid reduces and it thickens naturally.

BUTTER TOPPINGS FOR BEEF

A great way to serve beef is with a simply prepared herbed butter that you can prepare beforehand and serve straight from the fridge. You just place a little on top of the cooked steak to melt.

Here is a variety of simple preparations, made by mixing butter at room temperature with the other ingredients. You can serve two for variety and colour if you wish.

You roll it up in a cylinder in plastic food wrap, and put it in the fridge for ready use.

Garlic Butter

Mix in crushed garlic, and some chopped fresh parsley.

Green Wasabi Butter

Mix in some wasabi paste, chopped parsley, chopped coriander, and a little lemon rind.

Red Caper Butter

Mix in some chopped capers, minced red chilli, minced ginger, and some chopped dill.

'Beurre Café de Paris' (France) - Herbed Butter

This herbed butter is a real standout taste sensation. It looks complicated, but please do try it; you will not regret it. The original well-guarded exotic recipe for this classic, dating from 1941, was created by Freddy Dumont and served in the Restaurant Café de Paris in Geneva. It was designed to complement sirloin steak.

Only a few restaurants claim to have the original recipe, but many have tried to copy it. This is my simplified version that I think works very well.

It will enhance many meat or seafood dishes, including wonderful lobster medallions.

Ingredients

400gm salted butter
2 anchovy fillets
1 clove garlic, minced
½ red chilli, deseeded, and very finely chopped
1tsp tomato paste
1tsp Dijon mustard
1tsp capers
the zest and juice of a ½ lemon
4tsp Cognac
1tsp ground white pepper
¼tsp ground sweet paprika
¼tsp ground turmeric
¼tsp ground fenugreek seed
¼tsp ground coriander seed
¼tsp ground cardamom seed
3 stalks fresh flat-leafed parsley, very finely chopped
3 stalks fresh chives, very finely chopped
1 stalk fresh oregano leaves, very finely chopped
1 stalk fresh thyme leaves, very finely chopped
1 small eschalot (French shallot), very finely chopped
leaves of a 5cm stalk of fresh rosemary, finely chopped

Method

Mix everything except the butter very well together, put it into a covered glass bowl in a warm place, and let the mixture ferment slightly overnight.

Soften the butter, mix it in, then form the butter into a log inside some cling film. I find the best way is to then roll the log up in a clear acetate sheet and fit it inside a leftover cardboard tube from a roll of baking paper or similar, and store it in the freezer for use at a moment's notice. This recipe makes two 30cm (1 foot) tubes.

Then when you need it, simply cut off coins of frozen butter, place one on top of each piece of cooked meat, and place the meat under a very hot grill till the butter starts to brown on top but remains hard inside. Or, just let it melt over the top of the meat.

PRIME BEEF STEAK

'Filet de Boeuf en Croûte' (France) - Beef Wellington

This has got to be one of the best beef dishes of all time! It is quite expensive, but really great, and well worth it.

Its origin is disputed. It is arguably of French, English, or even New Zealand origin, but the basic pastry technique has been around for centuries.

Ingredients

1.5Kg whole tenderloin (eye fillet) of beef. $!!
extra virgin olive oil for frying
1 brown onion, peeled and finely chopped
1 clove garlic, peeled and finely chopped
1 green shallot, finely chopped
100gm brown mushrooms
some fresh parsley, sage, rosemary, and thyme (sing along while picking the leaves)
¼tsp salt and ¼tsp freshly ground black pepper
2 sheets quality frozen butter puff pastry
½ cup Red Wine and Mushroom Pâté (as in DIPS) or other quality pâté
1 egg, whisked with a fork

Method

Brown the eye fillet all over in olive oil in a frying pan and remove it to a plate, reserving any pan juices. Allow it to cool a little. Then fry the onion, garlic, shallot, mushrooms, herbs, salt and pepper in a little oil in the pan, driving off any moisture.

Spread the pâté all over the top of the fillet. Then spread over the onion mixture.

Wrap the whole thing up neatly in puff pastry, seam side down, place it in a baking dish, brush the top with the beaten egg, and bake it in the oven at $180^{0}C$ for about 45 minutes. It is traditionally served medium rare in the middle, but cook it to your liking.

Keep it warm and resting while you make some gravy as below to serve on the side. Then slice the beef to about 3cm thickness. You can also make small individual serves called Beef Tournedos if you wish. This is also the name of the centre section of the eye fillet which is very often sold specifically for this magnificent dish.

Rich Gravy

Make rich brown gravy from any pan juices left in the frying pan, along with:

1 cup of red wine
1 cup of beef stock
1tsp balsamic vinegar
1tsp Worcestershire sauce
1tsp soy sauce
1tsp sea salt
1tsp black pepper
Simmer these in the frying pan to thicken the sauce and reduce the volume a little.

Barry Bakes © 2013

'Fillet Mignon' with Garlic Sauce (France)

This is definitely one of the finest beef recipes of all time, in my opinion and to my taste, as the flavours of beef, bacon, butter, and garlic combine so well; they seem to be made for each other.

A chef named Tao, who used small individual cast-iron frying pans over a raging gas flame for the steaks in his restaurant, and cooked them in half oil and half butter, first served my wife and me this outstanding dish.

It was, I am sure, one of the very best steaks that I have ever eaten anywhere; and I have eaten quite a few!

Ingredients (Serves 4)

4 pieces eye fillet steak, 3.5cm (1½") thick, about 1.2Kg.
4 rashers bacon, with the rind removed
4 cloves freshly crushed garlic for rubbing the steak
olive oil and butter for frying
sea salt and black pepper
4 slices of toast, with crusts removed
50gm butter approximately for the sauce
2 cloves freshly crushed garlic for the sauce
chopped parsley to garnish

Method

Wrap the bacon rashers around the outside edges of the fillet steak and secure them with 4 toothpicks each. 'Mignon' in French means 'small', and the steaks are often cut from the smaller forward end of the tenderloin. Otherwise, they can be from the centre cut or 'tournedos'.

Spread crushed garlic (about 4 cloves) on both sides of the steaks along with a little oil and salt and pepper and cook to your liking in a very hot heavy-based frying pan in a mixture of butter and oil. The butter provides a little extra flavour, and the oil brings up the smoke point. The idea is to get the outside of the steak nice and crusty without overcooking the middle. That's why you need plenty of searing heat.

Remove the steaks from the pan, and place them each on a slice of toast (a crouton) on the serving plates.

Now quickly add the butter and crushed garlic for the sauce to the pan for a few seconds without burning it, and pour it over the steaks so that it runs down and soaks into the croutons.

Another twist of salt and pepper, and a sprinkling of chopped parsley over the top and you are ready to serve it with whatever vegetables you have prepared. Mashed potatoes and fresh green beans work well with this.

The king of steak dishes!

Pan-Fried or Barbecued Prime Beef Steak

As explained in the introduction to this section, the prime beef steak cuts are:
- Scotch fillet (rib-eye)
- Eye Fillet (tenderloin, undercut)
- Porterhouse (sirloin, strip loin, entrecote, New York cut)
- T-Bone (tenderloin and sirloin on the bone)
- Rump (from the hind quarters or butt of beef)

BARBECUE FRIENDLY

You can pan-fry the sliced steaks or cook them on the barbecue equally well.

Refer to the suggested cooking times to cook them to your liking.

Don't ruin a good bit of rump steak with anything else but a grinding of fresh black pepper and sea salt—that's what I reckon anyway; for what it's worth!

But, you could top your steak just with a nice savoury butter as previously explained. Now if you really enjoy a sauce on top, make ahead of time some of Bazza's Barbecue Sauce (see Sauces), or some other sauce such as the pan sauces described below, which can be made right there in the frypan after you remove the steak to keep it warm.

Mushroom Sauce

Fry a finely chopped onion in the pan drippings. Add 250gm chopped brown mushrooms, stirring for about 2 minutes. Add ½ cup of dry white wine, salt and freshly ground black pepper to simmer for a few minutes.

Red Wine Sauce

Add to the pan drippings 2 chopped shallots and a chopped clove of garlic to brown a little. Add a cup of dry red wine to deglaze the pan, 1tsp balsamic vinegar, 1tsp soy sauce, some chopped parsley, salt and pepper, and allow it to reduce a little.

Whisky Sauce

Add some plain flour to the pan drippings and stir it to brown. Add some boiling water, stirring to a smooth sauce. Add 1Tbsp whisky, a chopped shallot, some chopped parsley, juice of half a lemon, salt and pepper, and allow it to simmer for a couple of minutes.

Brandy Sauce

Add some crushed garlic and ½tsp ground black pepper to the pan drippings. Add 1Tbsp brandy (or Spanish sherry), 2tsp Worcestershire sauce (or 1 anchovy), 2tsp Dijon mustard, some chopped flat-leafed parsley and finally ¾ cup cream to simmer a little.

Green Peppercorn Sauce

Add about 2Tbsp drained green peppercorns (available in very small tins from the supermarket) as the first step to the Brandy Sauce recipe above and simmer for a minute or so.

ROAST BEEF

Roasting beef could mean placing the meat on a rack, in a roasting pan, rotating it on a spit or rotisserie, or cooking it in a camp oven, Dutch oven, or even using an underground cooking method.

In all cases the goal is simply to cook all sides evenly.

There are several temperature approaches for roasting meats correctly, depending on the equipment available and the cut of meat you choose.

High-temperature cooking

At true roasting temperature of 200°C (400°F) or more, the water inside the muscle is lost at a high rate. It is suitable if a small tender cut such as fillet or scotch fillet is used, and the cooking is finished before the juices escape. Especially is this true if you want to cook the meat to no more than rare or medium rare.

Low-temperature cooking (the 'Low and Slow' method)

A low-temperature oven, 100°C to 160°C (200°F to 325°F), is best when slow-roasting large cuts of meat, turkey and even whole chickens. This method results in less moisture loss and the result is tender meat. This is also great for the flavourful tougher cuts which benefit from the long cooking time.

Combination temperature cooking

The combination method uses high heat just at the beginning or the end of the cooking, with the rest of the cooking done at a low temperature. This method produces the golden-brown caramelisation and crust due to the 'Maillard' reaction, but retains more of the moisture. This is ideal for a large beef roast.

The meat is first fried quickly in oil at high temperature on the top of the stove to 'brown the meat', giving it good colour and flavour. You could also do the same at the end of cooking as well if it is not to your liking.

I like to use my large oven-proof stainless-steel covered roasting dish for this type of task. I can 'brown' the meat in it on top of the stove, and then slip it straight into the oven with the lid on. I can also take the lid off for a while at the end if it needs a little more colour.

Oven bags are sometimes now used for a similar purpose for roasts. Simply follow the instructions on the packet.

Note that the searing of meat in no way 'locks in' the moisture. Moisture loss in meat is simply a function of heat and time.

Basting of the meat with the pan juices during cooking can help a little to reduce the moisture loss in the meat.

After cooking, it is best to cover the meat and let it 'rest' for a while. The temperature actually goes up, and it continues cooking; so it will not get cold.

Roast Beef with Yorkshire Puddings (England)

This is a classic recipe that is absolutely mouth-watering, and up there with the very best recipes in the world, in my humble opinion. It uses the combination roasting method described previously.

Ingredients

2.5Kg bolar blade roast of beef (from the shoulder)
extra virgin olive oil for cooking
Potatoes, carrots, parsnips, pumpkin, sweet potato, chopped into medium sized pieces

Method

In a very hot oven proof dish, brown the meat well on all sides in a little olive oil. Slice an onion and spread it out under the meat, with the fatty side of the meat facing up so that it tends to marinate itself. Add about 1 cup of white wine to the baking dish, and some black pepper. Cover it and cook it for 4 hours in an oven preheated to 130^0C (270^0F). Take the lid off for the last hour to brown it up all over, and baste it with the pan juices at the same time to keep it moist.

Also, for the last hour of cooking, bake the vegies in a separate tray in the oven after rubbing them all over with olive oil. Increase the heat a bit while the meat is resting.

Yorkshire Puddings

This is the traditional light batter pudding made from the pan drippings after cooking the Roast Beef. Originally, a single pudding was cooked in the pan juices under the meat as it drained, and eaten first, in order to stretch the main course a little bit further. Nowadays, individual puddings are more common, cooked in a muffin pan. They are the perfect accompaniment.

Ingredients

2 eggs
1 cup (250ml) milk
1 cup plain flour
1tsp salt
3Tbsp fat from the roast beef (make sure to leave enough to make some nice gravy)

Method

To make the Yorkshire puddings, whisk together the eggs and milk in a bowl. Add the flour and salt and whisk until you have smooth batter. Cover and set the batter aside for 30 minutes to rest. Divide the drained fat from the roast beef among a six 120ml (1/2 cup) capacity non-stick muffin pan tray, heat the tray in the oven for a few minutes, and then pour in the batter. Raise the oven temperature and cook the puddings at 180^0C for about 15 to 20 minutes until risen and browned. You can cook these while the beef is resting and being carved. It is normal for them to have a depression in the centre, but they should be light and crisp. Leave the vegies in the oven to crisp up a bit. Make some gravy with the rest of the pan drippings according to the directions on the following page. Magnificent!

Standing Beef Rib Roast with Vegetables

It is called a standing rib roast, prime rib roast, or rack of beef, because it is rib-eye steak with the bones left in. This helps heat distribution, and also makes it very tasty as the fat and juices prevent the meat from drying out. Organic grass-fed beef, aged on the bone for 2 weeks, or similar, is magnificent, if you can find it. For this dish a large roasting pan with a rack that sits about 5cm (2 inches) above the base is ideal. Buy a large bone-in rib-eye (scotch fillet) roast. A piece of about 2.5Kg with the fat layer trimmed but left on should be about four ribs worth, depending on the age of the animal, and should serve 6 to 8 people. It is an expensive cut, but makes a spectacular dish for a special occasion.

Ingredients

2.5Kg rib roast
2 finely chopped cloves fresh garlic, chopped rosemary, chopped thyme, freshly ground black pepper
4 potatoes, a sweet potato (kumara), 2 parsnips, 3 carrots, and 2 onions, chopped into large pieces.

Method

Rub the meat all over with olive oil and place it bone side down on a raised rack in a roasting pan. Sprinkle the garlic, herbs and pepper over the top. Cook the meat for an hour on high, about 220^0C, and then turn it down to medium, about 180^0C.

At this point, put your vegies in the roasting tray under the meat, making sure to turn them over well to coat them in the fat and pan juices. Cook for about one more hour, or until the vegetables are cooked to golden, and the meat is cooked to about medium or the desired degree of doneness.

Take the meat out and cover it with aluminium foil to rest for 15 minutes or so. Don't worry; it will stay hot.

Also, take out the vegies and return them to the oven on a tray for a little more time to crisp up if needed. That will also keep them hot while you are carving the meat.

Carve the meat by slicing down between the ribs, or you may want to remove the meat from the bones entirely before you slice it, serving the rib bones separately. Carving the meat at the table is also good for its pose value.

Gravy

Meanwhile, make some gravy in the roasting pan by tipping off any excess fat, leaving a little fat and the meat juices, and any juice that has drained out of the resting meat. Add a half a cup of plain flour to the pan to brown, stirring it in. Then add about 3 cups of boiling water, or a little more, along with some salt and pepper, stirring the gravy until it is smooth.

Serve the meat with the vegies on a separate platter, and the gravy in a serving jug or gravy boat on the side.

'Boeuf à la Mode' (France) - Beef in the Style, Pot Roast

The Pot Roast has got to be one of the best meals of all time! The idea is similar to other roast recipes, but with a pot roast there is a bit more liquid in the pot, and the vegetables go straight in with the meat. It ends up with a different taste, flavoured with the vegies, herbs and other ingredients that you have added. The idea is to cook it in the oven in a dish with a tightly fitting lid. As I have already mentioned, I have a large stainless-steel roasting pan with a heavy lid that I use to brown the meat and vegies on the stove top, add the other ingredients, and slip it straight into the oven, all in the same pot. You could also cook this recipe for the whole day in a slow cooker.

You cook at a moderate temperature of about $180^{o}C$. Too high, and it will boil away to nothing and possibly burn; too low, and it will not produce the steam that keeps it moist and the meat tender. So you need to lift the lid to check the temperature occasionally, keeping it just bubbling along, and keeping the level of liquid to about 4cm, topping it up with water. Give it a stir as well, about half way through cooking time.

Ingredients (Serves about 4)

2Kg pot roast, rolled beef brisket roast, bolar blade roast, or topside roast
1 finely chopped onion, carrot, and celery stalk
400gm can of chopped tomatoes
2 bay leaves and some fresh sprigs of thyme or sage (or use dried herbs)
2 cloves garlic, chopped (or use 1tsp bottled minced garlic)
2tsp soy sauce and 1tsp Worcestershire sauce, 1tsp sea salt and 1tsp black pepper
2 cups good quality dry red wine (shiraz or similar)
4 potatoes, halved
4 carrots, halved

ONE POT MEAL

Method

Brown the meat on all sides in very hot olive oil in the pan on top of the stove. Add the finely chopped onion, chopped carrot, and chopped stalk of celery (the French mirepoix combination) to the same oil to brown for a few minutes. These vegies that you put in at the start will eventually cook down for the sauce, an important part of the flavour mix. Place the beef and vegetables in a covered casserole dish.

Add the tomatoes, herbs, garlic, sauces, salt and pepper, and the wine. Cook everything for about $2\frac{1}{2}$ hours in a $180^{o}C$ moderate oven or until the beef is tender. After about $1\frac{1}{2}$ hrs cooking time, add the potatoes and carrots to the pot.

When cooked, remove the meat to a plate to rest, and cover it in foil to keep it warm. Do the same with the vegetables. Strain the sauce into a saucepan (that's where it gets its name) and pour off any excess oil. Simmer the sauce for about 5 minutes to reduce the volume a bit. If the liquid is still a bit too runny, thicken it with a 'beurre manié' (pronounced burr-mahn-yay, 'kneaded butter') by mixing 1Tbsp butter and 1Tbsp flour in a bowl till smooth, and stirring it into the sauce. Simmer it for about 3 minutes to remove the floury taste. The idea is that the butter coats the flour, so that when it is whisked into the hot mixture, the butter releases the flour without forming lumps.

Slice the beef, spoon the sauce over the beef and serve it with the vegetables, perhaps with some additional greens as well.

BRAISED BEEF

To flavour braised beef dishes, a mixture of onion, carrot and celery is often fried early in the process. In French cooking these are given the name of 'mirepoix' (pronounced mihr-pwah), after the guy who invented it. The Italian version of the same thing is called a 'soffritto'. These are the aromatic vegetables, key to a whole range of flavoursome dishes, and are used in the following recipes. The first four dishes are excellent examples of recipes for braised beef dishes, or casseroles, with variations in just the cooking liquid used, and some other minor ingredients.

'Carbonnades à la Flamande' (Belgium) - Braised Beef in Beer

Ingredients

1Kg chuck steak or shin beef, cubed
½ cup extra virgin olive oil for frying
1 large onion, 1 stick of celery, and 1 large carrot, all finely chopped.
1tsp crushed ginger
1tsp crushed garlic
½ cup plain flour
1tsp cracked black pepper
1tsp ground cumin seed
1tsp dried mixed herbs (or fresh rosemary and thyme leaves if available)
2 bay leaves, dried or fresh
1 cup beer (preferably a Belgian ale, but a pilsener style of beer also works very well)
1½ cups of water
1Tbsp brown mustard seeds
1 anchovy fillet, chopped
½ tsp sea salt

ONE POT MEAL

Method

Brown the beef in a little olive oil in an oven-proof dish in batches, and remove it from the pan to a bowl.

Then fry the onions, celery, carrot, ginger, and garlic in the same dish in a little oil for a few minutes until the onion becomes transparent.

Sprinkle over the flour, pepper, cumin, and herbs and stir the mixture until the flour starts to cook.

Deglaze the pan with the beer (this gets the tasty bits off the bottom of the pot).

Add the water, mustard seeds, anchovy, and salt. Return the beef, and stir well.

Cover the pan, and cook the dish in the oven at $180^{\circ}C$ for 2 hours.

Garnish with some flat-leafed parsley.

Perhaps serve this with hand cut potato chips rubbed with olive oil and baked in the oven for the last hour of cooking time. Whacko!

'Bouffe Bourguignonne' (France) - Braised Beef in Red Wine

This is a classic recipe that combines a range of complementary savoury flavours.
It starts with the 'mirepoix' of aromatic vegetables as a flavour base.
This, I think, is my very favourite thing to eat in the whole, whole, whole world.

Ingredients

½ cup extra virgin olive oil for frying
1Kg chuck steak or shin beef, cubed
2 rashers of bacon, rind removed, and finely chopped (or use pancetta)
1 large onion, finely chopped
1 stick of celery, finely chopped
1 large carrot, finely chopped
1tsp crushed ginger
1tsp crushed garlic
½ cup plain flour
1tsp cracked black pepper
1tsp ground cumin seed
1tsp dried mixed herbs (or fresh rosemary and thyme leaves if available)
2 bay leaves, dried or fresh
1 cup dry red wine (250ml Bordeaux, or similar). Now you're cooking with wine!
1½ cups of water
1Tbsp dark soy sauce
1 anchovy fillet, chopped
1 small tin of whole champignons
8 small whole pickling onions (small brown onions, peeled)
½tsp sea salt

ONE POT MEAL

Method

Brown the cubed beef in a little olive oil in the dish in batches, and remove it from the pan to a bowl.

Then fry the bacon, onion, celery, carrot, ginger, and garlic in the same dish in a little oil for a few minutes until the onion becomes transparent.

Sprinkle over the flour, pepper, cumin, and herbs and stir the mixture until the flour starts to cook.

Deglaze the pan with the wine. (This gets the tasty bits off the bottom). For best results, use a wine that you would be happy to drink on its own.

Add the water, soy sauce, anchovy, champignons, pickling onions, and salt.

Return the beef to the dish, and stir it in well.

Cover the pan, and cook the dish in the oven at $180^{\circ}C$ for 2 hours.

Garnish with some flat-leafed parsley.

You can serve this with some Dauphinoise potatoes, pasta, or rice.

Braised Beef in Guinness (Ireland)

Ingredients

1Kg chuck steak or shin beef, cubed
½ cup extra virgin olive oil for frying
1 large onion, 1 stick of celery, and 1 large carrot, all finely chopped.
1tsp crushed ginger
1tsp crushed garlic
½ cup plain flour
1tsp cracked black pepper
1tsp ground cumin seed
1tsp dried mixed herbs (or fresh rosemary and thyme leaves if available)
2 bay leaves, dried or fresh
1 cup Guinness (what could I do with the rest I wonder? Hmmm...)
1½ cups of water
1Tbsp dark soy sauce
1 anchovy fillet, chopped
8 prunes, de-pitted
½ tsp sea salt

ONE POT MEAL

Method

Brown the beef in a little olive oil in the dish in batches, and remove it from the pan to a bowl.

Then fry the onions, celery, carrot, ginger, and garlic in the same dish in a little oil for a few minutes until the onion becomes transparent.

Sprinkle over the flour, pepper, cumin, and herbs and stir the mixture until the flour starts to cook.

Deglaze the pan with the Guinness (this gets the tasty bits off the bottom of the pan).

Add the water, soy sauce, anchovy, prunes and salt.

Return the beef to the pot, and stir well.

Cover the pan, and cook the dish in the oven at $180^{\circ}C$ for 2 hours.

Garnish with some flat-leafed parsley.

Serve this with some mashed murphies and perhaps some carrots and peas for an authentic and delicious Irish meal that is pretty hard to beat.

Guinness Pie

You could also try your hand at making an authentic Guinness Beef Pie, if you really want to show off; now that you have come this far.

Simply use some ready-made butter puff pastry sheets to line a deep pie dish and fill the pie with the mixture. You may need to thicken it a bit with about 3tsp cornflour mixed in with ½ cup of water.

This is a truly special thing to eat, to be sure, to be sure.

Braised Beef in Pedro Ximénez Sherry (Spain)

Ingredients

1Kg chuck steak, or shin beef, cubed
½ cup extra virgin olive oil for frying
1 chorizo sausage, sliced into 1cm pieces
1 large onion, 1 stick of celery, and 1 large carrot, all finely chopped.
1tsp crushed ginger
1tsp crushed garlic
½ cup plain flour
1tsp cracked black pepper
1tsp ground cumin seed
1tsp dried mixed herbs (or fresh rosemary and thyme leaves if available)
2 bay leaves, dried or fresh
1 cup good quality Pedro Ximénez Spanish Sherry (this is the grape variety)
1½ cups of water
1Tbsp dark soy sauce
1 anchovy fillet, chopped
2 red chillies, chopped
½tsp sea salt

ONE POT MEAL

Method

Brown the beef in a little olive oil in the dish in batches, and remove it from the pan to a bowl.

Then fry the chorizo until nicely seared and remove from the pan.

Then fry the onions, celery, carrot, ginger, and garlic in the same dish in a little oil for a few minutes until the onion becomes transparent.

Sprinkle over the flour, pepper, cumin, and herbs and stir the mixture until the flour starts to cook.

Deglaze the pan with the sherry (this gets the tasty bits off the bottom).

Add the water, soy sauce, anchovy, chillies and salt. Return the beef, and stir well.

Cover the pan, and cook the dish in the oven at 180°C for 2 hours.

Garnish with some flat-leafed parsley.

Serve with lightly fried flour tortillas or quesadillas with cheese.

Or, you could serve some Salsa Verde on the side.

'Salsa Verde' (Spain) - Green Sauce

Put into a blender a bunch of flat leaf parsley, a clove of garlic, a tablespoon of capers, the juice of one lemon, 1/3 cup olive oil, salt and pepper.
Serve on the side.

'Osso Bucco alla Milanese' (Italy) – Bone with a Hole

This is a classic Italian braised beef or veal dish from Milan, made from shin beef, which has a large marrow bone in the middle (the origin of the name). The gristle and marrow break down magically with long cooking, giving tender meat and fabulous flavour. Another similar dish is 'Spezzatino di Manzo' or Braised Beef, often made with chuck steak and sometimes veal, and sometimes with chunky vegetables added. It also starts with a 'soffritto' of onion, carrot and celery lightly fried in olive oil.
The French do a similar thing which they call 'Daube de Boeuf'.

Ingredients (serves 4)

1.5Kg (about 8) veal osso bucco shin slices on the bone, or use boneless gravy beef
50gm (1/3 cup) plain flour seasoned with 1tsp sea salt and 1tsp black pepper
1tsp dried mixed herbs
extra virgin olive oil for frying the meat
1 carrot, 1 onion, 1 stick celery, all finely chopped
400gm can of diced tomatoes
1 cup Chianti (or other full-bodied dry red wine)
4 sprigs fresh thyme
2 garlic cloves, crushed
2 dried bay leaves
8 pitted black olives
2tsp soy sauce
1 anchovy fillet

ONE POT MEAL

Method

Get a plastic bag and put in the veal shin pieces with the plain flour, salt and pepper, and mixed herbs. Twist the top and shake until the veal is coated in the seasoned flour. Then brown the veal pieces in a frying pan with some oil and remove them.

Then brown the chopped onion, carrot, and celery in the same pan with a little more oil if necessary, and remove this to a casserole dish with the veal pieces, the tomatoes, red wine, thyme, garlic, bay leaves, olives, soy sauce, and anchovy fillet, and cook it covered in the oven for about $2\frac{1}{2}$ hours at 180^0C until the meat almost falls from the bones.

Add a little water during cooking if it appears to be a bit dry. Season it with a little extra salt and pepper to taste. Great served with risoni pasta (rice pasta), or mashed potatoes and greens.

Make a traditional Gremolata by combining the following ingredients in a bowl, and sprinkling this over the veal to serve (in a similar way to the similar practice in French, Greek, and Cajun cuisines).

Gremolata (Italy)

$\frac{1}{2}$ cup chopped fresh continental parsley
2 garlic cloves, crushed, or very finely chopped
2tsp finely grated lemon rind

'Chilli Colorado con Carne' (Mexico) - Red Chilli with Meat

This dish combines the wonderful flavours of red chilli, ground cumin, beef, and onion.

It uses an unusual method (not well known) where the onions are added right at the end of cooking time to produce a very different and very appealing flavour.

Ingredients

1.5Kg chuck steak, cubed
½ cup red wine
¼ cup olive oil
2tsp ground red chilli
1tsp freshly ground black pepper
1Tbsp tequila (if available, or use sherry)
extra olive oil for frying
6 hot red chillies, chopped
3Tbsp fresh ground cumin
3 cloves garlic, crushed
3 cups beef stock
1tsp sea salt
½tsp freshly ground, or cracked, black pepper
3 brown onions, peeled and finely chopped

ONE POT MEAL

Method

Marinate the cubed beef in the wine, oil, chilli, pepper, and tequila for an hour.

Brown the steak in the olive oil in batches in a large, heavy saucepan.

Add the chillies, cumin, garlic, stock, salt and pepper, and cook it in the closed pot on the top of the stove for about 2½ hours till tender. Or, you may choose to cook it in the oven.

It should cook down to where it is fairly dry and there is not a lot of liquid left. For this reason, you will need to keep an eye on it so that it does not stick to the pot and burn.

About 15 minutes before the end of your cooking time, add the finely chopped onions to the mixture, and stir to combine well. Let this simmer with the lid off till you are ready to serve it.

One of the simplest and yet tastiest beef dishes you will ever eat, I reckon, IMHO!

Serve with some flour tortillas.

If you wish, you can roll up portions of the mixture in some flour tortillas, and cook them lightly in just a little olive oil in a frypan to make Chimichangas (this is a Spanish word that means 'thingamajig').

This food is pretty blooming rip; like a stocking on a chicken's lip.

A real Mexican delicacy.

Braised Beef with Dumplings (Australia)

This recipe is often called 'Braised Steak and Onions', or 'Bossy (the cow) in a Bowl', and when cooked with dumplings is very similar to the English dish 'Beef Cobbler', and also similar to the American version of it called 'Beef and Biscuits'.

Ingredients

1 Kg chuck steak or shin beef, cubed
½ cup extra virgin olive oil for frying
2 large onions, 1 large carrot, and 1 stick of celery, all finely chopped
1tsp crushed ginger and 1tsp crushed garlic
½ cup plain flour
1tsp ground cumin seed
1tsp dried mixed herbs (or fresh rosemary and thyme leaves if available)
2 bay leaves, dried or fresh
½tsp sea salt and ½tsp cracked black pepper
1 cup dry red wine (shiraz or cabernet sauvignon or similar)
1½ cups of water
1 dash of soy sauce
1 anchovy fillet, chopped

ONE POT MEAL

Method

A large ovenproof covered dish is ideal for this recipe. Otherwise use a frypan to start the cooking and a casserole dish to finish the cooking in the oven.
Brown the beef in a little olive oil in the dish in batches, and remove it from the pan. Fry the onions, carrot, celery, ginger, and garlic in a little more oil for a few minutes. Sprinkle over the flour, cumin, herbs, salt and pepper, and stir it till the flour starts to cook. Then add the wine, water, soy sauce, and anchovy, and return the beef to the pan. Cover and cook it in the oven at $180^{0}C$ for 2 hours.

Dumplings Ingredients (makes about 8)

2 cups S. R. Flour, plus extra for kneading
1tsp dried mixed herbs
¼ cup finely grated parmesan cheese (optional), or caraway seeds
½tsp fine sea salt
60gm cold butter and 1 cup full cream milk

Method

Mix the flour, herbs, cheese, and salt together in a large bowl. Rub the butter into the flour with your fingers until it resembles fine breadcrumbs. Make a well in the centre and mix in enough milk, working it with your hands, till you have firm dough, and then knead the dough on a lightly floured surface until it is smooth.

Roll it out to about 2½cm in thickness, and use a glass to stamp out rounds of dough. Place these on top of the braised beef, leaving a little space between each one to allow for expansion, and cook uncovered for the last 25 minutes of the above cooking time, or until the dumplings are browned on top. Garnish with some flat-leafed parsley.

Beef 'Stroganov' (Russia) – Shaved Beef with Sour Cream

This dish originated over a hundred years ago in Russia, where it seems that the Stroganov family originated. The recipe has varied quite a bit since then.

You may want to try a similar dish, often called 'Chicken Fricassee', made by using chicken strips with a similar cooking method.

Ingredients

600gm good quality rump or fillet steak, sliced thinly across the grain for tenderness
½ cup extra virgin olive oil for frying
1 onion, finely chopped
2 cloves garlic, crushed
400gm tin button mushrooms, drained and sliced
½ cup white wine
1 Tbsp tomato paste
300ml carton of sour cream
a dash of Worcestershire sauce
1 tsp Dijon mustard
1 tsp sweet paprika
1 tsp sugar
½ tsp sea salt
½ tsp ground white pepper
Finely chopped fresh parsley

ONE POT MEAL

Method

Brown the meat in batches in olive oil in a heavy-based frying pan over high heat, without overcooking it.

Remove it from the pan and set it aside.

Cook the onion in oil for 2-3 minutes, or until soft and translucent, and then add the garlic and stir briefly.

Add the mushrooms and cook for about 3 minutes, or until soft.

Deglaze the pan by adding the white wine (this gets the good stuff off the bottom).

Stir in the tomato paste, sour cream, Worcestershire sauce, mustard, paprika, sugar, salt and pepper.

Return the beef strips to the pan and stir until heated through and the sauce has thickened and reduced a little.

Sprinkle with chopped parsley as a garnish.

Serve this with whatever vegies work for you, or perhaps some rice.

OTHER BEEF RECIPES

Meat Loaf (England, Europe)

Ingredients

1Kg lean beef mince. You could also use a mixture of pork and veal mince.
1 cup breadcrumbs
1 brown onion and 1 clove garlic, both finely chopped
1Tbsp mixed herbs
1Tbsp tomato paste
1 egg
½ cup red wine
2tsp Worcestershire sauce and 2tsp soy sauce
1tsp sea salt and 1tsp freshly ground black pepper

Method

Mix together all of the above ingredients in a bowl and put the mixture into a shallow oven dish. Level it out, and bake it for about ½ hour in a moderate oven.
Serve these two recipes with tomato sauce (ketchup) or the Cumberland Sauce below.

Beef Rissoles (Australia, Denmark-'frikadeller', elsewhere)

Ingredients

1Kg lean beef mince (from a cow raised on a hillside - humour)
1 cup breadcrumbs
1 brown onion, very finely chopped
2 eggs
1Tbsp plain flour
some chopped flat-leaf parsley
sea salt and freshly ground black pepper

BARBECUE FRIENDLY

Method

Mix together all the above ingredients in a bowl, and roll portions of the mixture into patties about 5cm in diameter. Roll these in either plain flour or breadcrumbs, and cook in hot oil in a frying pan or on the barbecue hotplate till cooked through.

Cumberland Sauce (England)

The juice of 1 orange and 1Tbsp orange zest
1Tbsp brown sugar
200mg jar of red currant jelly
½ cup port or Pedro Ximénez Spanish sherry
1tsp minced ginger, 1tsp paprika, and 1tsp Hot English mustard
¼tsp sea salt and ¼tsp white pepper
Simmer the above ingredients for 20 minutes in a saucepan. Then thicken it with 2tsp cornflour mixed into ½ cup red wine, and simmer for a further 1 minute.

Beef 'Chop Suey' (China)

This contains the basic ingredients of what would resemble a Chinese Beef Chop Suey ('assorted pieces'). The original recipes may have contained all sorts of these assorted pieces.

The recipe also contains some noodles, so it might also be loosely called a Beef Chow Mein ('fried noodles'), a dish with many variations.

A very basic version of this was the only thing that I could cook in my bachelor days, and a potful of this stuff lasted me for quite a few meals.

My handwritten recipe came from my Mum, who originally obtained it from my sister-in-law Lynne, who I suspect got the basis of it from the back of a soup packet (don't knock it; there are many very workable recipes on packets and labels).

It actually tastes better than it sounds. In fact, if you were to roll up all of the ingredients in the cabbage leaves, you would have something similar to a dish called, 'Cabbage Rolls'.

It is very comestible provender indeed!

Ingredients

40gm butter
500gm minced steak
1 onion, peeled and chopped
1 carrot, peeled and chopped
1 stalk celery, peeled and chopped
1 clove garlic, peeled and chopped
100gm green beans, peeled
¼ cabbage, sliced (Savoy or Won bok)
1 small pkt rice noodles
½tsp ground cumin
½tsp ground coriander
½tsp fenugreek seed
½ tsp ground turmeric
½tsp sea salt
½tsp white pepper
2 cups water
1Tbsp dark soy sauce

ONE POT MEAL

Method

Brown the meat and onion in the butter in a large saucepan on top of the stove.

Add the carrot, celery and garlic to fry for a couple of minutes.

Add the rest of the ingredients.

Cook for 30 minutes, stirring often.

Serve the Chop Suey in bowls.

Extra soy sauce can be added if desired.

CLASSIC VEAL RECIPES

'Pörkölt' (Hungary) - Hungarian Goulash

A surprising amount of development has gone into this relatively simple recipe and the related ones, from the passing on of early varieties of paprika grown by the Romans and Turks. Painstaking breeding and much scientific research in recent times have yielded many varieties of the spice, which, like the tomato, is of the potato family, and have also given rise to production methods that are a Hungarian national tradition.

The dish uses lots of onions, lots of paprika, and a few tricks that need to be adhered to. The most popular variety of paprika used is a mild one called Noble-Sweet, although some people add some of the more pungent varieties to it as well.

Authentically, it is best dissolved in hot lard, but not at too high a temperature as it will burn the paprika, causing it to lose its colour and flavour.

As in Hungary, you can use any kind of meat that you wish with the same recipe.

Ingredients

1.5Kg cubed shin beef or veal
lard (or olive oil if you prefer)
4 large, finely chopped onions
4tsp sweet paprika
1tsp sea salt
1tsp freshly ground black pepper
1 chopped green capsicum
2 chopped tomatoes
1 red chilli, finely chopped
1 cup water or red wine
½ cup cream and ½ cup sour cream, mixed

ONE POT MEAL

Method

In a large covered pot or casserole dish fry the onions in the lard on the top of the stove using moderate heat with the lid on, until the onions are golden yellow. They take longer with the lid on, but the onion fibres break down, making the dish thick at the end, and also readily digestible. This is one of the tricks. There is no need to thicken the dish at the end of cooking.

Take the onions off the heat, and add the paprika, mixing it thoroughly, and add the water, or red wine.

Now add the cubed meat, and the salt and freshly ground black pepper.

Add the chopped green capsicum, the chopped tomatoes, and the chilli.

Cook the dish at a simmer for about 1½ to 2 hours, adding extra water if necessary to prevent it from burning.

As an alternative, you can add ½ cup of cream and ½ cup of sour cream at the end, but do not bring it to the boil again.

Veal 'Cordon Bleu' (France) – Blue ribbon

Ingredients

olive oil for frying
4 veal steaks (escalopes), pounded to about 5mm thickness with a meat mallet
4 slices of Gruyère (or Swiss) cheese
4 small slices of quality leg ham
plain flour for dusting, seasoned with salt and pepper
1 egg, whipped with a dash of milk using a fork
1 cup breadcrumbs

Method

Place a slice of cheese and a piece of ham on the end of each piece of veal.

Fold the veal over to encase the filling, and seal the edges with a little of the egg.

Using the meat mallet, lightly tamp around the edges to seal them.

Dip each piece in seasoned flour, then the egg, then breadcrumbs, to coat them.

Fry the veal escalopes in oil till golden and cooked through.

Serve with your choice of vegies.

BARBECUE FRIENDLY

'Wiener Schnitzel' (Austria) - Viennese boneless cutlet

In Austria, Wiener Schnitzel is protected by law, and must be made from veal.

There are many variations of this dish around the world. They are very versatile, with many options available to you for toppings or sauces.

Ingredients

olive oil for frying
4 thin veal steaks, about 5mm thick (or pound them a little thinner if you wish)
plain flour for dusting, seasoned with salt and pepper
1 egg, whipped with a dash of milk using a fork
1 cup breadcrumbs

Method

Dip each piece of veal in seasoned flour, then the egg, then breadcrumbs, to coat them.

Fry the veal steaks in oil till golden and cooked through.

Top with some gherkins and capers, and serve with quartered lemon on the side.

Or, pour over a lemon sauce, or mushroom sauce, or onion gravy (See Sauces).

BRAISED VEAL DISHES

'Stifado' (Greece) - Veal and Vegetable Stew

My friend, Helen, who came from the island of Lesbos in Greece originally, showed me this recipe. I am amazed at how really simple, yet how very tasty it is.

Ingredients

800gm thinly sliced boneless veal cutlets
½ cup extra virgin olive oil
1 onion, finely diced
1 stick of celery, finely diced
1 clove garlic, finely diced
½ cup white wine
1 cup tomato puree
1 cup water
a few fresh basil leaves
a few fresh flat-leafed parsley leaves
½tsp ground cumin seed
½tsp sea salt
½tsp freshly ground black pepper
2 carrots, chopped
150gm whole green beans, topped and tailed
4 potatoes, thinly sliced
300gm Greek fetta cheese

ONE POT MEAL

Method

Cook the veal slices in a large pot in the oil in batches till lightly browned.

Remove them from the pot.

Add a little more oil and lightly fry the onion, celery, and garlic till the onion is translucent.

Add the wine to deglaze the pan and stir gently (to get the tasty bits off the bottom).

Return the veal to the pot.

Add the tomato puree, water, basil, parsley, cumin, salt and pepper.

Cook this, covered, for about 30 minutes.

Add the carrots, layer the beans in a lattice across the top, and finally, lay the potato slices over the top in an overlapping pattern.

Grind a little more salt and pepper on top, and cook, covered, for 30 minutes more.

Serve the dish topped with some cubes of good Greek fetta cheese.

Fantastikos!

'Scaloppini di Vitello con Funghi' (Italy) - Veal and Mushrooms

Ingredients

800gm thin (1cm) veal slices, dredged in plain flour seasoned with salt and pepper
½ cup extra virgin olive oil and 25gms butter for frying
1 brown onion and 1 clove garlic, finely diced
½ cup dry white wine
3 sprigs of fresh thyme (or use 1tsp dried thyme)
½tsp sea salt and ½tsp freshly ground black pepper
½ cup cream
1 small can champignons (button mushrooms)
1 anchovy fillet, finely chopped
1Tbsp Dijon mustard

Method

Dredge the veal slices in seasoned flour, brown them in the oil in a frypan, and remove.
Add the butter to the pan, and lightly fry the onion and garlic till translucent.
Deglaze the pan with the wine, and add the thyme, salt and pepper, and the cream.
Add the champignons, anchovy, and mustard, and stir it together.
Return the veal to the pan to heat through. Serve garnished with chopped parsley.

Veal Marsala (Sicily)

Ingredients

800gm thin veal slices (1cm), dredged in plain flour seasoned with salt and pepper
½ cup extra virgin olive oil for frying
25gm butter
1 brown onion and 1 clove garlic, finely diced
½ cup Sicilian Marsala (or Portuguese Madeira, or Spanish Sherry)
3 sprigs of fresh thyme (or use 1 tsp dried thyme)
½tsp sea salt and ½tsp freshly ground black pepper
½ cup cream
1 small can champignons (button mushrooms)
1 anchovy fillet, finely chopped
1Tbsp Dijon mustard

Method

Dredge the veal slices in seasoned flour, brown them in the oil in a frypan, and remove.
Add the butter to the pan, and lightly fry the onion and garlic till translucent.
Deglaze the pan with the wine, and add the thyme, salt and pepper, and the cream.
Add the champignons, anchovy, and mustard, and stir it together.
Return the veal to the pan to heat through. Serve garnished with chopped parsley.
Note: Sicilian Marsala is a very fine, fortified wine of high quality, and does not contain eggs like some cheaper imitations.

Veal 'Scaloppine' with Lemon and Capers (Italy)

Ingredients

800gm thin (1cm) veal slices, dredged in plain flour seasoned with salt and pepper
½ cup extra virgin olive oil and 25gm butter for frying
1 brown onion and 1 clove garlic, finely chopped
½ cup dry white wine
3 sprigs of fresh thyme (or use 1tsp dried thyme leaves)
½tsp sea salt and ½tsp freshly ground black pepper
½ cup chicken stock
½Tbsp capers (available in a jar)
1 anchovy fillet, finely chopped
1 lemon, juiced

Method

Dredge the veal slices in seasoned flour, brown them in the oil in a frypan, and remove. They should only take about 5 minutes to cook.
Add the butter to the pan, and lightly fry the onion and garlic till translucent.
Deglaze the pan with the wine, and add the thyme, salt and pepper, and the stock.
When it has reduced a little, add the capers, anchovy, and lemon juice, and stir it.
Return the veal to the pan to heat through. Serve garnished with chopped parsley.

Veal 'Saltimbocca' (Italy) - Jump in the Mouth

Ingredients

800gm thin (1cm) veal slices (look for nice light-coloured meat), about 4
8 thin slices of prosciutto
½ cup extra virgin olive oil and 25gm butter for frying
1 brown onion and 1 clove garlic, finely diced
½ cup dry white wine
12 fresh sage leaves (or use dried sage leaves)
½tsp sea salt and ½tsp freshly ground black pepper
½ cup chicken stock
½Tbsp capers (available in a jar from the supermarket)
1 anchovy fillet, finely chopped
1 lemon, juiced

Method

Season the veal slices with a little salt and pepper, wrap 2 slices of prosciutto around each slice, and brown them in enough oil in a frypan till cooked through, and remove.
Add the butter to the pan, and lightly fry the onion and garlic till translucent.
Deglaze the pan with the wine, and add the sage, salt and pepper, and the stock.
When it has reduced a little, add the capers, anchovy, and lemon juice, and stir it.
Return the veal to the pan to heat through. Serve garnished with chopped parsley.

BREADS

INFORMATION ABOUT FLOUR

Here are a few facts about flour and the various types that are available.
Wheat is the most common grain used, but rice, corn, rye, and others are used.
The higher the protein content of the flour, the harder it will be, and the more suitable for breads. The lower the protein, the softer the flour, and the more suitable for cakes, biscuits and pie crusts. Check the figures on the packet.

WHOLEMEAL FLOUR

This is wheat flour that is ground on a traditional millstone using the whole grain.

PLAIN (ALL PURPOSE) FLOUR

This is fine flour milled from the inner part of the wheat kernel. It mostly comes pre-sifted, requiring a stir before levelling off when measuring. Steel roller mills are used.

SELF-RAISING FLOUR

This is a plain flour that has had baking powder and salt added to it. The leavening reacts during the cooking process to produce carbon dioxide, which aerates the mixture and makes it rise.

OO FLOUR

This is a superfine plain flour used especially for making pizzas and focaccia.

DURUM SEMOLINA FLOUR

Flour from durum wheat used to make pasta and couscous. It is yellow in colour and high in gluten.

CORNFLOUR

These days it can be made from corn, or also from light plain wheaten flour.
It is most often used for thickening certain sauces and dishes such as Chinese dishes, stews or casseroles.

Basic Batters

Plain Batter
1 cup plain flour
1 egg
1tsp oil
1¼ cups milk
1 pinch salt

Beer Batter
¾ cup plain flour
1 egg
2tsp melted butter
¾ cup flat beer
1 pinch salt

Tempura Batter
½ cup plain flour
½ cup cornflour
1tsp baking powder
1 cup soda water

THE SCIENCE OF BAKING POWDER

Here is some food science that may be over the head of some of you folk mentioned on the front cover, but there are probably some geeks out there who will find this mildly interesting (nonetheless, please keep reading, you might learn something).

Baking powder contains three things. The first is a base (an alkali), usually bicarbonate of soda (sodium hydrogen carbonate), which is also called baking soda. The second is an acidic ingredient, such as cream of tartar (potassium bitartrate) or calcium phosphate. And third is a starch, such as corn flour or rice flour, to keep the mixture of the other two dry. All three ingredients are powders, and are packaged together.

Incidentally, cream of tartar is tartaric acid which is a by-product of the wine-making industry, and sodium bicarbonate can be found in natural deposits, and so both have been used in cooking for a very long time.

The most common baking powder currently used in Australia is Ward's™ baking powder. It contains rice flour rather than corn flour so is gluten free and is phosphate based.

Acids are souring ingredients. When a recipe contains other souring ingredients, such as sour cream, yoghurt, or milk soured with lemon or vinegar, chocolate, fruits, honey, golden syrup or molasses, then usually plain baking soda is used rather than baking powder. If you use baking soda without other acidic ingredients, the taste can be bitter. Baking powder is used in baking cakes, scones, biscuits where there isn't any other acid or souring component, and the taste is neutral.

Self-raising flour contains plain flour and bicarbonate of soda and either cream of tartar or a phosphate. If a recipe says plain flour and bicarbonate of soda, then other ingredients in it are acting as a souring agent and using self-raising flour will not work. Self-raising flour cannot be substituted for plain flour without altering the recipe.

If you want to make your own self-raising flour, then you add to each cup of plain flour 2tsp baking powder, or, $1\frac{1}{4}$tsp cream of tartar and $\frac{1}{2}$tsp bicarbonate of soda (baking soda).

What really happens in cooking (concentrate really hard now) is this:

When you mix a liquid into the dry ingredients, a chemical reaction starts between the bicarbonate of soda and the acid, giving off bubbles of carbon dioxide that make the existing bubbles in the mixture larger.

Where you see the expression, 'cream the butter and the sugar', you need to make sure to do that well, because that makes the initial bubbles. The baking powder then adds carbon dioxide to the bubbles. For this reason you need to cook the mixture straight after mixing in the liquids.

There are some double-acting baking powders that have a second reaction when they get to a high temperature, as they contain an extra acid such as calcium aluminium phosphate, or sodium aluminium sulphate. I prefer not to use these aluminium-containing chemicals in my food.

Garlic Naan (India, Iran)

Ingredients

1 sachet of 8gms dried yeast mixed into ¾ cup warm water
2 cups plain (all purpose) flour
1tsp castor sugar
1tsp salt
1tsp crushed garlic
2Tbsp olive oil
2Tbsp plain yoghurt

Method

Mix the yeast in the water and leave it to stand for 15 minutes.
Mix the liquid into the sifted dry ingredients of flour, sugar, and salt.
Add the garlic, olive oil, and yoghurt, and mix together into dough.
Knead the dough till smooth on a floured surface, and store it in a warm place for an hour in a greased bowl or until it has doubled in size. Punch it down and knead it again for 5 minutes. Divide the dough into 6, and roll each out into 20cm rounds on a lightly oiled surface. Cook each piece in a very hot heavy frying pan both sides until puffy.

Chapattis (India)

Ingredients

½ cup milk, plus 1 egg, plus 1Tbsp olive oil
1 cup plain (all purpose) flour
1 cup whole meal flour
1tsp castor sugar
1tsp salt
½ tsp baking powder

Method

Mix together the milk, egg, and oil. Pour this into a bowl containing the dry ingredients of flour, sugar, salt, and baking powder, and mix this together to make dough.
Knead it on a smooth work surface, using a little extra flour until you have smooth dough, and cover it for half an hour. Divide the dough into about 8 pieces, and roll each out on an oiled surface to make rounds of about 20cm diameter and 2mm thick.
Place them one at a time in a heavy, hot frying pan and evenly cook them for about 1 minute each side until golden and slightly charred, using a drizzle of extra oil in the pan if needed. Flip them back quickly again, and they should puff up a little.
Cover them with a napkin to keep them moist until you are ready to eat.

Rotis (Fiji)

Into 3 cups of plain flour, rub about 2Tbsp butter or olive oil. Mix in enough hot water to make dough. Knead the dough until smooth, roll it into balls and roll them flat. Cook them in a little olive oil in a hot pan until puffy.

These are very similar to Parathas and many other regional unleavened flatbreads. The deep-fried version is known as Puri, which is often stuffed with assorted fillings.

Rotis (Thailand)

The famous Thai rotis can be made by mixing some soft dough from 3 cups plain flour, 1tsp salt, 1Tbsp caster sugar, 1Tbsp milk, 1 egg and about ¾ cup of water. Roll the dough into 3cm balls, drizzle with some extra light olive oil, and rest them for about an hour. Then press them flat, slap, rotate and turn them on a benchtop or board until very thin. Twirl them to a circular shape, or fold square containing egg or banana, and shallow fry.

Cheesy Crust Focaccia with Rosemary and Garlic (Italy)

Ingredients

3 cups of plain bread flour
1tsp sugar
1tsp of good quality sea salt flakes
1 cup warm water or a little more
4tsp olive oil
7gm sachet of dried yeast
tasty cheese, sliced into long fingers
extra oil for topping
some fresh rosemary leaves
3 cloves fresh garlic, very finely sliced
good quality sea salt flakes (such as Maldon salt, Himalayan salt, Australian Lake salt)

> Centuries-old Focaccia, meaning 'baking hearth', is always made using good olive oil

Method

Combine one cup of flour, sugar, and salt.
In a jug combine the warm water, oil and yeast, and let it activate for a few minutes.
Gradually add more flour as you stir the liquid into the dough, and continue stirring until the dough is thick and stretchy.
Dust a pan with flour and knead the dough for five minutes.
Place the dough in a well-oiled bowl covered in cling wrap, in a warm place, and let it rise for thirty minutes or more until it doubles in size.
Stretch it out onto an oiled tray, poking it with your fingers to make little dents. Bring the edges up the sides a bit, so that you can slide the cheese fingers into it.
Put the cheese edge on, and roll the pastry over it, enclosing the cheese.
Brush the top of the focaccia with the extra oil.
Sprinkle over the rosemary leaves, and the garlic. Sprinkle salt flakes over the top.
You could add some chopped olives or a few thin tomato slices, but it is usually best to keep it fairly plain. Bake it in the oven for about 30 minutes at $180^{0}C$.

Damper (Australia)

Damper was originally very rough bush bread made by Australian stockmen and early colonials who carried the basic staples of plain flour, salt, sugar, and tea with them, and supplemented this with whatever meat they could catch themselves in the bush.
So, damper, the name of which came from the idea of damping down the coals to cook, or maybe even damping the appetite, was made just with flour, salt, and water.
It was pretty tough and often black from the coals of the fire in which it was cooked for about thirty minutes. They may have taken some clues from aboriginal women who cooked a similar thing from seasonal grains and nuts. Small loaves gained the name of Johnny Cakes. Some of the bushies would also knead it on a cardboard box, and either cook it in the fire coals, on a sheet of tin or wire mesh, wrapped around a stick, or perhaps in a frying pan with the bacon fat.
A little later, it had baking soda added to it to give it a bit of a lift. Later again, butter and milk were added when available, and damper became a little like a large scone. It is pretty much the same recipe as for Irish Soda Bread, with the Irish settlers or convicts possibly having some influence on the development of the recipe.
The Irish Spotted Dog is similar, but with the addition of an egg and some sultanas.
Here is a delicious modern Damper used by bush-bashers everywhere:

Ingredients

3 cups S.R. Flour
1tsp sea salt
50gm butter
½ cup milk
½ cup water or a little more

Method

Rub the butter into the mixture of flour and salt until it resembles breadcrumbs.
Add the milk and water and knead it until you have firm dough.
Note: The same result was often achieved by melting the butter in the liquid before mixing it into the dry ingredients.
Bake it whole in the oven at $180^{\circ}C$ on a greased tray for about half an hour or so, until it sounds hollow when tapped.
You can also cook it in a camp oven (cast iron cooking pot) over hot coals, with a shovelful of hot coals placed on top of the lid.

Plain Scones (Scotland)

Make about 12 scones using the above recipe. Cut the dough into rounds with a drinking glass, and bake the scones on a lightly greased tray at $180^{\circ}C$ for about 12 minutes.
In the USA, similar small bread is known as Biscuits, which are usually cooked with fat.
You can make great Herb Scones to accompany a casserole by adding chopped chives and parsley, or even some grated cheese.
For Wholemeal Date Scones, use instead 1½ cups Wholemeal S.R. Flour and 1½ cups White S.R. Flour, and add ¾ cup chopped pitted dates, and 1tsp mixed spice.

Crêpes (France)

Ingredients (makes about 12)

1 cup plain flour
2 cups milk
3 eggs
butter for cooking

Method

Sift the flour into a bowl, and add the milk and eggs, whisking until well combined.
Heat a medium size, non-stick frying pan over medium heat. A 22cm crêpe pan is best.
Put a knob of butter into the pan to melt, swirling it around.
Pour a ladle of batter into the pan, swirling it to cover the whole base with a layer.
Cook them for about 2 minutes until light golden, turn over, and cook for 1 minute.
Transfer to a plate and cover to keep warm. Repeat with the remaining batter.
A variety of sweet or savoury fillings can be made for Crêpes.
Dessert crêpes options might include:
- Sprinkling with sugar and squeezing over some lemon juice.
- Serve with fruit (maybe brandied cumquats) and ice cream.
- Serve with strawberries and pour over chocolate sauce or topping.

For savoury crêpes, please see Duck and Pork.

Pancakes (International)

These are also known as pikelets, hotcakes, flapjacks, and drop scones, and by many other regional names as well.
Basic pancakes, it is thought, may possibly be the earliest known cereal food.

Ingredients (Makes about 8)

1 cup S. R. Flour
1 cup milk
1 egg
¼ cup sugar
butter for cooking

Method

Mix the pancake batter using the above ingredients. Fry spoonfuls of batter in butter in a frying pan until golden both sides.
Some sweet toppings might include:
- Butter, jam, and whipped cream.
- Sliced bananas and maple syrup.
- Fruit and plain yoghurt.
- Fried apple, banana, or pineapple, with whipped cream

You can also make some delicious apple pikelets (memories of my childhood come flashing back) by adding some finely chopped apple to the pancake mixture.

CAKES, SLICES AND BISCUITS

CAKE INGREDIENTS

Generally speaking, eggs add structure, volume, flavour and moisture to a cake. Butter provides flavour, tenderness and volume. Sugar provides sweetness, colour, and slows down gluten development for tenderness. The liquids dissolve the salt and sugar, add colour and flavour, activate the baking powder, and produce steam to help the cake rise.

TRUE SPONGE CAKE

A true sponge cake contains separated eggs, no butter, and no baking powder. It contains lots of eggs and sugar, but no raising agents. It relies on the quantity of air beaten into both the yolks and the whites of the eggs, and the expansion of that air in baking. It requires a moderate oven of about 165^0C.

Cream of tartar, or another acid, appears to be a desirable ingredient of sponge cakes, and essential to angel food cakes, to retain cake volume to the end of cooking.

Good Old-Fashioned Lemon Sponge

Ingredients

6 eggs, separated into yolks and whites
1 cup caster sugar
the grated rind (zest) of one-half of a lemon
1 Tbsp lemon juice
1 cup plain cake flour
$\frac{1}{4}$ tsp salt

Method

Beat the egg yolks with an electric mixer until thick and a lemon-colour.

Add $\frac{1}{2}$ cup of the sugar gradually, and continue beating.

Add $\frac{1}{2}$ of the lemon juice and the lemon rind, and beat it in.

In a separate bowl, beat the egg whites until stiff. Add the other $\frac{1}{2}$ of the lemon juice and the other $\frac{1}{2}$ cup of sugar, and continue beating until stiff peaks form.

Fold the egg whites into the yolks with a silicone spatula (or similar).

When the whites are partially mixed with the yolks, carefully cut and fold in the flour that has been mixed and sifted with the salt.

Bake one hour in a slow oven, in an angel cake (tube) pan or until a toothpick inserted comes out clean.

Invert the cake to cool completely before removing it from the pan.

ANGEL FOOD CAKE

This type of cake uses separated eggs, but uses the whites only, no butter, and no baking powder.

It was originally named as an opposite of the chocolate 'Devil's Food Cake'.

No butter is used in these cakes, as it would affect the egg whites' ability to stop the cake from sinking.

A special angel cake tin that has a centre tube is often used.

Angel Food Cake

Ingredients

9 egg whites
1tsp cream of tartar
1 cup sugar
7/8 cup flour
1/8tsp salt
1tsp vanilla essence

Method

Beat the whites of the eggs to froth, add the cream of tartar and beat till the eggs are stiff but not dry, then gradually add the sifted sugar, beating after additions.

Sift the flour with the salt five times and fold it into the mixture. Add the vanilla.

Bake in an ungreased angel cake tin in a moderate oven of 165^0C for forty-five minutes.

Be careful not to jar or disturb it while baking.

Remove from the oven, turn the pan upside down on a wire netting or with a knife handle or some other small article inserted under the edge of the pan to permit steam to escape, and let it stand until the cake falls out.

GÉNOISE SPONGE CAKE

This is an Italian cake often used in the famous Tiramisu dessert, and takes its name from the city of Genoa. It is also the basis for many filled cakes in the French style.

It uses whole eggs, beaten with the sugar over a little heat, and no baking powder, relying on the air beaten into the batter to make it rise.

It is used to make layer cakes, rolled sponge cake, and cake fingers.

Basic Vanilla or Chocolate Génoise Sponge

Ingredients

6 eggs
1 cup castor sugar
1tsp vanilla essence
1tsp salt
1 cup sifted plain flour

Method

Preheat your oven to $180^0 C$.

Grease with butter and line with baking paper a 23cm springform cake pan. The paper will stick to the butter and hold it in place while you get the batter in. This also makes it easier to remove the cake, and makes washing up a little easier.

Place the eggs, sugar, vanilla, and salt in a mixing bowl on top of a double boiler. Heat over simmering water until mixture is warm to the touch. Make sure that the bowl does not touch the water.

Remove the bowl from the heat.

Beat mixture with an electric beater on medium speed until cool. The batter will triple in volume and be thick and fluffy. It should leave trails in the mixture.

Carefully fold the sifted flour into the egg mixture in three additions until the flour is just combined. Do not over fold or the mixture will lose its volume.

Pour the batter into the prepared cake pan. Bake for about 30 minutes until springy to the touch.

Allow the cake to cool completely. Run a knife around edges of pan to loosen cake. Cover with a serving plate and invert both pan and plate. Gently remove pan.

Serve cake as is, or frosted, or use it as a base for other dessert recipes.

To make a chocolate cake, just substitute some of the flour with cocoa powder.

Barry Bakes © 2013

CHIFFON CAKE

Invented by Harry Baker in 1927, it was called the 'cake discovery of the century'.

This type of cake uses separated eggs, and vegetable oil, and baking powder to make it rise.

The high oil and egg content makes it a very rich, light and moist cake that does not dry out as quickly as butter cake, as oil is liquid at cool temperatures. This also means that it is suited to refrigerating or freezing, using interesting fillings.

The secret is the use of vegetable oil which also seems to affect the foam structure of the beaten eggs.

Lemon Chiffon Cake

Ingredients

1¾ cups cake flour
1 Tbsp baking powder
1 tsp salt
1/2 cup white sugar
1/2 cup vegetable oil
6 egg yolks
3/4 cup water
1 Tbsp lemon zest
6 egg whites
½ tsp cream of tartar
3/4 cup white sugar
1 cup heavy whipping cream
2 1/2 cups lemon pie filling
8 slices lemon

Method

Preheat your oven to 180 degrees C. In a large bowl, combine the flour, baking powder, salt, and 1/2 cup sugar. Add oil, egg yolks, water, and lemon rind. Beat with an electric mixer until smooth. In a small bowl, beat the egg whites and cream of tartar until peaks form. Gradually add 3/4 cup sugar, and beat until very stiff and shiny peaks form. Fold 1/3 of the whites into the batter, then quickly fold in remaining whites until no streaks remain. Turn batter into an ungreased 25cm tube pan.

Bake for 60 minutes or until a toothpick inserted in the centre comes out clean. Invert the cake and cool completely in pan. When cool, loosen edges and shake pan to remove the cake.

To make the filling, beat cream to stiff peaks and fold in lemon filling. Chill until stiff. To assemble the cake, slice it horizontally into 3 equal layers. Fill layers with 1/3 cup of filling. Spread remaining filling on top layer. Decorate with lemon slices.

BUTTER CAKE

A Butter Cake uses the creaming method, where the butter and sugar are creamed together, and it also uses baking powder, or self-raising flour.

It is a development of the old recipe for Pound Cake where equal quantities of butter, sugar, eggs and flour were used; originally a pound of each.

Sometimes when the old kitchen scales were used, the eggs replaced the weights, and the other ingredients were balanced to an equal weight.

The modern use of self-raising flour or baking powder produces a lighter result.

In the UK this cake is known as a Victoria Sponge, named after Queen Victoria, who often liked to have some with her afternoon tea. It is sometimes just called Plain Cake or Madeira Cake because it was sometimes consumed while drinking Madeira wine.

Basic Butter Cake

Ingredients (2 layers)

250gm (9oz) unsalted butter, softened
250gm (9oz) or 1½ cups castor sugar
1tsp vanilla extract
4 medium eggs (70gm)
250gm (9oz) or 2 cups sifted S.R. Flour
To make a chocolate cake, reduce the flour to 1½ cups and add ½ cup cocoa
Raspberry jam and whipped cream for filling

Method

Preheat the oven to $180^{0}C$. Grease and line two 20cm cake tins with baking paper.

Beat the butter, sugar, and vanilla together with an electric mixer until smooth and creamy (about 10 minutes). It should look almost white.

Then, one at a time, add the eggs and beat until combined.

Fold in the flour and cocoa (if using it), until just combined. If the mixture looks a little thick, you can add a splash of milk.

Divide the mixture between the tins and bake for 30 minutes, or until a toothpick inserted comes out clean. The centre of the cake should be springy when pressed.

Cool for 10 minutes before turning them out onto a wire tray.

Spread the jam and cream on the bottom layer and sprinkle the top layer with icing sugar.

Chocolate Icing (if using)

2/3 cup cream
200gm milk chocolate
To make the icing, heat the cream and chocolate in a sauce pan on low heat, and stir until creamy. Take it off to cool, and then whisk the mixture until thick and spreadable.

OTHER CAKES

Grandma's Boiled Fruit Cake

Ingredients

500gm mixed Fruit
½ cup Cognac or brandy
1 cup water
125gm butter
½ cup pure maple syrup
1 cup brown sugar
1tsp bicarbonate of soda
1Tbsp boiling water
2 eggs, lightly beaten
1½ cups S. R. flour
1 cup plain flour
½tsp ground cinnamon
½tsp ground nutmeg
½tsp ground ginger

Method

Soak the fruit overnight in the Cognac or brandy.

Put the fruit, water, butter, maple syrup, and sugar in a saucepan, bring it to the boil, and then take it off the heat. Add the bicarbonate of soda mixed with the boiling water.

Cool the mixture for about 30 minutes, and then add the lightly beaten eggs, mixing in thoroughly.

In a bowl, mix together well the sifted flours and the spices.

Pour in the fruit mixture and fold it together.

Put the mixture into a 23cm round or square cake tin, greased and lined with baking paper.

Bake it at 160°C in the oven for about 1¼ to 1½ hours.

Remove it from oven, allow it to cool in the tin, and then remove the cake.

This recipe makes a moist fruit cake with tender fruit.

In Australia, it used to be the practice that when a cake didn't quite work out the way that you wanted, you simply served it as a dessert and poured custard over the top. One evening many years ago, my uncle Ossie, personally incensed at this custom, was heard to very loudly protest before the whole family at the dinner table, 'When I have cake, I have cake; and when I have puddin', I have puddin'!'

Fruit and Pumpkin Cake (Australia)

This is an old family recipe that was given to me by Leslie, my brother's sister-in-law, who is also my wife's ex-sister-in-law's cousin, and also the cousin of my wife's cousin's husband (tricky, this food caper). It's a little unusual, in that there are no eggs, butter, or sugar in this recipe.

Ingredients

360gm mixed fruit (sultanas, raisins, etc.)
1 cup apricot nectar (or juice from canned apricots)
1tsp honey
1½ cups S. R. Flour
1 cup cooked and mashed pumpkin
1tsp mixed spice
1tsp baking soda

Method

In a saucepan, bring the fruit, nectar and honey to the boil and simmer for 3 minutes. Allow it to cool and then add the rest of the ingredients, stirring well.
Bake in a greased loaf tin at 150°C for about an hour. Allow it to cool in the tin for 10 minutes. Pour 1Tbsp sherry over the top of the cake.

Sultana Cake

Cream together 250gm sugar with 185gm butter. Add 3 eggs, one at a time, beating in well each time. Fold in 3 cups S. R. Flour and a pinch of salt a bit at a time with 2/3 cup of milk. Add a little vanilla essence (real essence is best) and 1½ cups of sultanas and mix well. Put the mixture into a cake tin greased with butter and dusted with flour and bake in a moderate oven until cooked, about 1¼ hours.

Pecan Cake

Beat together well 180gm butter and a cup of sugar. Add three eggs, one at a time, and 1tsp vanilla essence, mixing well. Gently mix in 2½ cups S. R. Flour, ¾ cup milk, and 1 cup crushed pecan nuts (or walnuts). Put the mixture into a round cake tin lined with baking paper, and decorate the top with slices of pears or peaches. Drizzle a little honey over the top and bake at 180°C for about 1 hour.

Carrot Cake

Melt together 100gm butter, 100gm raw sugar and 3Tbsp honey. Mix in with 225gm wholemeal flour, a grated carrot, 1Tbsp lemon juice, 2tsp cinnamon and 1½tsp baking powder. Bake in a greased baking tin for 1 hour. Optional topping can be made by mixing together 50gm cream cheese, 25gm butter, 100gm icing sugar and 1tsp vanilla essence. Spread this on when the cake has cooled.

Chocolate Torte (Austria)

A torte is a rich, usually multi-layered, filled cake. This is my take on a cake similar to an Austrian delicacy called Sacher Torte. This is one of those products where the original closely-guarded secret recipe has been the subject of legal battles.

Ingredients

150gm dark chocolate (60% cocoa solids)
150gm butter
1 cup castor sugar
4 eggs, separated into yolks and whites (do not allow any yolk in the whites)
1 cup plain flour, sifted
1tsp lemon juice
¾ cup smooth apricot jam

Method

Melt the chocolate in a stainless steel bowl over a saucepan of simmering water and allow it to cool a little.

Meanwhile, in another bowl and using electric beaters, cream the butter and half a cup of the sugar together until it is pale and creamy.

One at a time, beat in the egg yolks until combined.

Stir this mixture into the chocolate mixture.

Add the flour and stir it in.

In a separate clean bowl, beat the egg whites till soft peaks form, gradually add the other half a cup of sugar and the lemon juice, and beat the whites till stiff peaks form.

Fold the egg whites lightly into the chocolate mixture.

Pour the mixture into a greased 23cm spring-form cake tin lined with baking paper.

Bake at $180^0 C$ for about 30 minutes.

When cooked, let it cool for 10 minutes in the pan, and then turn it out upside down on a cooling rack.

When it is cooled, cut the cake in half horizontally, fill it with the jam, and ice it using the mixture below.

Chocolate Icing

150gm dark chocolate

150ml thickened cream

Melt the chocolate with the cream over low heat in a saucepan, and when it has cooled slightly, ice the cake on the top and down the sides.

Allow it to set at room temperature for about two hours.

Orange Cake

Ingredients

3 eggs, beaten
½ cup milk
½ cup vegetable oil
½ cup orange juice
2 tsp grated orange zest
2 cups S. R. Flour
½ tsp salt
1 cup castor sugar

Ingredients for Orange Butter Frosting

6 Tbsp butter, softened
2 cups castor sugar
2 Tbsp orange juice
1 tsp vanilla extract
1 tsp grated orange zest

Method

Preheat oven to 180°C. Grease and line with baking paper 2x20cm cake pans.

In a medium bowl, whisk together the eggs, milk, oil, orange juice and zest.

Sift the flour, salt and sugar into a large bowl, and make a well in the centre.

Add half of the egg mixture, and mix on low speed until the dry ingredients are incorporated. Increase to medium speed and beat for about one minute to aerate and develop the structure. Scrape down the sides of the bowl.

Add the remaining egg mixture in 2 lots, beating for about 30 seconds after each addition to incorporate the egg and strengthen the cake's structure.

Put the cake batter into the prepared pans and smooth off the tops.

Bake for about 35 minutes or until the cakes are golden brown and a toothpick inserted in the centre comes out clean. If you find that the cakes are browning too much, cover them with a piece of foil.

Remove the cake from the oven, and allow it to cool for about 10 minutes.

To make the frosting, cream the butter until smooth, gradually beating in the sugar until light and creamy.

Beat in the 2 Tbsp orange juice to bring it up to spreading consistency.

Stir in the vanilla and orange zest.

Chocolate Mud Cake

Ingredients

250gm butter, chopped
200gm dark chocolate, chopped
1 cup caster sugar
1 cup hot water
2tsp vanilla essence
2 eggs lightly beaten
1½ cups S. R. Flour
½ cup plain flour
½ cup cocoa

Method

Melt the butter, chocolate, and sugar in the hot water in a large bowl until the mixture is smooth; then let it cool down for a few minutes.

Add the vanilla and the eggs. Stir to combine. Add the two types of flour and the cocoa and stir until smooth. Pour the cake mixture into a prepared cake pan, and bake it at 180^0C for about 45 minutes or a little more, till cooked.

Chocolate Ganache

150gm dark chocolate, chopped
½ cup thickened cream

Put the chocolate and cream in a small saucepan over low heat and stir until smooth. When it cools down enough to thicken to a spreadable consistency, spread it over the cake. It will then set in a few more minutes.

Orange and Poppy Seed Cake

Ingredients

1 large whole thoroughly washed (they are often waxed) and unpeeled Navel orange, with the tough top and bottom skin trimmed off, and cut into rough pieces
125gm butter, softened
3 eggs
1tsp vanilla essence
½ cup castor sugar
½ cup milk
½ cup poppy seeds
2 cups S. R. Flour

Method

Process the orange pieces in a food processor. Then add the butter, eggs, vanilla, sugar, milk, and poppy seeds till well mixed. Add the flour and mix till well combined. Pour the mixture into an 18cm cake pan that has been greased and lined with baking paper, and bake in the oven at 180^0C for about 45 minutes or until cooked.

MUFFINS

Chocolate Muffins

Ingredients

2 cups S. R. Flour
1 cup caster sugar
½ cup cocoa powder
½ cup chocolate buttons (or choc-chips)
1 cup plain Greek-style yoghurt (or 100gm softened butter)
½ cup milk
1 egg
1tsp vanilla essence

Method

Mix the flour, sugar, cocoa and chocolate in a bowl and make a well in the centre.

Mix together in a separate bowl the yoghurt, milk, egg, and vanilla.

Pour the yoghurt mixture into the dry mixture and stir until they are just combined.

Pour into paper cases in a 12 muffin tray and bake at $180^{o}C$ for 15-20 minutes.

Banana Muffins

Use the above recipe, but substitute 2 chopped ripe bananas for the chocolate and cocoa, and mix them in with the yoghurt, milk, egg, and vanilla mixture.

Orange Muffins

Ingredients

2 cups S. R. Flour
1 cup caster sugar
100gm softened butter
½ cup milk
1 egg
½ cup orange juice
a little grated orange zest

Method

Mix the flour and sugar in a bowl and make a well in the centre.

Mix together in a separate bowl the butter, milk, egg, orange juice and rind.

Pour the butter mixture into the dry mixture and stir until they are just combined.

Pour into paper cases in a 12 muffin tray and bake at $180^{o}C$ for 15-20 minutes.

Blueberry Muffins

Ingredients

2 cups S. R. Flour
1 cup caster sugar
1tsp ground cinnamon
1 cup plain Greek-style yoghurt (or 100gm softened butter)
½ cup milk
1 egg
1 cup frozen blueberries

Method

Mix the flour, sugar, and cinnamon in a bowl and make a well in the centre.

Mix together in a separate bowl the butter, milk, egg, and blueberries.

Pour the yoghurt mixture into the dry mixture and stir until they are just combined.

Pour into paper cases in a 12 muffin tray and bake at 180^0C for 15-20 minutes.

Apple Muffins

Using the above recipe, substitute 1 cup canned pie apple for the fruit.

Cherry Muffins

Using the above recipe, substitute 1 cup canned pitted cherries.

Pesto Muffins

Here are a couple of savoury muffin recipes.

Ingredients

2 cups S. R. Flour
1Tbsp caster sugar
1Tbsp olive oil
1Tbsp basil pesto
1 cup milk
1 egg
1tsp sea salt and ½ tsp black pepper

Method

Mix the ingredients together. Put the mixture into a greased muffin tray and sprinkle a little grated parmesan on the top. Bake for about 20 minutes or until browned and firm.

Pizza Muffins

Using the recipe above, substitute the pesto with 1Tbsp tomato paste, 1Tbsp chopped sun-dried tomatoes, 1Tbsp chopped and pitted black olives, 1 chopped anchovy fillet, 1 chopped red chilli, and 1tsp mixed herbs.

SLICES

Chocolate Brownies (United States)

These seem to have appeared in Australia in the last twenty years. They are nothing short of wicked. Chocoholics go crazy over these.

Ingredients

200gm block of good quality dark chocolate (60% cocoa solids)
200gm butter
2tsp vanilla essence
4 eggs
1 cup caster sugar
1 cup plain flour

Method

Melt the butter and chocolate together gently in a saucepan, add the vanilla, and allow the mixture to cool a little.
Meanwhile, whisk the eggs and sugar together in a bowl till light and creamy.
Mix in the flour, then the chocolate mixture.
Pour the mixture into a 23cm square cake tin, lined with baking paper.
Cook for about 40 to 45 minutes at 180^0C till the outside starts to firm up. The inside will not be properly set yet.
Allow them to cool and set for a few hours before slicing, or eat them warm.

Chocolate and Caramel Slice (Australia)

Ingredients

1½ cups plain flour
125gm butter
½ cup caster sugar
½ cup maple syrup
400gm can sweetened condensed milk
80gm butter
200gm block milk chocolate
2tsp vegetable oil

Method

Process the flour, butter, and sugar and press into a 23cm tin lined with baking paper. Bake for 15 minutes at 180^0C.
Heat the syrup, condensed milk, and butter in a saucepan for about 10 minutes until caramelised. Pour over the base, cook for a further 10 minutes, and cool completely.
Melt the chocolate gently with the oil in a saucepan, and pour it over the top of the caramel layer.
Refrigerate when cooled a little. Cut into squares before the chocolate sets hard.

Raspberry Coconut Slice (Australia)

This is a very old style of slice that has been around for generations. I remember my grandmother making this one. It is a quick, no-fuss recipe similar to a Bakewell tart.

Ingredients

100gm butter
½ cup caster sugar
1 egg
½ cup self-raising flour
½ cup plain flour
½ cup raspberry jam

Coconut Topping Ingredients

2 eggs
½ cup castor sugar
2 cups desiccated coconut

Method

Cream the butter, sugar, and egg together with an electric mixer until light and fluffy. Stir in the flour til smooth. Spread the mixture in to a 23cm square cake tin that has been lined with baking paper. Spread the raspberry jam over the base.
Mix together the topping ingredients and spread on top (that's why it's called topping). Bake in the oven at 180^0C for about 30 minutes.

Chocolate Coconut Slice (Australia)

Ingredients

1 cup self-raising flour
1 cup caster sugar
1 cup desiccated coconut
125gm butter, softened
2Tbsp cocoa powder
1 egg

Icing

1 cup icing sugar
2Tbsp cocoa powder
2tsp butter, softened
2Tbsp hot water

Method

Mix all of the ingredients in a bowl and press into a 23cm tin lined with baking paper. Bake for 20 minutes at 180^0C and let it cool for a while.
Ice with the chocolate icing after mixing all of the ingredients together, and sprinkle some extra coconut over the top. Refrigerate.
This recipe is one from my sister-in-law, Lynne.

Macadamia Slice (Australia)

Ingredients

1 cup macadamia nuts, coarsely chopped
1 cup rolled oats
1 cup desiccated coconut
1 cup plain flour
1 cup sultanas
½ cup sugar
2 eggs
125gm butter, melted
1Tbsp honey

Method

In a mixing bowl, mix together the nuts, oats, coconut, flour, sultanas, and sugar.
In a separate bowl, whisk the eggs and then whisk in the butter and honey.
Pour the egg mixture into the dry ingredients and mix well.
Press the mixture into a flat pan and cook it at $180^{0}C$ for about 25 minutes.

Muesli Slice (Australia)

Ingredients

½ cup toasted muesli
½ cup rolled oats
½ cup desiccated coconut
½ cup raw sugar
½ cup flaked almonds
½ cup sultanas
½ cup S. R. Flour
½ cup honey
½ cup butter, softened
½ cup olive oil

Method

In a mixing bowl, mix all the ingredients together well down to the flour. Then stir through well the honey, butter, and oil. Tip the mixture into a baking tray lined with baking paper, and bake at $180^{0}C$ for about 30 minutes. When cooled, slice into squares.

Toasted Breakfast Muesli

First bake for about 4 minutes, 2 cups rolled oats, 1 cup wheat bran, 1 cup wheat germ, and 2tsp ground cinnamon mixed through. Then, bake for about 2 minutes, 1 cup (100gm) sunflower seeds, pepitas, and pine nuts mix (available from the supermarket), 1 cup roasted pistachio nuts, 1/2 cup sesame seeds, 1/2 cup slivered almonds, and 1/2 cup desiccated coconut. Then, add in to the other baked ingredients, 1 cup sultanas, 1 cup raisins, 1 cup dried cranberries, and a few chopped dates and prunes.

'Baklava' (Turkey, Middle East)

Ingredients

1 cup chopped walnuts

1 cup chopped pistachio nuts

1 cup chopped mixed nuts (almonds, brazil nuts, pecans, hazelnuts)

1tsp ground ginger

1tsp ground cinnamon

½tsp ground cloves

½ cup breadcrumbs

2tsp lemon rind

250gm butter, melted

375gm packet of filo pastry (from the fridge, not freezer, section of the supermarket)

Syrup Ingredients

1 cup castor sugar

1 cup water

1 cup honey

Method

Preheat the oven to 180°C and toast the nuts for 5 minutes.

Mix the nuts with the ginger, spices, breadcrumbs, lemon rind, and a little of the melted butter.

Now trim the pastry sheets to the size of the oven dish you will be using.

Grease the dish lightly with a little butter, put 2 sheets of pastry in the bottom, and arrange the trimmed sections of pastry as well in the bottom.

Using a pastry brush, lightly brush the sheets with some melted butter.

Spread half of the nut mixture over the pastry.

Arrange half of the remaining pastry sheets over the dish next, lightly buttering every third pastry sheet.

Spread the remaining nut mixture over the pastry in the dish.

Arrange the remaining pastry sheets, buttering every third sheet lightly.

Tip any remaining butter over the top and brush it evenly.

Now carefully cut the whole dish down to the base into diamond shapes.

Bake it in the oven for 40 minutes until golden brown, and remove it from oven.

Now heat the syrup ingredients of castor sugar, water, and honey together till hot.

Pour the mixture over the baklava, and when it is cooled, and the honey mixture has been absorbed, refrigerate it for a couple of hours before eating.

BISCUITS

'Biscotte Uovo' (Italy) Sicilian Egg Biscuits

This is my attempt to recreate old Mama Maria's great homemade Sicilian biscuits.

Ingredients

250gm butter, softened
4 eggs
4 cups plain flour
¼ tsp salt
½ cup milk, or a little more
1 cup sugar
½ cup water

Method

Beat the eggs into the butter one at a time. Then add the flour and salt to the egg mixture. Use enough milk to make firm dough. Put in the fridge for an hour. Then roll out sausage shapes, and form them into various designs, some twists, some knots, and some doughnuts. Bake them on an oven tray for about 25 minutes at $200^{0}C$ until cooked. After cooling for a while, dip them into a hot melted sugar and water mixture.

Anzac Biscuits (Australia)

These were a nutritious, long-shelf-life staple of Australian WW1 soldiers.
Note: The more usual term in the USA for this type of product is 'cookies'.

Ingredients

1 cup rolled oats
1 cup plain flour
1 cup brown sugar
½ cup desiccated coconut
125gm butter
2 Tbsp golden syrup (or maple syrup)
1 Tbsp water
1 tsp bicarbonate of soda

Method

Mix together the first four ingredients in a mixing bowl.
Melt the butter gently in a saucepan, and add the syrup, and the water with the bicarbonate of soda mixed into it. It will bubble a bit, but don't panic.
Mix the liquid into the dry ingredients.
Form small balls of mixture and put them on a baking tray lined with baking paper.
Flatten them out a bit.
Cook them in the oven at $180^{0}C$ for about 10 minutes till they are golden brown.
Don't worry if they are a little soft, as they will firm up when they cool down.

Shortbread Biscuits (Scotland)

Shortbread gets its name from the 'short' dough which is crumbly in texture and high in butter, and traditionally follows the formula of 1 of sugar / 2 of butter / 3 of flour. These are absolutely delicious. Use some self-restraint, please.

Ingredients

225gm (1 1/2 cups) plain flour
75gm (1/2 cup) cornflour that is made from corn, not wheat
250gm (1 cup) butter, at room temperature
100gm (1/2 cup) caster sugar

Method

Using your hands, rub the butter into the flour until you have a breadcrumb texture.
Mix in the caster sugar well.
Knead the dough until smooth, wrap it in cling wrap and refrigerate it for ½ hour.
Roll out the dough to 5mm and cut out shapes with a cookie cutter or a glass.
Place them on baking trays lined with baking paper. Bake at 160^0C for about 25 minutes.

Ginger Nut Biscuits (New Zealand)

Ingredients

125gm (1/2 cup) butter, softened
1 cup brown sugar
2 cups S. R. Flour
3tsp ground ginger
1tsp ground cinnamon
½tsp ground nutmeg

Method

Whisk together the butter and sugar till smooth.
Mix the flour and spices together well in a separate bowl.
Mix both lots together and roll into small balls.
Place them on baking trays lined with baking paper and flatten them a little with a fork.
Bake at 180^0C for about 20 minutes.

Cinnamon Biscuits

Follow the recipe above, but replace the spices with 3tsp ground cinnamon.

Peanut Biscuits

Follow the recipe above, but replace the spices with 1 cup roasted peanuts.

Chocolate Chip Bikkies

Follow the recipe above, but replace the spices with ½ cup cocoa and ½ cup chocolate chips. Otherwise known as Computer Biscuits—both have chips in them.

Chocolate Macarons (France)

These are fiddly, with a high failure rate. Macaron is the name for a meringue biscuit using almond meal, whereas Macaroon is the name usually used for a meringue biscuit that uses coconut. There is a French method, this one, and a trickier Italian method which uses a very hot sugar mixture.

Ingredients

200gm (2 cups) ground almond meal
160gm (1 cup) caster sugar
2 Tbsp cocoa powder
5 egg whites (about 210 gm from 70gm eggs)
½ cup caster sugar
2 tsp lemon juice

> **Egg Weight Facts**
> 10% egg shell
> 60% egg white
> 30% egg yolk

Chocolate Ganache

100ml whipping cream
200gm good quality dark chocolate (60% cocoa solids)
20gm butter, softened

Method

Mix together in a bowl the almond meal, sugar, and cocoa powder.

In a separate dry bowl whip the egg whites till soft peaks form. Then add the sugar and lemon juice gradually while whipping till the egg whites are firm and glossy.

Then fold in the dry almond mixture and stir with a spatula till the mixture becomes runny enough to fall from the spatula. This means that it is losing some air, but don't worry because this consistency is needed—just enough air without having too much.

Using a disposable piping bag with a 1cm hole, pipe the mixture onto baking paper placed on a baking tray making circles about 3-4cm across.

Hold the tray up and bang it on the bottom a couple of times to settle the mixture slightly. The macarons should end up reasonably flat on top when cooked.

Now let the whole thing rest on the bench for about 15 minutes or so to allow the mixture to form a skin, which then tends to lift as they cook, making a 'foot' on the biscuits. The top should start to look dry. Meanwhile, pre-heat the oven to $180^{\circ}C$.

Bake for about 15 minutes till just firm on top. Take them out of the oven, slide the paper off the hot tray to stop them cooking, and allow them to cool down.

Make the chocolate ganache by heating the cream in a saucepan till simmering. Then take it off the heat, add the chocolate, stirring, then the butter, stirring till smooth. With spoonfuls of warm mixture, sandwich the macaroons together.

Options

For coloured macarons, leave out the cocoa powder and add some food colouring to the meringue mixture, or divide the mixture and make two colours.

Or, you could fill the macarons with pastry cream, or lemon curd.

CHICKEN

ROAST CHICKEN

Roast Chicken with Herb Stuffing

Ingredients

1.5Kg free-range chicken
olive oil for rubbing over the chicken

Stuffing Ingredients

2 cups breadcrumbs (from 2 day old sourdough bread preferably)
1 stalk of celery, including some leaves, very finely chopped
1 red onion, very finely chopped
2 peeled cloves garlic, finely chopped
2 Tbsp fresh herbs (flat-leaf parsley, sage and thyme), finely chopped
1 egg
the juice of one lemon and some of the zest
1 Tbsp extra virgin olive oil
1 tsp salt and 1 tsp freshly ground black pepper

Method

Rub the chicken with oil. Stuff it with the mixture shown, after checking that the giblets haven't been placed back inside the chicken. You don't want them.
Roast it at $180^{\circ}C$ in the oven for about 2 hours till it is golden.
Serve with roasted vegetables and simple gravy made in the pan with the juices.
QUICK TIP: If you really want roasted chicken, I suggest that you go down to the chicken shop or supermarket and buy a freshly cooked, hot, stuffed chicken that is ready to go. It'll be just as good as, or maybe better than, the one you do yourself!

Roasted Herbed Chicken Pieces

1.5Kg chicken pieces
½ cup lemon juice, freshly squeezed, and a little lemon rind
2 cloves garlic, chopped (or crushed garlic)
1 Tbsp extra virgin olive oil
1 Tbsp chopped fresh rosemary leaves, 1 Tbsp chopped fresh flat-leaf parsley, 1 Tbsp chopped fresh sage leaves, and 1 Tbsp chopped fresh thyme leaves
1 tsp crushed ginger
1 tsp crushed chilli
1 tsp sea salt and 1 tsp freshly ground black pepper

Method

Put the chicken pieces in a large baking dish.
Mix together the rest of the ingredients, and rub them all over the chicken pieces.
Roast for about 45 minutes in a $200^{\circ}C$ oven or until golden and cooked through.

BRAISED CHICKEN THIGH FILLETS

The first three recipes here are French and Italian versions of pretty much the same kind of dish, with some variations. They use thigh fillets, which are the drumsticks with bones and skin removed, very tasty, and quite economical.

You could also cook this on top of the stove if you wish, or even all day in a slow-cooker.

I think these are some of the all-time best chicken dishes!

'Coq au Vin Rouge' (France) - Braised Chicken in Red Wine

Ingredients

1Kg chicken thigh fillets, boned and skinned, cut into large pieces
olive oil for frying
2 rashers bacon, chopped
1 onion, chopped
1 carrot, chopped
1 stalk celery, chopped
2 spring onions, chopped
2 cloves garlic, chopped
2 anchovy fillets
2 Tbsp plain flour
½ bottle dry red wine (shiraz, cabernet, merlot, or similar)
1 cup chicken stock
some fresh oregano, thyme, and Italian parsley (flat-leaf)
2 bay leaves
½ tsp black pepper
small tin of champignons
6 small pickling onions, whole peeled

ONE POT MEAL

Method

Brown the chicken pieces in oil in a large oven-proof pot or casserole and remove them.

Brown the bacon, onion, carrot, and celery in the pot.

Add the spring onions, garlic, and anchovies to cook lightly.

Add the flour and stir till cooked, about ½ minute.

Add the wine to deglaze the pot, stirring the flour off the bottom of the pot.

Return the chicken to the pot and add the stock, herbs, bay leaves, pepper, champignons, and the pickling onions.

Cover, and cook for one hour in a moderate $180^{0}C$ oven.

'Coq au Vin Blanc' (France) - Braised Chicken in White Wine

Ingredients

800gm chicken thigh fillets, boned and skinned, cut into cubes of about 2cm
½ cup olive oil for frying
1 leek, chopped
a knob of butter
2 rashers bacon, chopped (or ham or prosciutto)
1 carrot, chopped
1 stalk celery, chopped
2 spring onions, chopped
2 cloves garlic, chopped
2 Tbsp plain flour
2 cups dry white wine (sauvignon blanc is perfect)
1 cup chicken stock
some fresh oregano, thyme, and Italian flat-leafed parsley
2 bay leaves
½ tsp salt
½ tsp black pepper
small tin of champignons
6 small pickling onions, whole peeled

ONE POT MEAL

Method

Brown the chicken pieces in oil in a large oven-proof pot or casserole and remove them.

Sauté the leek in the butter till soft and remove it from the pot. The word sauté in French means 'jumped', so the idea is to keep the food moving so that it will cook evenly at the same temperature. The butter, which goes so well with leeks, will not burn either.

Brown the bacon, onion, carrot, and celery in the pot with a little extra oil if needed.

Add the spring onions and garlic to cook lightly, without burning.

Add the flour and stir till cooked, about ½ minute.

Add the wine to deglaze the pot, stirring the flour off the bottom of the pot.

Return the chicken to the pot and add the stock, herbs, bay leaves, salt and pepper, champignons, and the pickling onions.

Cover, and cook for one hour in a moderate 180°C oven, or this will simmer quite well in a pot on the top of the stove.

Option

You can use this mixture to make a nice chicken pie if you wish, just by putting it in some puff pastry sheets in a pie dish, and returning it to the oven till the pastry is cooked and lightly browned on top.

Chicken 'Cacciatore' (Italy) - Hunter's Chicken

This recipe was originally made using rabbit.
It is similar to the French recipe, 'Chicken Chasseur', also meaning 'hunter's chicken', which is often made with white wine and brandy.

Ingredients

1Kg boneless chicken thighs, skinless, trimmed of excess fat, chopped into pieces
½ cup olive oil
1 large onion, chopped
1 carrot, peeled, finely chopped
1 celery stick, finely chopped
100gm sliced pancetta, chopped (or bacon)
2 spring onions, chopped
2 garlic cloves, crushed
1 small tin sliced button mushrooms (champignons)
2 Tbsp plain flour
1 cup Chianti, dry red wine (or white wine if you prefer it)
1 cup pitted kalamata olives
1 anchovy fillet
some fresh oregano, thyme, and Italian flat-leafed parsley
2 bay leaves
½ tsp sugar
400gm can diced tomatoes
1 cup chicken stock
1 packet Risoni pasta (small pasta resembling rice)

ONE POT MEAL

Method

Fry the chicken pieces in a large oven-proof pot in olive oil until browned all over, and remove them from the pot.

Add the onion, carrot, celery, and pancetta to the pan with enough oil to cook for a couple of minutes until the onion is softened and translucent.

Add the spring onions, garlic and mushrooms and cook for a further minute or so.

Stir in the plain flour to cook for about half a minute, and then add the wine to deglaze the pot, allowing it to simmer for a couple of minutes, stirring.

Return the chicken to the pot and add the olives, anchovy, herbs, bay leaves, sugar, tomatoes, and stock.

Cover and cook for one hour in a moderate 180^0C oven.

Serve with boiled Risoni pasta according to the packet directions, and garnish with some chopped parsley.

Chicken 'Chermoula' (Tunisia)

Note: A tajine is both the name of a type of North African dish, and the name of the clay cooking implement. It has a conical lid that enables condensation to return to the base of the pan while cooking. Some tajines will withstand stove-top temperatures for browning the meat in the base, while others are only suitable for use in the oven.

Ingredients

800gm chicken thigh cutlets (about 8), skinned, boned, and roughly chopped
Chermoula paste as shown
¼ cup olive oil for frying
1 brown onion, thinly sliced
1 cup dry white wine
400gm can diced tomatoes (or 3 fresh tomatoes, chopped)
8 dried apricots, halved
8 pitted dates, halved
½ cup pistachio nuts, hulled
chopped parsley to garnish
small packet Couscous

Chermoula Paste
1Tbsp extra virgin olive oil
½ cup finely chopped flat-leaf parsley
½ cup finely chopped coriander leaves
2 garlic cloves, crushed
2 fresh long red chillies, finely chopped
1tsp ground cumin seeds
1tsp turmeric
1tsp sweet paprika
1tsp cinnamon
1tsp sea salt
1tsp freshly ground black pepper
1 large lemon, juiced
the grated zest of half of the lemon

Method

Marinate the chicken pieces in the Chermoula paste for about 3 hours if possible.
Scrape the marinade off the chicken roughly so that it doesn't burn when fried. Retain the marinade.
Brown the chicken well on both sides in the oil in a large pot or tajine until golden, and remove it from the pot.
Fry the onion in a little more oil if necessary in the pot until starting to colour.
Add the wine to deglaze the pan (to lift the tasty bits off the bottom) and add some extra fruity flavour.
Now add all of the leftover marinade to the pot.
Add the tomatoes, apricots, and dates to the pot.
Cover and cook it in the pot or tajine, in the oven or on top of the stove, at a low temperature (about 160^0C in the oven), for about an hour.
Top with some hulled and salted pistachio nuts and a little chopped parsley.
Serve with some plain couscous (Tunisian national dish), cooked according to the packet directions.

Harissa (Tunisia) Chilli Paste

In a mortar and pestle, crush 6 deseeded and chopped fresh long red chillies, 2 cloves garlic, and 1tsp salt in 1Tbsp good quality extra virgin olive oil. Add 1tsp caraway seeds, 1tsp cumin seeds, and 1tsp coriander seeds that have been lightly toasted in a hot frying pan, and grind to a smooth paste. This dish is a popular accompaniment.

'Sate Ayam' (Indonesia) - Chicken Sate with Peanut Sauce

Ingredients for the Skewers

1.5Kg chicken thigh fillets, trimmed and cubed
1Tbsp peanut oil
1Tbsp coconut cream
1Tbsp soy sauce
2tsp minced red chilli
2tsp minced ginger
½tsp salt and ½tsp white pepper

BARBECUE FRIENDLY

Method

In a large bowl, mix together all the above ingredients and marinate the chicken for an hour. Thread the chicken onto bamboo skewers and grill the chicken over hot coals until just cooked through. Cover the ends of the skewers in foil to stop them from burning. A charcoal-burning satay cooker or tapas grill is ideal; you can cook at the table. Or, if not, you can suspend the skewers by their ends over a barbecue grill using two supports of suitable size. Serve with the Sambal Kacang (sate peanut sauce) as a dipping sauce.

Sambal Kacang

Ingredients

¼ cup peanut oil
1 French shallot, or brown onion, finely chopped
1 anchovy fillet, finely chopped
2tsp sugar
2 red chillies, chopped very finely
2 cloves of garlic, very finely chopped
1tsp minced ginger
1tsp chopped lemongrass
1tsp ground cumin
1tsp ground coriander
1tsp ground turmeric
½tsp ground white pepper
½tsp sea salt
¼ cup kecap manis (or dark soy sauce)
the juice of one Tahitian lime
400ml can coconut cream (less the 1Tbsp used in the marinade above)
1 cup roasted peanuts, crushed (beer nuts with the reddish inner skins are excellent)

Method

In the peanut oil, fry all of the above ingredients down to the salt for a few minutes. Add to the mixture the kecap manis, lime juice, coconut cream, and the peanuts. Simmer until the mixture reduces a little, and the coconut oil comes to the top. Simmer the sauce a little longer in its own oil, and serve with the skewers.

Chicken Mignons with Fresh Herb Stuffing (France)

Ingredients (Serves 4)

800gm chicken thigh fillets (about 8), boned and skinned
8 pieces of prosciutto (1 for each fillet)
toothpicks for securing the mignons
2tsp olive oil to rub the outside
8 cubes of butter, about 2cm of a packet

Stuffing Ingredients

2 cups breadcrumbs (from 2 day old sourdough preferably)
1 stalk of celery, including some leaves, very finely chopped
1 red onion, very finely chopped
2 peeled cloves garlic, finely chopped
2Tbsp fresh herbs (flat-leaf parsley, sage and thyme), finely chopped
1 egg
the juice of one lemon and some of the zest
1Tbsp extra virgin olive oil
1tsp salt and 1tsp freshly ground black pepper

Method

Make the stuffing by mixing all of the ingredients together (or use a blender).

Lay the chicken thigh fillets on a cutting board, and place some of the stuffing inside each fillet (the fillets are usually whole, with the thigh bone pulled out), along with a cube of butter in each.

The butter will drizzle through the stuffing into the chicken during cooking, mix with the garlic, bread and herbs.

Roll the pieces of prosciutto around each fillet with the stuffing inside to encase the ends of the fillets with the flaps tucked under. Secure the fillets with toothpicks.

This will make 8 mignons (meaning 'small'), enough for four people.

Place them on an oven tray, and using your fingers, rub the outside of the mignons all over with a little olive oil to assist the cooking process.

Bake them at $180^{\circ}C$ for about 40 minutes, or until cooked through.

Serve them standing up, with perhaps a potato dish and some asparagus that you have placed in the tray for the last 10 minutes of cooking time. Voila! (French for 'behold!')

My father-in-law, Dave, used to tell about the chicken farmer who decided to try breeding chickens with four legs, because people seemed to favour eating the drumsticks.
The chicken breeding experiment was quite successful; the problem was that he then couldn't catch them.

Chicken, Leek and Potato Pie

My daughter Melissa lovingly makes this pie for her husband Peter, with a cute little pastry heart on the top!

Ingredients

About 500gm cubed chicken thigh fillets (or use leftover roasted chicken meat)
1 brown onion, finely chopped
1 leek, trimmed, washed, finely chopped
1 green shallot, finely chopped
1 clove garlic, crushed
100gm brown mushrooms, chopped
1 knob of butter
1 Tbsp plain flour
½ cup dry white wine
1 cup hot water
2 large potatoes, peeled, finely diced
1 carrot, peeled, finely diced
½ cup frozen peas
½ cup thickened cream
1tsp dried mixed herbs
1tsp ground coriander seed
1tsp ground cardamom seed
1tsp sea salt
1tsp freshly ground black pepper

Method

Brown the cubed chicken breasts in a frying pan and remove from the pan.

Then fry the chopped onion, leek, shallot, and garlic in the pan and remove.

Then, fry the chopped mushrooms and remove from the pan.

Add a little butter to the pan, then the flour to cook for a minute while stirring constantly so that it does not burn.

Then add the white wine to deglaze the pan and make a roux (lifting the tasty bits off the bottom of the pan). Add the cup of hot water.

Stir this until the roux is smooth.

Add the potatoes, carrot, peas, and then the cream on low heat, and stir to combine.

Return the chicken, onion mixture, and mushrooms, and add the herbs, spices, salt and pepper to heat through, while stirring.

Pack the chicken mixture in puff pastry sheets in a pie dish, about 1½ sheets of pastry for the bottom and 1½ sheets for the top, to bake for about an hour in the oven until the pastry is cooked and golden.

'Doro Wat' (Ethiopia) - Chicken in Red Pepper Paste

Similar to an Indian curry in many respects, this recipe has the unique step of dry frying the onion mixture.

Sometimes it is served with hard-boiled eggs on top.

Ingredients

1.2Kg skinless chicken thigh fillets, roughly chopped
the juice of 2 lemons
2tsp sea salt
2 onions, peeled and chopped
2 cloves garlic
3cm piece ginger root, chopped (or 3tspn crushed ginger)
¼ cup olive oil
Berberé spice mix
1 cup dry red wine
½ cup water

ONE POT MEAL

Method

Marinate the chicken pieces in the lemon juice and salt in a non-reactive bowl for 30 minutes.

Meanwhile, blend to a paste the onions, garlic, and ginger. Fry them without oil in a dry frying pan on low heat, stirring constantly, till the liquid is gone and it smells uniquely smoky, but not burnt. This will take about 10 minutes.

Add the oil, then the Berberé spice mix to fry for about one minute. Take care not to burn the spices.

Add the wine and water, and stir to combine the flavours while bringing it to the boil.

Put the chicken pieces into a tajine, or casserole dish, pour over the sauce mixture, and cook it in a moderate oven for about 45 minutes. Check halfway through and add a little water if it is getting too dry. Serve with Naan bread or similar (See Bread)

Berberé Spice Mix

2tsp sweet paprika
2tsp red pepper flakes (or 1 dried chilli, crushed)
1tsp cayenne pepper (hot chilli powder)
1tsp fenugreek seeds
½tsp ground cumin
½tsp ground cardamom
½tsp ground fennel seeds
½tsp ground cloves
½tsp ground nutmeg
½tsp turmeric
½tsp ground black pepper
½tsp sea salt

CHICKEN BREAST FILLETS

Chicken breast fillets are readily available, are reasonably economical, easy to work with, and open to a wide variety of upmarket, healthful recipes. Here are some very good ones.

Chicken in Prosciutto (Italy)

Ingredients

2 large skinless chicken breast fillets
4 sage leaves
4 slices prosciutto
potatoes, sweet potatoes, pumpkin and other vegetables, largely chopped for baking
some extra virgin olive oil for cooking
frozen peas or beans, or other greens

Marinade Ingredients

2tsp Dijon mustard
2tsp minced chilli
2tsp minced garlic
2tsp lemon juice
2tsp olive oil
¼tsp sea salt
¼tsp ground white pepper

Method

Marinate the chicken breasts for 30 minutes in the marinade ingredients listed.

Place two sage leaves on top of each chicken breast.

Wrap 2 slices of prosciutto around each chicken breast and fold them under to secure the ends.

Spread any remaining marinade mixture over the chicken.

Put the chicken in an ovenproof dish and bake it uncovered along with the veggies for about 45 minutes or until the chicken is cooked through.

Slice the chicken breasts if desired (sliced they will serve 4).

Serve with baked vegies, as below, and green beans or asparagus.

Baked Vegetables

Place the potatoes and vegetables in an ovenproof dish and rub them all over with olive oil using your fingers. Sprinkle over some sea salt.

Bake them in the oven for about 60 minutes at 180^0C till golden.

Boil the greens very quickly in water, to serve with the dish.

'Cotolette alla Bolognese' (Italy) - Chicken Parmigiana

You need a flavourful tomato sauce with onion, garlic, and herbs, for this dish.

And I use three cheeses for the topping, which provides just the right tang, I think.

Interesting Detail: The five basic tastes detected by the nose, mouth and tongue, as currently understood, are: sweet, salty, sour, bitter, and umami (savoury).

Parmesan cheese is very high in glutamate, and so has a strong umami taste. When combined with foods like mushrooms, seafood, and some others, umami seems to have some synergistic taste results.

Ingredients

6 chicken breast fillets, pounded flat (chicken scaloppine), or use thigh fillets
1 egg, lightly beaten with a splash of milk, and salt and pepper
1 cup breadcrumbs with ½ cup grated Parmesan cheese added
extra virgin olive oil for frying
½ cup grated Mozzarella cheese
½ cup grated Tasty cheese
½ cup grated Parmesan (Parmagiano-Reggiano) cheese (please, not the powdered stuff)

Tomato Sauce Ingredients

1 onion, very finely chopped
2 cloves minced garlic
700gm jar of Passata or Provista Sugo Italian cooking sauce (available at supermarket)
1tsp sea salt
1tsp freshly ground black pepper
small handful finely chopped flat leaf parsley
small handful fresh basil

Method

Coat the chicken scaloppine well in the egg mixture and then the breadcrumb mixture.

Fry them in a frying pan in oil until lightly golden and remove from the pan.

In the same pan, fry the onion and garlic till it is just starting to colour, and then add the tomato sauce, salt and pepper and herbs.

Cook the sauce for about 20 minutes, or until fragrant and fairly thick.

Place the chicken fillets in a layer in the bottom of a baking dish, and pour the sauce over the whole lot.

Then sprinkle over the Mozzarella, Tasty, and Parmesan cheeses.

Bake in the oven at 180^0C for about 15 minutes, or until heated through and the cheese has developed a nice crusty topping.

Your guests will be all over this; like seagulls on a sausage roll.

Chicken in Macadamia Nuts (Australia)

Macadamia nuts are native to north-eastern Australia, the world's largest commercial producer, and are considered to be the world's finest nut. They contain a higher percentage of healthy monounsaturated oils than any other natural product.

Tests indicate that including macadamia nuts in the diet can help to reduce blood pressure, lower undesirable LDL cholesterol, lower blood triglycerides, and despite being high in fat can, when eaten in moderation, contribute to weight loss due to being extremely high in monounsaturated oils, soluble fibre, important vitamins and minerals, and anti-oxidants. There is also evidence of some synergistic activity between the constituents that provides health benefits.

Ingredients (serves 4)

extra virgin olive oil for frying
2 large chicken breast fillets
1 egg, lightly beaten
1 cup salted macadamia nuts, ground finely

Method

Lay the breasts flat and slice them through horizontally to make four thin fillets.

Beat the egg with a little milk, and dip the chicken into the egg mixture.

Dip the chicken into the macadamia nuts to coat all over.

Brown the chicken slowly in the oil until cooked through. Be careful to not overcook it though, or it will be as dry as a chook's tit.

You may want to serve the chicken with a sauce such as the one below.

Roasted Capsicum Sauce (Italy)

Ingredients

2 large red capsicums (bell peppers), halved lengthways
2 cloves fresh garlic, crushed
1 Tbsp extra virgin olive oil
½ tsp sugar
½ tsp sea salt
½ tsp ground white pepper

Method

Grill (broil) the halved red capsicums (red bell peppers) until the skin blisters and starts to blacken. Put them in a plastic bag for 10 minutes to loosen the skin, and then peel them.

Slice the capsicums finely and add them to the garlic already lightly frying in the olive oil. Add the sugar, salt and pepper. Do not burn the garlic or it will become bitter-tasting. Fry the capsicums very lightly and remove them from heat.

Process the capsicums to a bright red smooth paste, and serve it on the side of the chicken.

Chicken Kiev (Russia)

There is argument about whether this dish originated in the Ukraine, with its capital in Kiev, or in Russia. Regardless, it's a classic dish not found a lot on modern menus, and one that I think is much underrated. But, some things can go wrong in the preparation.

- If you flatten out the breasts with a meat mallet and roll the garlic butter up inside, it is easy to get tears in the meat that will let the garlic butter leak out.
- This can also mean you have a large lump of meat to cook, and if you fry it you may end up with the inside not properly cooked and the outside burnt.
- Many resort to baking it, or frying it a little first so as to get it cooked through properly. But the crust is usually not as crisp as it could be.
- Some use toothpicks to hold it together, which can result in nasty surprises in the mouth.
- Often, a lot of extra ingredients are added which detract from the dish.

I believe that the method below provides an easy solution to all of these problems.

Ingredients

2 large breasts of chicken
4tsp minced garlic
4 knobs plain salted butter
½ cup finely chopped flat-leaf parsley
a little plain flour seasoned with salt and pepper
1 egg, with a splash of milk, lightly beaten with a fork
1 cup breadcrumbs
extra virgin olive oil for frying

Method

Lay the breasts flat on a cutting board, and, using a sharp knife cut each one horizontally through the middle so that you end up with four fillets about 2cm thick. Then carefully make a slice with your knife down the side of each fillet without cutting all the way through, to create a pocket in each one. Stuff each fillet with 1tsp garlic, a knob of butter, and a little parsley.

Now glue the opening in each piece together by putting your finger in the flour and the egg and running it down the edge of the opening. Then use a meat mallet to lightly tamp the edge together.

Roll each piece in the flour, then the egg and the breadcrumbs to coat them all over. If you have any egg and breadcrumbs left, do it again, making sure to seal up the cut edge.

Pan-fry the Kievs in hot oil in a frying pan till golden and cooked through. This method ensures that each piece is thin enough to fry properly.

Filling options for some variations on the dish

As an alternative, you may want to try one of these filling mixtures:
Traditional English, with breadcrumbs, finely chopped onion, crushed garlic, fresh thyme, fresh sage, chopped parsley, grated lemon rind, salt and pepper, and an egg.
Greek, with lightly cooked spinach, onion, garlic, fetta cheese, and a dash of nutmeg.

Chicken with Green Peppercorns (France)

Green peppercorns have a unique flavour that goes well with chicken or beef, and are usually available in very small tins from the supermarket.

They are the unripe fruits that become black peppercorns when mature and dried. White peppercorns are the ripe fruits with the skin removed.

This recipe is one of the very best things that can be done with chicken breast fillets.

Ingredients

2 whole chicken breast fillets, sliced lengthways into about 8 pieces
extra virgin olive oil for frying
1 Tbsp butter
1 small brown onion, very finely chopped
1 clove garlic, very finely chopped
1 green shallot (scallion), chopped
2 Tbsp canned green peppercorns, drained
½ tsp ground coriander seed
½ tsp sea salt
a sprig of rosemary leaves
1 Tbsp brandy or sherry
¾ cup dry white wine (sauvignon blanc or chardonnay)
¾ cup cream

Method

Fry the sliced chicken breast fillets in oil in a frying pan until browned on all sides, and remove from the pan.

Add the butter, chopped onion, garlic, and shallot to the pan to fry until they are soft.

Add the green peppercorns, coriander, salt and rosemary leaves.

Add the brandy, and then the white wine to deglaze the pan. Stir until smooth.

Return the chicken pieces to the pan.

Turn down the heat to low and then stir in the cream till the mixture is smooth.

Simmer on low until the chicken is cooked through and the sauce is smooth.

Serve with your choice of vegies.

Options

You could add some champignons along with the peppercorns if you wish.

Or, you could turn this into a beautiful Chicken and Peppercorn Pie by chopping the chicken a little smaller, and using some butter puff pastry sheets for the pie crust.

Fill the pastry with the mixture, sprinkle over some sesame seeds, and bake it at 180^0C until the pastry is cooked and golden.

Jerked Chicken with Banana Relish (Jamaica)

Jerk recipes, usually for chicken or pork, are based on two main ingredients, red hot chillies and allspice (pimento berries, native to the Caribbean).

Ingredients

2 large chicken breast fillets, sliced lengthways into 4 pieces
extra virgin olive oil, for cooking

Jerk Paste Ingredients

juice of 1 Tahitian lime
1 shallot, finely chopped
1 green jalapeno chilli, finely chopped
1Tbsp extra virgin olive oil
1Tbsp balsamic vinegar
1Tbsp Jamaican rum (or another spirit)
2tsp crushed hot chillies (available in a jar)
2tsp crushed garlic
2tsp crushed ginger
2tsp honey
2tsp ground allspice (pimento)
1tsp freshly ground black pepper
1tsp ground cinnamon
1tsp ground nutmeg
1tsp dried thyme

ONE POT MEAL

Method

Lay the breasts flat on a cutting board and slice each horizontally to get 4 pieces.

Marinate the chicken in a paste made by mixing together all the above ingredients, and putting it all in a plastic zip-lock bag in the fridge for several hours, or overnight.

Brown the chicken all over in a little olive oil in a heavy frypan, turn the heat down to low, add any leftover marinade, put the lid on, and cook it through (about 15 minutes). Or, alternatively, you could slip it into the oven for ¾ hour. Serve with the Relish.

Banana Relish

Ingredients

1 brown onion, finely chopped
3 bananas, thinly sliced crossways
the juice of 1 orange
1tsp sugar
1tsp ground coriander seed

Method

Sauté the onion in the oil, and add the other ingredients.

Cook for a few minutes, and serve on the side of the chicken.

Chicken Provençal (France)

Ingredients

2 whole chicken breast fillets, sliced lengthways to make about 8 pieces
extra virgin olive oil for frying
1Tbsp butter
1 French shallot, or small brown onion, very finely chopped
1 clove garlic, very finely chopped
2 slices prosciutto, roughly chopped
small can champignons (button mushrooms), drained
12 cherry tomatoes, whole
12 pitted kalamata olives
6 green beans, peeled and halved
½ red capsicum (bell pepper), finely sliced
½tsp sea salt
½tsp freshly ground black pepper

ONE POT MEAL

Method

Brown the chicken pieces in some oil in a large frying pan until golden all over.
Add the butter, onion, garlic, and prosciutto to fry along with the chicken till fragrant.
Add the mushrooms, tomatoes, olives, beans, capsicum, salt and pepper.
Sauté covered for about 5 minutes, until the chicken is just cooked through.
Give it a shake occasionally. Do not overcook the vegetable ingredients.

Mustard, Ginger and Lemon Chicken (France)

Ingredients

2 whole chicken breast fillets, sliced lengthways to make about 8 pieces
the juice of one lemon, and a little of the lemon zest
2tsp Dijon mustard
1tsp crushed garlic
1tsp minced ginger
2Tbsp extra virgin olive oil for frying
1Tbsp butter
1 French shallot, or a small brown onion, very finely chopped
½ cup dry white wine
½tsp sea salt and ½tsp ground white pepper

Method

Marinate the chicken pieces in the lemon juice, mustard, garlic and ginger for ½ hour, then remove them, dry them with paper towel, and fry them in the oil in a frying pan till well browned on all sides. They will be almost cooked at this stage.
Add the butter and the onion to fry for a minute or two, and then add the white wine. Return any leftover marinade to the pan, add salt and pepper, cover, and cook for a few minutes more before serving with the sauce poured over the top.

MARINATED CHICKEN DRUMSTICKS

Chicken Drumsticks with Garlic (Greece) 'Kotopoulo sti Shara'

Marinade Ingredients

1.5Kg chicken drumsticks
1Tbsp extra virgin olive oil
½ cup dry white wine
juice of one lemon
1tsp crushed garlic
1tsp crushed red chilli
1tsp hot mustard
1tsp dried oregano
1tsp ground coriander seed
1tsp sea salt
1tsp ground black pepper

BARBECUE FRIENDLY

Method

Marinate chicken drumsticks for about 3 hours if possible

Barbecue the drumsticks for about ¼ hour each side, or until cooked and golden.

Or, bake them in the oven for 45 minutes, if the barbecue is busy with other stuff.

Honey Soy Chicken Drumsticks (China)

Marinade Ingredients

1.5Kg chicken drumsticks, or chicken pieces
1Tbsp extra virgin olive oil
1Tbsp honey
2tsp soy sauce
½ cup dry red wine (or dry sherry)
1tsp crushed garlic
1tsp crushed red chilli
1tsp minced ginger root
1tsp ground coriander seed
1tsp dried thyme
1tsp sea salt
1tsp ground black pepper

BARBECUE FRIENDLY

Method

Marinate chicken drumsticks for about 3 hours if possible.

Barbecue the chicken for about 20 minutes each side, or until cooked through.

Or, you can bake the chicken with the marinade in a moderate oven for 45 minutes.

Sprinkle over the top some lightly toasted sesame seeds (heated in a dry pan).

CURRIES

INFO ON SPICES

To have on hand the spices you will need, you have several options open to you. The most basic is just to buy a curry powder off the shelf, which contains a roasted blend of spices suitable for a half-reasonable curry. You could purchase an off the shelf curry paste in a jar, available in a wide variety of spice blends. When freshened up in a little hot oil at some point in the cooking of the dish, they produce quite a respectable curry.

You can also use good quality individual dry spices that are available in the supermarket, my preferred method; providing flexibility in which ones you use, and in what quantity. This way they are always on hand, and you can learn a little bit about them as well. If you use these dry spices, some recommend that you freshen them up by lightly roasting them in a dry frying pan first. Or, allowing them to fry in some oil during some part of the cooking process, say with the browning of some onions, will do the same thing for you and is quick and easy. This is a good practice that I use and find successful.

Spice combinations vary greatly. Masala simply means a spice blend. Garam masala is usually a fragrant blend of cumin, coriander, cardamom, cinnamon, cloves and nutmeg, and a Tandoori masala is a North Indian spice blend that is pretty much the same as the blend for a chicken tikka, or butter chicken curry, as I see it.

Curries are now the number one dish in the U.K. with many people being of Indian or Pakistani origin, and the popularity of the dishes is increasing generally, not only there, but worldwide. They are not difficult to cook, once you get the hang of it, and provide some very easy one-pot meals. There is wide variation in recipes found in cookery books and many have been greatly Westernised as well.

The following two spice blends serve the purpose for the curry recipes in this book, from Northern and Southern India, Sri Lanka, Indonesia, Malaysia, and Thailand. Simply mix them in a cup and add them at the appropriate time in cooking.

Various aromatics and herbs are added in addition, as required by the recipe, and salt and pepper are listed separately. This keeps everything very simple to prepare.

Basic Spice Blend
1tsp ground cumin seed
1tsp ground coriander seed
1tsp ground cardamom seed
1tsp ground fenugreek seed
1tsp ground turmeric

Aromatic Spice Blend
1tsp ground cumin seed
½tsp ground coriander seed
½tsp ground cardamom seed
½tsp ground fenugreek seed
½tsp ground turmeric
½tsp ground cinnamon
½tsp ground nutmeg
½tsp ground cloves
½tsp ground fennel

BEEF CURRY

Beef 'Rendang' (Indonesia) - Spicy Beef Stew

Originally made with water buffalo, it seems. It's definitely one of my favourites.

Ingredients

1.5Kg shin beef or chuck steak cut into 3cm cubes
2 large brown onions, sliced
aromatic spice blend (mix together in a cup)
3 cloves garlic (minced or finely chopped)
3 finely chopped red chillies (or 1Tbsp sambal oelek)
2cm piece of finely chopped green ginger root (or use 1Tbsp minced ginger)
6cm piece of finely chopped lemon grass (bottom part with the outer removed) or bottled lemon grass
400ml can coconut cream
1 cup water
1Tbsp kecap manis (Indonesian soy sauce containing palm sugar, garlic, and star anise) or use soy sauce
1 anchovy fillet
1tsp sea salt
1tsp ground black pepper
2 kaffir lime leaves
1 cup desiccated coconut, dry fried with no oil in a frying pan until it is lightly browned. This ingredient is called 'kerisik', and gives the Rendang its unique taste.

Aromatic Spice Blend
1tsp ground cumin seed
½tsp ground coriander seed
½tsp ground cardamom seed
½tsp ground fenugreek seed
½tsp ground turmeric
½tsp ground cinnamon
½tsp ground nutmeg
½tsp ground cloves
½tsp ground fennel

ONE POT MEAL

Method

Brown the steak in oil in batches in a large pot and remove it to a bowl.

Fry the onions in oil in the pot until lightly golden. Then add the garlic, chillies, ginger, and lemon grass to fry for a minute until fragrant.

Now mix in the spice blend to fry for a minute in the oil till fragrant. These aromatics and spices are the ingredients of what is often referred to as a Rendang curry paste.

Return all of the meat to the pot.

Add the coconut cream, water, kecap manis, anchovy fillet, salt and pepper, and simmer in the pot on the stovetop, uncovered, for about 1 hour.

Season with a little extra salt and pepper to taste if needed, and add the lime leaves and the kerisik.

Simmer for about 1 hour more or a little longer, stirring regularly, until the oil 'splits' from the coconut milk, the meat begins to fry in the oil, and it starts to brown and thicken. It will end up quite dry.

Be careful not to burn it; stir it constantly at this point.

Serve with rice and/or chapattis, or Naan bread (See Breads).

Beef Madras (Southern India)

This is a basic tomato-based curry, and one of the first types to be used in the West. The city of Madras is now known as Chennai.

Ingredients

1.5Kg shin beef or chuck steak cut into 3cm cubes
olive oil for frying
2 large brown onions, sliced
1 stalk celery, chopped
2 finely chopped cloves garlic (or minced garlic)
2 finely chopped red chillies (or minced chilli)
2cm piece grated green ginger root (or minced ginger)
aromatic spice blend (mix them together in a cup)
1 cup beef stock
400gm can chopped tomatoes
1 anchovy fillet
1tsp sea salt
1tsp ground black pepper
2 fresh (not dried) curry leaves if available (or substitute 2 bay leaves)

Aromatic Spice Blend
1tsp ground cumin seed
½tsp ground coriander seed
½tsp ground cardamom seed
½tsp ground fenugreek seed
½tsp ground turmeric
½tsp ground cinnamon
½tsp ground nutmeg
½tsp ground cloves
½tsp ground fennel

Method

Brown the steak in oil in batches in a large pot and remove.

Brown the onions in oil in the pot until light golden brown. Then add the celery, garlic, chillies, and ginger to fry for a minute.

Add the spice blend and stir for about 30 seconds until fragrant.

Return the beef to the pot.

Add the beef stock, tomatoes, anchovy, salt and pepper, and leaves.

Cook the dish, covered, on the top of the stove for 1½ hours.

Serve with some Naan bread. I tell you; you'll be as full as a butcher's dog!

This dish also tastes very good as leftovers the next day!

Options

You can add extra chillies if you prefer it a little bit hotter.

Or, you can make this into a beef and vegetable curry simply by adding the following vegetable ingredients when the tomatoes go in:

1 chopped carrot
1 chopped parsnip
3 chopped potatoes
100gm green beans, halved

ONE POT MEAL

'Massaman' Beef Curry (Thailand)

This curry reportedly originated with Muslims in Thailand, who had close connections with the Arab traders.

It uniquely contains potatoes, coconut cream, and peanuts as its flavour identity.

As with many Thai dishes, you are looking for the combination of sweet, sour, salty, and spicy flavours. In addition to a curry, a full Thai meal will typically include a soup, a stir-fry, rice, and various salads or accompaniments.

Ingredients

1.5Kg shin beef or chuck steak cut into 3cm cubes
olive oil for frying
2 large brown onions, sliced
1 stalk celery, chopped
2 finely chopped cloves garlic (or use minced garlic)
3 finely chopped red chillies (or use minced chilli)
2tsp chopped lemon grass
2cm piece grated green ginger root (or minced ginger)
aromatic spice blend (mix the spices together in a cup)
500gm new potatoes, halved
1 cup beef stock
400gm can coconut cream
1 anchovy fillet (available in small jars)
2 bay leaves
2 kaffir lime leaves
juice of one Tahitian lime
2tsp sugar
1tsp sea salt and 1tsp freshly ground black pepper
2 green shallots, finely chopped
½ cup roasted peanuts

Aromatic Spice Blend
1tsp ground cumin seed
½tsp ground coriander seed
½tsp ground cardamom seed
½tsp ground fenugreek seed
½tsp ground turmeric
½tsp ground cinnamon
½tsp ground nutmeg
½tsp ground cloves
½tsp ground fennel

ONE POT MEAL

Method

Brown the steak in oil in batches in a large pot and remove.

Brown the onions in oil in the pot until light golden brown. Then add the celery, garlic, chillies, lemon grass and ginger to fry for a minute.

Add the spice blend and stir for about 30 seconds until fragrant.

Return the beef to the pot.

Add the potatoes, stock, coconut cream, anchovy, leaves, juice, sugar, salt and pepper.

Cook the dish, covered, on the top of the stove for 1½ hours.

Serve with steamed rice, Naan bread, or delicious Thai-style Rotis (see Breads).

Garnish with the green shallots and the roasted peanuts.

This dish also tastes exceptionally good as leftovers the next day, when the flavours will have soaked well into the potatoes.

LAMB CURRY

'Rogan Josh' (Northern India) - lamb cooked in butter

Ingredients

ghee (clarified butter), or olive oil, for frying
1Kg lamb leg, or shoulder, cut into 3cm cubes
2 large sliced brown onions
2 chopped cloves of garlic
2cm piece green ginger root (or minced)
2 chopped red chillies
1 stalk celery, chopped
1 anchovy fillet
aromatic spice blend (mix it up in a cup)
1 cup natural yoghurt
1tsp sea salt
1tsp freshly ground black pepper
3 fresh curry leaves if available (not dried leaves as they are not very good. Substitute if necessary 2 bay leaves)

> **Aromatic Spice Blend**
> 1tsp ground cumin seed
> ½tsp ground coriander seed
> ½tsp ground cardamom seed
> ½tsp ground fenugreek seed
> ½tsp ground turmeric
> ½tsp ground cinnamon
> ½tsp ground nutmeg
> ½tsp ground cloves
> ½tsp ground fennel

Method

Brown the lamb in ghee (or oil) in batches in a large pot and remove.

Brown the onions in ghee in the pot until light golden brown.

Add the garlic, ginger, chillies, celery, and anchovy to fry for a minute.

Mix in the spice blend and stir for about 30 seconds until fragrant.

Return the lamb to the pot, and turn the heat to low.

Add the yoghurt, salt and pepper, and leaves.

Cook the dish, covered, on low heat on the top of the stove for 1½ hours.

Serve with rice and chapattis, or Naan bread (see Breads)

> **ONE POT MEAL**

'Saag Gosht' (Northern India) - Lamb and Spinach Curry

This recipe uses the one above as the base recipe, but with the following variations.

To the spices, add 1tsp brown mustard seeds.

When the yoghurt is added, also add 1 chopped stalk of coriander (cilantro), along with about 200gm of baby spinach leaves.

> **Safety Tip**
> Make sure that you don't inhale too much curry powder—you could end up in a korma.

'Kofta' Curry (Southern India) – Meatballs in Tomato Sauce

This is my version of the Indian classic dish that has been carried almost worldwide.

Ingredients

½ cup extra virgin olive oil for frying
1Kg good quality lamb mince
1 egg
2 medium brown onions, finely chopped
1 slice bread
aromatic spice blend (mixed in a cup)
2 cloves of garlic, chopped (or 1tspn minced)
2cm piece ginger root, chopped (or 1tspn bottled)
2 red chillies, chopped (or 1tspn minced)
1 cup tomato puree
3 fresh curry leaves, or 2 bay leaves
½tsp salt
½tsp ground black pepper
1 cup water
¾ cup natural yoghurt

> **Aromatic Spice Blend**
> 1tsp ground cumin seed
> ½tsp ground coriander seed
> ½tsp ground cardamom seed
> ½tsp ground fenugreek seed
> ½tsp ground turmeric
> ½tsp ground cinnamon
> ½tsp ground nutmeg
> ½tsp ground cloves
> ½tsp ground fennel

Method

Mix together the lamb mince, the egg, one finely chopped onion, a slice of bread that has been soaked in water and squeezed out, and half of the spice mix.

Roll the mixture into 3cm balls and fry them both sides in a heavy frypan in some oil till lightly brown. Remove them from the pan.

Fry the other onion in oil until translucent, and add the remaining spice mixture to fry for a minute or so.

Add the garlic, ginger, chillies, tomato puree, leaves, and salt and pepper to cook for another minute or so.

Add the water, stir it to a nice consistency, and place the meatballs evenly in the sauce.

Simmer the dish, uncovered, on the top of the stove for about 20 minutes until the meatballs are nicely cooked and the sauce has become thick.

Remove from the heat, add the yoghurt, stir gently, and cook for a few minutes more till heated through.

Serve with Naan bread, chapattis, or rice.

> **ONE POT MEAL**

PORK CURRY

Pork 'Vindaloo' (Portugal, West Indies)

The name originally stems from the Portugese words for 'wine' and 'garlic'.

Ingredients

1Kg pork leg or shoulder fillets cut into 3cm cubes
olive oil for frying (or ghee)
2 large sliced brown onions
2 chopped cloves of garlic (or use minced)
2cm piece of grated green ginger root (or minced)
4 chopped red chillies (or use minced)
1Tbsp brown mustard seeds
1tsp ground allspice
3 fresh curry leaves (not dried) if available
(substitute instead if necessary 2 bay leaves)
1tsp salt
1tsp ground black pepper
1 cup dry white wine
2 cups water
4 large potatoes, peeled and quartered

Aromatic Spice Blend
1tsp ground cumin seed
½tsp ground coriander seed
½tsp ground cardamom seed
½tsp ground fenugreek seed
½tsp ground turmeric
½tsp ground cinnamon
½tsp ground nutmeg
½tsp ground cloves
½tsp ground fennel

Method

Brown the pork in oil (or ghee) in batches in a large pot and remove.

Brown the onions in oil in the pot until light golden brown.

Add the garlic, ginger, chillies, mustard seeds, allspice, to fry a little.

Mix in the spice blend to cook for another minute and stir until fragrant.

Return the pork to the pot.

Add the curry leaves, salt and pepper, white wine, and water.

Cook the dish, covered, on the top of the stove for 1½ hours.

Add the potatoes half way through cooking time.

Serve with some Naan bread.

You can also serve an Apple Raita on the side if you wish to complement it.

ONE POT MEAL

Apple 'Raita' (India)

Mix together:

300gm carton natural yoghurt
1 coarsely grated Lebanese cucumber
1 coarsely grated Granny Smith apple
¼ cup lemon juice

CHICKEN CURRY

Chicken 'Tikka Masala' (North India) – Spicy Chicken

The recipe to make Chicken Korma or Tandoori Chicken will be very similar to this one.

Ingredients

800gm chopped chicken thigh fillets
olive oil for frying
1 large brown onion, finely chopped
1 stalk celery, finely chopped
2 fresh red chillies, finely chopped
2 cloves of fresh garlic, finely chopped
1Tbsp fresh grated ginger (about 2cm piece)
juice of 1 lemon
1 cup plain yoghurt Greek style
½ cup cream
400gm can of crushed tomatoes
1tsp sea salt
1tsp freshly ground black pepper
3 fresh (not dried) curry leaves if available (substitute if necessary 2 fresh kaffir lime leaves or 2 bay leaves)

Aromatic Spice Blend
1tsp ground cumin seed
½tsp ground coriander seed
½tsp ground cardamom seed
½tsp ground fenugreek seed
½tsp ground turmeric
½tsp ground cinnamon
½tsp ground nutmeg
½tsp ground cloves
½tsp ground fennel

ONE POT MEAL

Method

Toss the chicken pieces in the spice blend to coat them all over.

Brown the chicken both sides in oil in a large frying pan and remove.

Fry the onion, celery, chilli, garlic, and ginger in oil until lightly cooked.

Return the chicken to the pan.

Add the lemon juice, yoghurt, cream, tomatoes, salt and pepper, and leaves.

Cook for 30 minutes uncovered in the pan. Serve with rice and pappadums.

Chicken 'Makhani' (North India) – Butter Chicken

Butter Chicken, a favourite Westernised version of this curry, is very similar to the above recipe.

Follow the recipe above, but with the following variations:

At the same time as you add the yoghurt, add 100gm crushed raw cashew nuts that have been dry roasted a little in a frying pan (or use already roasted cashews).

Then, near the end of cooking time, add 30gm butter.

Chicken and King Prawn Green Curry (Thailand)

Ingredients (serves 4)

½ cup extra virgin olive oil for frying
800gm skinless chicken thigh fillets (about 8), quartered, or 1Kg skinned drumsticks
basic spice blend as shown
1 large brown onion, finely chopped
1 stalk celery, finely chopped
2 cloves of garlic, chopped (or 1tsp crushed garlic)
2cm piece ginger root, chopped (or 1tsp bottled)
2 jalapeno chillies, chopped, or 2 long green chillies
2 fresh curry leaves if available (or 2 bay leaves)
2 fresh kaffir lime leaves
2 green shallots, finely chopped
small handful of fresh flat-leafed (Italian) parsley
1 stalk fresh coriander leaf (cilantro)
1 stalk lemon grass, chopped (or 1tsp bottled)
1 anchovy fillet, chopped
1 lime (or lemon), juiced
1 green capsicum (bell pepper), chopped into chunks
50gm green beans, chopped in half
50gm broccoli florets
½ cup water
200ml can coconut cream (half of a 400ml can)
1tsp sea salt and 1tsp cracked pepper
16 peeled green (raw) king prawns (usually available frozen), defrosted

Basic Spice Blend
1tsp ground cumin seed
1tsp ground coriander seed
1tsp ground cardamom seed
1tsp ground fenugreek seed
1tsp ground turmeric

ONE POT MEAL

Method

Roll the chicken drumsticks or fillets in the spice blend and fry them both sides in a heavy frypan in some oil till lightly browned. Remove from the pan.
Fry the onion in oil until translucent, and add any remaining spices for a minute or so.
Add the aromatics of celery, garlic, ginger, and chillies to cook for another minute.
Return the chicken to the pan, and add the rest of the ingredients (except the prawns).
Simmer the dish, uncovered, on the top of the stove for about 30 minutes, until the chicken is nicely cooked through and the sauce has thickened a little.
Add the prawns for 3 minutes only, and serve with yellow coconut rice, or steamed rice.

Yellow Coconut Rice

Fry a small chopped onion and a clove of crushed garlic along with 1tsp ground turmeric in a little oil till fragrant, not browned. Add 1 cup rice and give it a stir to coat. Add 1 cup of water and 200ml coconut cream (perhaps the other half of the 400ml can) and bring this to the boil.
Reduce the heat to low, cover, and cook for about 15 minutes.
Let it sit for a few minutes and then stir it with a fork to separate the grains.

Chicken 'Tikka' (South India) – Chicken Pieces

This is my version of the famous Southern Indian recipe with Chinese influence called 'Chicken 65', which has as many explanations for the name, and as many variations, as there are restaurants. Having an unusual method of preparation, it is worth the effort.

Ingredients

800gm chicken thigh fillets, cut to bite size
olive oil for frying
1 egg
3 Tbsp cornflour

Stir fry ingredients

½ red onion, very finely sliced
½ tsp crushed garlic
½ tsp crushed ginger root
½ tsp crushed red chilli
½ tsp salt
½ tsp ground white pepper
2 tsp brown mustard seeds
2 curry leaves if they are available
2 dried red chillies, chopped, for flavour
2 stalks coriander leaves for a unique flavour
8 baby spinach leaves
aromatic spice blend
½ cup plain yoghurt

Marinade Ingredients
juice of one lemon
½ tsp crushed garlic
½ tsp crushed ginger root
½ tsp hot red ground chilli

Aromatic Spice Blend
1 tsp ground cumin seed
½ tsp ground coriander seed
½ tsp ground cardamom seed
½ tsp ground fenugreek seed
½ tsp ground turmeric
½ tsp ground cinnamon
½ tsp ground nutmeg
½ tsp ground cloves
½ tsp ground fennel

Step 1 Marinate and Grill

Marinate the chicken pieces in the marinade ingredients for at least 1 hour.
Place the chicken pieces on a shallow tray and grill them under the stove griller (broiler) for about 4 minutes until partially cooked and lightly seared to give them a slightly smoky taste (the authentic method would be to use an Indian clay tandoor oven).

Step 2 Batter and Fry

Dip the chicken pieces in a batter made by mixing the egg and cornflour. In a frypan, fry the chicken pieces in batches in 1cm deep oil until golden, turning them as needed, remove them from the pan, and drain them on kitchen paper. At this stage, you can leave it for a while if you wish.

Step 3 Stir Fry and Reduce

In just a little oil in the same pan (or in a different pan if you want to continue frying another batch) stir fry the ingredients listed (except for the yoghurt), for 1 or 2 minutes, and return the chicken to the pan to heat through. Reduce the heat a little now and add the yoghurt. Reduce the mixture until it is fairly dry.
Serve with wedges of lemon and some Naan or Chapatti bread. Amazing and different!

SEAFOOD CURRY

Seafood Curry with King Prawns and Chick Peas (Sri Lanka)

Chick Peas (Garbanzo beans, or Ceci beans) are an ancient legume that is high in protein. While a little boring when used in some recipes, here they add some texture and provide good food value.

Curry Ingredients (Serves about 6)

1Tbsp olive oil
1 brown onion, finely chopped
1 stick celery, finely chopped
1 carrot, finely chopped
1tsp crushed garlic
1tsp crushed chilli
1tsp ground ginger
1tsp brown mustard seeds
aromatic spice blend
400gm can chick peas, drained
1 cup water
2 kaffir lime leaves
2 fresh curry leaves
1.2Kg butternut pumpkin, peeled, cut into pieces
1tsp sea salt
1tsp ground black pepper
400ml can coconut milk

Aromatic Spice Blend
1tsp ground cumin seed
½tsp ground coriander seed
½tsp ground cardamom seed
½tsp ground fenugreek seed
½tsp ground turmeric
½tsp ground cinnamon
½tsp ground nutmeg
½tsp ground cloves
½tsp ground fennel

ONE POT MEAL

Seafood Ingredients

200gm boneless white fish, cut into 6 portions (please check thoroughly for bones)
1 fresh cleaned calamari (squid) tube sliced into rings, soaked in milk for 15 minutes
18 frozen peeled green (raw) king prawns, thawed by running cold water over them

Method

Lightly brown the onion, celery, and carrot in the oil.
Add the garlic, chilli, ginger, mustard seeds, and spices, to fry for half a minute.
Add the chick peas, water, lime leaves, curry leaves, pumpkin, salt and pepper, and simmer for 30 minutes.
Remove the leaves and blend the mixture with a stick blender till smooth and soupy.
Add the coconut milk and simmer uncovered for 5 more minutes, stirring occasionally.
The curry is now complete and should be a nice golden colour.
Meanwhile, lightly fry the seafood in a small amount of olive oil in a frypan.
The white fish will take the longest. When cooked, remove it from the frypan.
Next cook the squid for about 1 minute each side, and remove.
Then cook the prawns for about 2 minutes each side
Serve the curry in 6 bowls, apportioning the seafood among them and placing it on top.

VEGETABLE CURRY

'Dum Aloo' (India) Potato Curry

Ingredients

1 brown (yellow) onion, finely chopped
1tsp crushed garlic
1tsp grated ginger root
1tsp brown mustard seeds
1tsp minced red chilli
spice blend
1Kg chopped potatoes (about 1½ cm cubes)
1 cup plain yoghurt
1tsp sea salt
½tsp ground black pepper

> **Basic Spice Blend**
> 1tsp ground cumin seed
> 1tsp ground coriander seed
> 1tsp ground cardamom seed
> 1tsp ground fenugreek seed
> 1tsp ground turmeric

> **ONE POT MEAL**

Method

Fry the onion till it is just starting to colour, and then add the garlic, ginger, mustard seeds, and chilli to fry for a couple of minutes. Add the spice blend to fry for a minute. Stir in the chopped potatoes to coat in the spices, and stir while cooking for a little while. Add the yoghurt, salt and pepper. Cover and cook until fairly dry, about ¼ hour.

'Aloo Methi' (India) – Potato with Fenugreek Leaves

Make the potato curry according to the above recipe. Add 1 small bunch kasuri methi leaves (fenugreek leaves) when the yoghurt goes in. If unavailable, substitute some celery leaves. The fenugreek leaves have a unique flavour that goes well with potatoes.

'Dhal' (India) Lentil Curry

Cook some red lentils in water about 20 mins and drain. Dry fry some mustard seeds, cumin, coriander, turmeric and a little cinnamon and nutmeg in a dry frying pan. Add some oil and fry some onions, ginger, garlic and chilli. Add to the lentils and blend.

Eggplant Curry with Yoghurt

2 large eggplants
1 chopped onion
2 cloves chopped garlic
1tsp each ground cumin, ground coriander, turmeric, fenugreek, nutmeg, black pepper.
juice of 1 lemon
1 cup plain yoghurt

Pierce the whole eggplants once and bake for 1 hour in the oven. When cooled a little, chop the flesh into cubes. Fry the onions and garlic, and add the spices to cook a little. Add the lemon juice, eggplant, remove from the heat, and stir through the yoghurt.

DUCK

ROAST DUCK

'Canard à l'Orange' (France) Roast Duck in Orange Sauce

For this classic dish, I find that a whole fresh duckling is best. It is cheaper than buying duck breasts, and a whole duck will serve about six people.

Method for Roasting the Duck

Always roast the duck in a hot oven of about 190°C. A 2½Kg duck will take 2½ hrs. For a crispy skin, wipe the uncooked duck dry with kitchen paper and sprinkle a little salt on the skin. Place the duck on a rack in a baking tray so the fat can drain freely. Ensure the vent end of the duck is always open, allowing the heat to cook the meat from the inside as well. Never stuff the cavity of a whole duck as this prevents hot air entering the duck cavity. If you wish, a few herbs, some orange zest, or some star anise placed inside will make for a good aroma and add to the flavour. Duck, as with all meats and poultry, should rest after cooking, to allow the juices to settle. It is also easier to handle and carve. To serve, put some sauce on the plate with the orange slices to the side, and place the duck portions on top of the sauce to prevent the nice crispy skin from going soggy. Or, if you like, you can serve the orange sauce separately in a jug. Put some carrots or potatoes cut in half in with the duck for the last hour of cooking. Save the duck fat from the baking dish after cooking and use it for making the best ever chips, as it is very high in monounsaturated fat, has a high smoke point, and is one of the few fats that can be re-used. Or, mix some of the fat with some minced garlic to make Gascony Butter for spreading on croutons. You can also make some crepes to wrap up any leftover duck meat with a green shallot and some Hoi Sin sauce. Yum!

Orange Sauce Ingredients

1/2 cup sugar
1/3 cup water
1/4 cup red wine vinegar
3 cups orange juice
2 cups chicken stock
1/4 cup of Cointreau orange liqueur
1Tbsp honey
salt and white pepper
a sprig of thyme and some chives, chopped
1 Navel orange, sliced thinly into rounds
1Tbsp cornflour mixed with a little water

Method

Boil the sugar and water until it starts to caramelize. Add the liquids and herbs and spices and simmer until the sauce is reduced by about half. Add the orange slices to cook a little, and thicken the sauce by stirring in the cornflour mixture.

EGGS

BASIC EGGS

Fried eggs

Get some fresh cackleberries, and break them into some hot light oil in a frying pan. Spoon any excess oil over the yolks to cook them sunny side up, or you may want to flip them when the underside is cooked. About 4 minutes should give you medium eggs. Non-stick egg rings can be used in the pan or on the hotplate if you prefer your eggs to be round and neat. The whites should be properly cooked, and not runny.
My wife, Correen, likes her googs with their eyes closed, or even blindfolded.

Poached Eggs

Bring some water to the boil. Crack your henfruit, one at a time, into a small bowl or cup. Swirl the water with your spoon to make a whirlpool, and slide the egg in. About 4 minutes cooking should give you semi-soft eggs.

Eggs Benedict

These are made by placing poached eggs, shaved ham, avocado, baby spinach leaves, and some quick Hollandaise sauce (below) on an English muffin:
Melt 200gm butter in a saucepan with 1Tbsp water and 1tsp white vinegar. Do not let it burn. Then slowly drizzle the butter mixture into a blender containing 4 egg yolks and 2Tbsp lemon juice, salt and pepper.

Boiled Eggs

Place the whole eggs in a saucepan, and cover with cold water. Cover and bring the eggs to the boil over high heat. Reduce the heat to medium, and simmer gently for 4 minutes for medium boiled eggs (2 for soft, 6 for hard). Remove the eggs with a spoon.

Coddled eggs

Boil the water first, and gently place the whole eggs in the water. Remove the water from the heat when it gets to a light boil again, and let the eggs cook in the water for 6 minutes for medium eggs. Remove the eggs with a spoon.

Scrambled Eggs

Break your yolkers into a bowl, add a splash of milk, and whisk them up.
Tip them into a frypan greased with some butter.
Stir them gently with a plastic spoon while cooking, until creamy curds form.
You can add, if you wish, some grated cheese or chopped green shallots to the mixture.

FRITTATA

These frittata recipes are tops. Quick and easy, tasty and versatile, they will provide the basis for a quick meal for four.

Egg and Bacon Frittata (Italy)

Ingredients

3 rashers of bacon, chopped
20gm butter
1 small brown onion, chopped
6 eggs
¾ cup cream
salt and freshly ground black pepper
2 green shallots, chopped
grated parmesan cheese

> **Safety Tip**
> Be careful not to drop the eggs.
> That's why chickens lay them.

Method

Fry the bacon in the butter until browned and remove it from the frying pan.
Fry the onion in the butter and fat until it starts to brown.
Pour in the lightly whisked eggs, cream, salt and pepper and cook on low heat until the edges are starting to set, about 4 minutes.
Top with the cooked bacon and shallots and cook for about 4 minutes more, until the eggs are almost set.
Sprinkle on a little grated parmesan cheese and put the whole pan under the griller for about 3 minutes until the egg is set and the top is golden.

Basil, Bacon, and Ricotta Frittata

Cook the frittata as above, but use only one rasher of bacon, and add a cup of ricotta cheese and some fresh basil leaves to the top.

Chicken, Spinach and Feta Frittata

Cook as above, but instead of bacon, add a cup of cooked chicken meat, some fresh baby spinach leaves and about 100gm of crumbled feta cheese to the top.

Ham and Cheese Frittata

Cook as above, but instead of bacon, add 4 slices chopped ham and a cup of grated cheddar cheese to the top.

Smoked Salmon and Caper Frittata

Cook as above, but instead of bacon, add 2 slices of chopped smoked salmon, some capers, and a couple of chopped rocket leaves.

OTHER EGG RECIPES

'Spanakopita' (Greece) Spinach Pie

This dish is a Greek classic. The Greeks often eat either Spanakopita (spinach pie) or Tyropita (cheese pie) as a mid-morning snack, as breakfast is not commonly eaten. I think I could happily live on this for quite a while.

Ingredients

2 tablespoons olive oil
2 brown onions, finely chopped
400gm baby spinach leaves, washed (or use spinach or silver beet leaves)
4 shallots, chopped
½ cup broad-leafed parsley, chopped
¼ cup dill leaves, chopped
4 eggs, lightly beaten
1tsp black pepper
¼tsp sea salt
300gm Greek feta cheese, crumbled
375gm packet chilled filo pastry (from the refrigerator, not freezer, section)
150gm butter, melted
½ cup hard cheese, grated (parmesan or pecorino Romano are suitable)

Method

Heat olive oil in a large frying pan over medium heat and add the onion to cook, stirring for 5 minutes until soft, and put aside.

Lightly whisk the eggs in a bowl, and add the salt and pepper.

Preheat oven to 180°C. Grease a large 30cm x 38cm base baking dish with oil.

Place one pastry sheet on the workbench. Brush with melted butter with a pastry brush. Top with 2 pastry sheets. Brush with butter. Continue to layer the pastry, brushing every second layer with melted butter, until you use half the sheets to line the base of the baking dish.

Now layer the filling of spinach leaves, fried onions, chopped shallots, parsley, dill, and crumbled feta, and pour over the egg mixture evenly. Season with the salt and pepper.

Use the remaining pastry sheets to cover the spinach filling, brushing every second sheet as before. Brush the top with butter. Sprinkle over the parmesan cheese. Bake for 40 minutes or until golden brown and crisp. Allow it to cool in the pan for 15 minutes. Cut it into squares to serve about 8, depending on how much you want to steal for lunches the next day.

Refrigerate whatever is left over, covered. You can reheat it or just serve it cold.

This is really good Greek tucker!

Bacon and Egg Quiche (somewhere in Europe)

Similar to a Frittata, which is Italian, but with a pastry case, a quiche is considered to be French. But the name apparently was borrowed from the German 'kishe', and these types of recipes go back over 600 years in England. Who knows where it's from!

Often the pastry case is blind baked first using pastry weights, supposedly to stop the pastry sagging, bubbling, shrinking, or going soggy. In my experience, it seems to be a waste of time and effort and totally useless - like teats on a bull. Not needed.

Ingredients for simple shortcrust pastry

1½ cups plain flour
a pinch of salt
60gm butter, chopped
½ cup sugar
½ cup milk

Ingredients for the filling (Serves four)

1Tbsp olive oil
4 rashers of smoked bacon, chopped into small pieces
1 onion, finely chopped
1 green shallot (the skinny kind), chopped
a few sprigs of parsley, chopped
a few sprigs of dill
6 eggs
½ cup milk
½ cup cream
1tsp sea salt
1tsp freshly ground black pepper
1 cup grated tasty cheese

> **Safety Tip**
> When in France, you don't eat more than one egg at a time; because one egg is 'un oeuf'.

Method

Put the flour and salt into a bowl and add the butter, crumbling it up with your fingers until you have a breadcrumb feel to it.

Stir in the sugar and then stir in enough of the milk to make firm dough. Wrap this in plastic wrap and put it in the fridge for a half an hour to rest.

Then roll out the pastry to about 5mm and place it on a 25cm pie plate, crimping the edges nicely to decorate.

Meanwhile, fry the bacon and onion in the oil in a frypan till just starting to colour and then when it has cooled a little, put it in the pastry case.

Sprinkle in the chopped green shallot and the parsley and the dill.

In a bowl, whisk the eggs with the milk, cream, salt and pepper, and pour the mixture into the case. Sprinkle the cheese over the top.

Bake the quiche in the oven at 180^0C for about 30 minutes or so, until it is cooked.

Options

You could also add champignons, olives, anchovies, spinach, or sun-dried tomatoes.

'Omelette au Fromage' (France) Cheese Omelette

Omelettes are pretty basic food and can be cooked quickly. They have been around for centuries and every cuisine seems to have an equivalent. The Chinese version is called Egg Fu Yung, which is sometimes deep-fried.

The word seems to have originally derived from the Latin for 'thin plate'.

With a whisk, lightly mix together 2 eggs and a dash of milk, salt and pepper.

Pour into a 20cm non stick pan greased with melted butter. As the omelette cooks draw some of the cooked egg away from the edge with the whisk and tilt the pan so that the uncooked part runs to the edge. This will aid even cooking. It should only take about one minute.

Before the top is fully set, sprinkle a bit of chopped parsley and some grated cheese on the top. Or, you could use some chopped green shallots, cooked mushrooms, sun-dried tomatoes, or other filling as well.

Fold the omelette over in half in the pan, and when it appears to be cooked, slide it on to a serving plate.

It should be light in texture, golden on the outside, and slightly underdone on the inside, but not runny.

Savoury Bread and Butter Pudding

Sauté an onion, a leek and a couple of green shallots in a little butter in a pan.

Whisk together a couple of eggs, some grated cheese, some milk, a little French mustard, and salt and pepper.

Now butter and cut diagonally about 8 slices of bread. Layer some bread, some onion mixture and some egg mixture and repeat till all of it is used.

Sprinkle a little Parmesan cheese over the top and bake in the oven for about $\frac{3}{4}$ hour.

Bacon and Egg Casserole

Line a casserole dish with buttered bread slices, with the butter facing out.

Fill up the middle with a mixture of bread cubes, cooked bacon pieces, grated cheese and a chopped spring onion.

Pour over the top a mixture of 2 eggs, milk, a little mustard, salt and pepper.

Bake in the oven for $\frac{1}{2}$ hour.

Welsh Rarebit

Mix together some grated cheese, butter, mustard, a dash of Worcestershire sauce, an egg, salt and pepper, and a splash of beer.

Spread generously on toast and grill until melted and browning.

In Yorkshire they put some bacon rashers and a poached egg on top.

FAST FOOD

A WORD ABOUT FAST FOOD

'Fast food', otherwise described by many as 'junk food', has developed a bad name, due to the unhealthy nature of many fast foods, and a positive worldwide trend towards more healthy eating. But 'fast food' needn't be unhealthy; although it often is.
As a long-time 'junk food' aficionado, I have included here a collection of my favourite recipes, which have been refined over the years to resemble my favourite take-away (take-out) foods, but which have a difference. All of the recipes here are genuinely healthy, are made with basic whole foods and natural healthy fats that are used in moderation, and are often steamed, baked, or grilled; instead of fried. Enjoy!

BONZER TAKE-AWAY-FOOD-SHOP TUCKER

Steamed Dim Sims (Australia, believe it or not)

Dim Sims (not dim sum) originated in 1945 with the Australian chef William Wing Young. To make your own, start with about 2 cups of plain flour, add 1tsp olive oil, ½tsp salt and 1/3 cup or so of warm water to make dough when mixed and kneaded. Roll the dough flat and thin, and cut it into about 10cm circles with a large drinking glass. Or, you can buy ready made fresh dumpling or wonton wrappers from the refrigerated section of the supermarket or Asian grocer (won ton wrappers are yellow and contain eggs).
Make a filling for the Dim Sims by mixing together 500gm pork mince, 1 cup of shredded Chinese Won bok cabbage, 2 very finely chopped shallots, 2tsp minced garlic, a 1cm piece of grated fresh ginger, ½tsp of sesame oil, ½tsp Chinese five spice, 1tsp freshly ground white pepper, 2tsp dark soy sauce and an egg to bind it all. Put a little of the filling into each round of pastry and pinch the edges up. Steam them in batches in a stainless steel or bamboo steamer lined with baking paper, for about 20 minutes. This mixture will make about 40 Dim Sims. Yum! Serve with soy sauce, or chilli paste (below).

Bazza's Healthy Baked Spring Rolls

Brown a chopped onion and then some pork and veal mince in olive oil and a little sesame oil in a pan. Add 1tsp crushed garlic, 1tsp minced ginger, 1tsp chopped lemon grass, 1 anchovy, finely chopped carrot, celery, Asian greens, some ground coriander, salt and pepper, and cook this for a while. When cooled a little, roll small portions of the mixture in spring roll wrappers by folding in the ends first and then rolling them up (these are available from the supermarket frozen food section). Place them on a tray, and bake them in the oven for about 20 minutes until cooked. Serve with soy sauce or chilli paste.

Chilli Paste (Indonesia) 'Sambal Ulek'

Fry about 10 finely chopped hot red chillies in a little oil in a frypan till fragrant. Add 1Tbsp white wine vinegar, 1tsp sugar, 1tsp sea salt and cook for another minute. Process the mixture to a paste. It will keep in the fridge for a few days if necessary.

Baked Potato Chips (Everywhere)

You'll notice that I haven't called these 'French Fries'. That's because they're not French, and they're not fried. They are healthy, and very, very tasty!

Chop up potatoes lengthwise into about 1cm strips. Waxy, low starch potatoes are the best, such as Sebago, King Edward or Pink Eye. Rinse them and dry them off thoroughly with a tea towel or paper towels. This is the secret, because you want the heat of the oven to be used in baking the chips; not wasted in evaporating the moisture.

Put them in a baking dish and rub them all over with plenty of good quality extra virgin olive oil using your fingers. This will also help the heat to penetrate the chips.

Sprinkle liberally with good quality sea salt, and bake them in a hot oven at about 220°C for 45 minutes or until spectacularly golden brown. Or, if you have something else in the oven at a lower temperature, then about an hour at 180°C should do it.

Turn them with a spatula at a little more than half way through cooking time, when they start to release from the dish. This recoats them with whatever oil is left in the dish.

'Potato Scallops' (Australia) aka 'Potato Cakes'

These are almost an institution in Australia, and good ones are to die for.

500gm large old potatoes, peeled, and sliced to 3mm thickness (use a mandolin)
2 cups self-raising flour
1 teaspoon sea salt flakes
¼ teaspoon white pepper
1½ cups water
1 cup extra virgin olive oil

> **Safety Tip**
> Only eat one on an empty stomach; after that it won't really be empty.

Method

Put the flour, salt and pepper into a bowl.

Dry the potatoes and drop them into the flour to coat. Remove them to a plate. Gradually add water to the flour, mixing with a whisk to a fairly thick coating batter. Coat the potato slices with the batter till well covered, and place them into some shallow hot oil in a pan, a few at a time, until golden. Drain, and sprinkle with sea salt.

Fried Chicken (United States)

Put some plain flour and, literally, a little bit of every herb and spice you can find in the pantry in a plastic bag, with some sliced chicken breast fillets, twist the bag at the top and shake it to coat the chicken. Dead chook easy!

Put the chicken pieces in a roasting pan with a little extra virgin olive oil drizzled over the top, and bake them in the oven at 180°C for 45 mins, turning once.

This tastes just like the unhealthy versions that are deep fried in a pressure cooker!

Chicken Nuggets (United States)

Follow the recipe above, but simply chop up the chicken a little smaller. You could also use chicken thigh fillets for this. They will only need about 30 minutes cooking time.

PIES, PASTIES AND SAUSAGE ROLLS

Homemade Aussie Meat Pie (Australia, of course)

Ingredients for the Filling

1.5Kg chuck steak (or shin beef, oyster blade, or topside, or minced beef)
2 lamb kidneys, chopped (optional for a Steak and Kidney Pie)
2Tbsp extra virgin olive oil for frying
2 medium sized brown (yellow) onions, finely chopped
1Tbsp beef booster
1Tbsp dark soy sauce
1Tbsp Worcestershire sauce (or use 1 chopped anchovy fillet)
1tsp dried mixed herbs
1tsp sea salt and 1tsp freshly ground black pepper
2 cups water, also later ½ cup water with 3tsp cornflour added as a thickening agent

Ingredients for the Homemade Shortcrust Pastry

3 cups plain flour (about 450gm)
a pinch of salt
100gm butter
100ml water
½ cup extra virgin olive oil (about 115gm)

Method

Keep in mind that the cheapest cuts of beef make the tastiest pie, but you will usually need to cook them a little longer to make them tender. To make individual pies, it is better to use half cubed steak and half beef mince, as it is easier to fill the pies. First fry the onions and meat in the olive oil. When nicely browned, add the beef booster, soy sauce, Worcestershire sauce, herbs, salt, pepper, and water, and cook the mixture, covered, on the top of the stove for an hour. The equal quantities of soy sauce and Worcestershire sauce produce a pie that tastes just like a famous Aussie meat pie. Thicken the mixture by stirring in the cornflour in water before filling the pie case(s). For the shortcrust pastry, rub the butter into the dry ingredients till it is crumbly, and add the water and oil till you have firm dough. Do not overwork it. Put it in the fridge for an hour to rest; this makes the pastry elastic and easy to roll. Roll it out to about 3mm thickness, and use it to line a large pie dish, and make a cover. Or, this will make about 8 small pies. The trick with shortcrust pastry is making it 'short'. You will need a delicate pastry that is flaky, but strong enough to hold the filling. The more butter, the shorter and flakier. The general rule with shortcrust pastry is that the fat is half the quantity of flour. Handle it as little as possible, and use cool ingredients. You don't want to stretch the gluten in the mixture, as this makes it tough. It is the opposite to bread and pasta which needs to be worked. Shortcrust pastry will not rise in baking, as there is no leavening agent, so sift the flour as well, to incorporate some air and make it light. You could also buy ready-made shortcrust pastry sheets for the base, and puff pastry sheets for the top, from the supermarket. Fill the pie(s), and bake them for about 40 minutes in the oven at $180^{0}C$, or until golden brown.

Meat and Vegetable Pasties (Britain) – aka 'Oggies'

Pasties originated in Cornwall or Devon, but are found throughout Britain. Cornish tin miners evidently carried the 'Oggy' recipe to countries such as the United States, South Africa, and Australia. Debate exists over the exact ingredients, and whether the seam should be at the side, making a D shape, or at the top. They were sometimes made with the pastry ends extended so that miners could eat them and throw away the dirty bits on the end (probably a good idea, since the tin ore often contained arsenic).

The Cornish Pasty Association restricted the use of the name, 'Cornish Pasty' in 2011, by gaining 'Protected Geographical Indicator' (PGI) status in Europe.

One secret of the Cornish pasty is the use of the swede, a yellow turnip, or rutabaga, a cross between a cabbage and a turnip. Poor English and Welsh farmers used to make pasties just with vegies including swede and leek, when there was little meat, and did quite well. I remember my mother and grandmother, of English and Welsh descent, commonly using swede in soups, stews, pies, and pasties. Another secret of pasties is that, unlike meat pies, the filling ingredients are all raw, with no additional flavourings.

Ingredients

250gm veal, beef or lamb mince (or traditionally, finely diced skirt steak)
1 large chopped potato (a waxy variety preferably)
1 large chopped onion
1 stalk chopped celery
1 small chopped carrot
1 small chopped swede
1Tbsp chopped parsley
1tsp sea salt and 1tsp freshly ground black pepper

Method

Mix the ingredients together after chopping up the vegies very finely.

Place a mound of filling on each pastry round, and dust a little plain flour over the top, along with a small dollop of butter to produce gravy inside the pasties. Fold the pastry over and crimp the edges together, using some beaten egg or milk to seal them. Pierce a couple of small holes in the top to let the steam out, and brush some of the egg over the top. Bake them for about 45 minutes at $180^{0}C$ or until well cooked through.

Homemade Shortcrust Pastry

2 cups plain flour (preferably strong bread flour)
1tsp baking powder
a pinch of salt
125gm butter chopped into cubes
½ cup water

Rub the butter into the dry ingredients till crumbly, gradually add the water till you have firm dough, and put it in the fridge for an hour.

Roll out pieces of dough to 3mm thickness, and cut 15cm circles using a bread and butter plate as a template. Or, you can buy frozen shortcrust pastry sheets.

Homemade Sausage Rolls

Sausage rolls are another fast food favourite, and they are quite tasty and healthy when made this way. The ingredients, method, and taste are not dissimilar to those of the famous English pork pies; however these ones require a little less labour.

This recipe contains diced apple as the secret ingredient, keeping the mixture moist.

Ingredients

600gm good quality pork and veal mince
1 cup breadcrumbs
1 finely chopped brown onion
1 Granny Smith apple or similar, cored, peeled, and finely diced
1tsp extra virgin olive oil
1tsp mixed herbs
1tsp ground cardamom seed
1tsp ground coriander seed
1tsp sea salt
1tsp white pepper
3 sheets frozen butter puff pastry (not the margarine variety, please)

Method

Use your hands to mix together well the ingredients down to the salt and pepper.

Lay the three sheets of puff pastry out on a bench top with the plastic layer still on the underneath side. This is a good trick for cleanliness, and also makes it easier to separate them later.

The pastry sheets will begin to thaw out and will be able to be handled easily by the time that you have the mixture in place on top of the pastry.

Divide the mixture into six portions and place two on each sheet of pastry.

Form the mixture into two sausage shapes on each sheet of pastry, a little way in from the edges of the sheets.

Fold each sheet over towards the middle to make two long logs and press to seal the edges down where they meet in the middle. Peel the plastic sheets from off the top of the pastry, but do not fully remove them till after you have cut the rolls into pieces.

Cut the pastry up the middle of the two logs, and cut the sausage rolls crossways into four pieces. This will give you eight sausage rolls from each sheet of pastry, making 24 sausage rolls in total.

Remove the sausage rolls from the pieces of plastic, and place them on two oven trays on sheets of baking paper. This prevents them from sticking to the trays.

Bake them in the oven for almost an hour, until cooked through and browned.

Keep in mind that the ingredients are raw, and so need to be fully cooked.

Serve with some good quality tomato sauce (ketchup) in a jug (or the bottle). Yum!

BURGERS

The hamburger probably originated from simple recipes in Germany known as Hamburg Steak. There are now countless variations of the burger. Wrap your laughing gear around one of these beauties.

> BARBECUE FRIENDLY

The Great Aussie Sourdough Burger (Australia)

Make some patties using lean beef mince, an egg, 1 finely diced onion, and a pinch of mixed herbs, a little finely chopped parsley, salt and pepper. Flatten them out to about 1cm and cook them on the hotplate till done. At the same time cook the same quantity of eggs, bacon rashers, and servings of fried onions to go on the burgers.

Toast and butter some thick slices of sourdough bread (really healthy) or rolls, and put on plates. Place on one side some lettuce, a slice of tomato, a slice of red onion, and a slice of cooked canned beetroot. When the other ingredients are cooked, put them on the other side with salt and pepper. Serve with tomato sauce (ketchup) or barbecue sauce (see Sauces for Bazza's Barbecue Sauce). Absolutely bloomin' marvellous!

Or, switch the patty for a slice of Scotch fillet steak, and you have a Steak Sandwich.

The Big American Burger (United States)

This is my recipe for a combination that resembles a favourite American-style burger. Make some patties using lean beef mince, an egg, salt and pepper, and cook them on the hotplate until done. Put them on toasted hamburger rolls with iceberg lettuce, finely sliced dill cucumbers, finely chopped red onion, a slice of cheese (not the plastic stuff), and some special sauce made by mixing together the following ingredients:

1 cup Whole Egg Mayonnaise
¼ cup Sweet Mustard Pickles
¼ cup Red Tomato Relish
¼ cup French Dressing

Lamb and Haloumi Burgers (Greece)

Make lamb patties by mixing together some lean lamb mince with a little finely chopped onion, an egg, a little finely chopped or dried oregano, salt and pepper. Flatten them a little and fry them on the barbecue in a little olive oil. At the same time, fry some slices of haloumi cheese both sides, and some red capsicum (bell pepper) slices. Put these on toasted grain bread rolls spread with some Roasted Eggplant Dip (See Dips for Baba Ganoush). Or, make a yoghurt dressing by mixing some plain yoghurt, chopped dill cucumbers, chopped shallots, chopped parsley, capers, chopped garlic and lemon juice.

Beef 'Bulgogi' Burgers (Korea) - fire meat

Marinate very finely sliced beef rump in a mixture of soy sauce, rice cooking wine, chopped garlic, chopped chilli, chopped shallots, sugar, salt, pepper and a dash of sesame oil, for about 3 hours. Cook the beef on a hot barbecue plate until just cooked. Serve this on fresh crusty bread rolls with some fresh salad ingredients of your choice.

PIZZA AND FOCACCIA

There's nothing unhealthy about a well-made pizza with fresh ingredients, often containing many elements of the highly-acclaimed Mediterranean diet. You can use pita bread for the base, buy ready-made pizza bases from the supermarket, or you can make enough dough for 2 pizzas in a bread making machine according to the recipe in your manual, or you can make your own dough. I recommend this last option, making your own dough, using the method for making dough found in the following Focaccia recipe.

This should make enough dough for three medium-sized pizzas; a good feed.

It is great fun and very satisfying to see your own perfect pizzas come together.

Method

Divide the dough amongst three oiled pizza trays, spread it out evenly, and top it with your favourite toppings. Cook the pizzas for about 20 minutes in a 230^0C oven, and then get stuck into them, along with a glass or two of whatever it is that you like to drink.

Capricciosa Pizza (Italy, Traditional) 'Mischievous'

Top with tomato puree, ham or pepperoni salami, grated mozzarella cheese, chopped mushrooms, pitted black olives (either Italian or kalamata), and anchovy fillets.
To me, this is the best authentic combination. Cook for 20 minutes in a hot oven.

Napolitano Pizza (Italy, Traditional) from Naples

Top with tomato puree, grated mozzarella cheese, sliced red onion, sliced mushrooms, salt and pepper. Cook for 20 minutes in a hot oven.

Chicken Pizza (Turkey)

Marinate a thinly sliced double chicken breast in lemon juice, olive oil, garlic and mint.

Drain the chicken, brown it in a frying pan in a little oil, and remove it from the pan.

Return the marinade to the pan and cook some onions with a small tin of tomatoes until thickened.

Top the dough with the tomato mixture, some baby spinach leaves, the chicken meat, and fetta cheese, and cook in a hot oven for about 20 minutes.

Squeeze over some lemon juice.

Some other Gourmet Pizza Combinations

- Grated mozzarella cheese, flaked parmesan cheese, sliced garlic, and parsley.
- Grated mozzarella cheese, crumbled fetta cheese, cherry tomatoes, and basil.
- Tomato puree, Spanish chorizo with smoked paprika, pitted olives, and chives.
- Thinly sliced potato, crumbled gorgonzola cheese, and fresh dill.

Cheesy-Crust Focaccia with Rosemary and Garlic (Italy)

Ingredients for the Dough

1 cup warm water or a little more
1tsp sugar
one 7gm or 8gm sachet of dried yeast
4tsp cold-pressed extra virgin olive oil
3 cups of OO flour or plain bread flour
1tsp of good quality sea salt flakes

Method for the Dough

In a jug combine the warm water, sugar, and yeast, and let it activate for a few minutes. You should see it bubble a little as the yeast works on the sugar.

Add the oil to the jug and stir. It will not combine, but this just mixes it in a little.

Put the flour and salt into a mixing bowl, mix together, and make a well in the middle. (The salt is not put in with the yeast, as salt kills yeast.)

Pour the contents of the jug into the flour, and stir it with a wooden spoon until it is reasonably well combined. Add a little more water if needed.

Dust the bottom of the bowl with a little flour and knead the dough for about five minutes until it is thick and stretchy. It may still be a little sticky.

Tip a little oil under the dough in the bowl, cover it in cling wrap, then wrap it in a tea towel in a warm place, and let it rise for thirty minutes or more until it approximately doubles in size.

Extra Ingredients for Assembling the Focaccia

tasty cheese, sliced into long batons
some good quality extra virgin olive oil for drizzling over the top
1 sprig of fresh rosemary leaves
2 finely sliced cloves of fresh garlic
good quality sea salt flakes for sprinkling on top

Method for Assembling the Focaccia

Stretch out the dough into an oiled tray or baking dish, poking it with your fingers to make little dents all over it (for the oil to puddle).

Put the cheese edge on the dough by pushing the cheese batons into the edge of the dough, and rolling the edge of the pastry over the top of the cheese.

Brush or drizzle the top of the dough with the oil, add the rosemary leaves and garlic by sprinkling them over the top.

Sprinkle over the sea salt flakes.

You could add some olives or a little finely sliced tomato; but keep it fairly plain.

Bake it for 30 minutes at 180^0C. Don't overcook it or it will dry out.

If this isn't good authentic food, I'll go hopping.

MEXICAN FOOD

Tortillas are the basis for a lot of Mexican food. Flour tortillas are from the north of Mexico, and corn tortillas are from the south. They are rolled up with fillings to make burritos, fried to make nachos, fried and rolled with fillings to make tacos, or dipped in chilli sauce and fried and rolled to make enchiladas. You can also dry fry them to make quesadillas, or fold and bake small portions of dough with fillings to make empanadas. Homemade flour tortillas can be made by beating together 4 cups plain flour, 1tsp salt, 1Tbsp olive oil, and 2 cups water. Roll balls of dough flat and lightly fry them in oil.

Quick Nachos (Mexico)

Arrange a packet of corn chips around an oven dish, top with some 'Chilli con Carne', a can of refried beans, a jar of taco sauce, some grated cheese and some sliced jalapeño chillies. Bake in the oven for ten minutes and top with some light sour cream.

Make the 'Chilli con Carne' (sometimes referred to as a Bowl of Red) by frying some lean mince, chopped onion, and chopped garlic. Add lots of red chilli, some salt and pepper, and a tin of chopped tomatoes. Cook for half an hour. Add a small can of red kidney beans and cook for a further half an hour.

Quick Tacos (Mexico)

Fill some ready-made Taco shells with Chilli con Carne, chopped tomatoes, chopped iceberg lettuce, chopped jalapeños, grated cheese, and some lite sour cream.

Burritos (Mexico)

Refresh ready-made flour tortillas by heating quickly in a dry frypan and roll them up with a hot cooked beef or chicken mixture such as Chilli con Carne or Chilli Colorado (see Beef) along with chopped tomato, lettuce, guacamole (see Dips), and grated cheese. You can make some nice Dead Chook Burritos by rolling up meat from a roasted chicken with some jalapeños, a small tin sweet corn, salt and pepper. Roll them up and put them in an oven dish, sprinkle on some grated cheese, and bake them for about 20 minutes.

Quesadillas (Mexico)

Cook two flour tortillas in a dry non-stick frypan (using no oil) with some grated cheese and some chopped jalapeño chilli peppers between them. Cook the bottom until just slightly brown, flip them over, and cook the other side. A great snack, or combine it with guacamole, Chilli con Carne, and refried beans.

Empanadas (Mexico)

Mix 2 cups plain flour, 1Tbsp butter, a pinch of salt, and about ½ cup of water to make soft dough. Roll this flat and cut out pastry circles about 6 cm across. Put a spoonful of Chilli con Carne filling in each circle and fold them in half to seal them. Bake them for about 20 minutes.

FISH AND SEAFOOD

FOR A SEAFOOD BANQUET

This seafood platter would suit a special occasion. Serve around a bed of potato mash, with the XO sauce, and some fresh crusty white bread. All three are prepared by giving the seafood a shake in a plastic bag containing plain flour seasoned with salt and pepper, and a little dried thyme. You can use the same bag. Put them straight onto the barby or into a pan with a little hot oil. Cook for about 2 minutes only, turning half way through.

Simple Scallops

Coat and cook some scallops as above.

BARBECUE FRIENDLY

Calamari Rings

Cut the calamari tubes into rings by slicing crossways. Coat and cook as above.

Seasoned Prawns

Coat and cook green some green prawns as above.

XO Seafood Sauce (pronounced 'ixo')

Ingredients

½ cup extra virgin olive oil
6 frozen prawns, thawed and finely chopped
1 onion, finely chopped
50gm prosciutto, very finely chopped
2 cloves garlic, finely chopped
2 fresh long red chillies, finely chopped
2 dried long red chillies, finely chopped
2 anchovy fillets in oil, finely chopped
1tsp minced ginger
1tsp sugar
1tsp salt and ½tsp white pepper
½ cup Shaoxing rice cooking wine
1 green shallot, very finely chopped

This is my simplified version of the famous Hong Kong sauce which was named after the spirit Cognac for the prestige, and is reputedly the 'Emperor of Sauces'.

Method

Fry the prawns in the olive oil till starting to colour, about 2 minutes, and remove them from the oil with a slotted spoon. Fry the onion in the oil until it starts to turn golden, and add the prosciutto, garlic, chillies, dried chillies, anchovies, ginger, sugar, salt and pepper. Add the rice cooking wine and shallot, and return the prawns to the pot. Cook for about 30 minutes more to reduce the liquid and develop the flavours.
Use this sauce hot, and store any leftover sauce in the fridge for up to a week.

FISH STEAKS AND FILLETS

Always serve your fish fillets boneless. This makes for easy eating and also prevents you from choking somebody. Here's a tip for you! If you get fillets of fish that should be boneless, and they aren't, just get a small pair of pointy-nosed pliers and carefully pull out all of the bones!

Crispy-skinned Atlantic Salmon (Thailand)

Dry the skin side of the fillets thoroughly and sprinkle liberally with salt to remove any moisture, leaving them sit for 10 minutes or so. Scrape off the salt and pat them dry again.

Make a spice mixture of freshly ground black pepper, finely ground sea salt, a pinch of sweet paprika, a pinch of ground fennel, and a pinch of ground coriander seed. Rub this into the skin side of the fillets.

Fry the salmon fillets in extra virgin olive oil with the skin-side down in a very hot non-stick pan for 3 to 4 minutes until the skin is crispy, holding them down with a wooden spatula for the first minute to prevent them from curling. Then turn the fillets after sprinkling on a little of the spice mixture, to cook the other side for about 2 minutes until cooked but still a little pink in the middle. Then turn off the heat, drain excess oil, and turn the fish back on to the skin side to finish crisping it.

Place each fillet on a bed of grilled zucchini and asparagus, drizzle over the pan sauce, garnish with finely chopped parsley, and serve with a side salad.

Red Wine Reduction Pan Sauce

1 Tbsp butter
1 tsp crushed garlic
1 tsp crushed ginger
½ cup red wine
1 Tbsp balsamic vinegar
1 Tbsp kecap manis (or dark soy sauce)
1 Tbsp sweet chilli sauce
1 kaffir lime leaf
salt and pepper

Method

In a small frying pan, fry the garlic and ginger very lightly in the butter on medium heat, and add the other ingredients.

Reduce the sauce while the rest of the dish is cooking till it is thickened a little, and then remove the leaf.

Serve the sauce drizzled over the fish, or in a gravy boat.

Beer-Battered Barramundi with Tartare Sauce

The barramundi, also known as Asian sea bass, Giant perch, or Pla kapong in Thailand, has a reputation for being a beautiful eating fish.

It is plentiful in northern areas of Australia where it grows to upwards of 50kilos in the ocean and major estuaries. I have enjoyed some beautiful Barramundi in Port Douglas in northern Queensland and also Adelaide River in the Northern Territory.

The word is from an Australian aboriginal language and means, 'river fish with large scales'.

It features on many restaurant menus as 'Barramundi in Beer Batter', and is in my opinion, up there with the best in fish eating enjoyment. It has to be wild caught barramundi though, as the farmed variety often tastes very much inferior.

Ingredients

1Kg fresh wild boneless barramundi fillets, cut into large pieces
plain flour for dusting
1 egg
1 can or stubby (375ml) of cold beer
1 cup plain flour
1tsp sea salt flakes

BARBECUE FRIENDLY

Method

First, dust the fish pieces in plain flour.
Whisk together the egg, beer, flour, and salt and then dip the fish pieces in the batter. Pan-fry till golden in some light olive oil; or you can cook them on a barbecue hotplate.
Serve with the Tartare sauce as shown and lemon wedges.

'Rémoulade' (France) - Tartare Sauce

Ingredients

1 cup whole egg mayonnaise
1 lemon, juiced
1 French shallot (or small brown onion), very finely chopped
1 green shallot, very finely chopped
1 finely chopped pickled dill cucumber
1 finely chopped anchovy fillet
1Tbsp Dijon mustard
1Tbsp chopped capers
1Tbsp chopped flat-leafed parsley
1Tbsp chopped fresh chives
½tsp sea salt
½tsp white pepper

Method

Mix together all of the sauce ingredients and serve on the side.

Coral Trout with White Wine Cream Sauce

The Coral Trout is an especially good fish for use in this recipe.

However, you can use snapper, dory, or flake (shark) or any firm-fleshed, boneless white fish that you prefer for this recipe.

Ingredients

1Kg fish fillets, with all bones removed (you don't want to choke anybody!)
plain flour
1tsp sea salt flakes
1tsp white pepper
1tsp dried thyme
light olive oil for frying

Method

Dust the fish fillets in flour seasoned with salt and pepper, and a little dried thyme.

The quickest method is to put it all in a plastic bag and give it a shake.

Fry the fish in some light oil till crusted and lightly browned, and cooked through.

Serve with the white wine cream sauce and lemon wedges, or the flaked almond sauce.

White Wine Cream Sauce

Fry a finely sliced French shallot (or a small brown onion) in some butter for a few minutes in a pan along with a finely chopped green shallot and 1tsp minced garlic.

Add 1 cup Sauvignon Blanc white wine (or Riesling, or Chardonnay) to reduce a little bit in volume in the pan.

Season this with ½tsp sea salt flakes and ½tsp white pepper.

Add ½ cup cream to the pan, and some finely chopped parsley.

Stir this with a wooden spoon till slightly thickened, and pour over the cooked fish.

Flaked Almond Sauce

In a little butter in the frying pan sauté flaked almonds, add some lemon juice, parsley, salt and pepper, and spoon over the fish to serve.

This sauce is great with many fish dishes. It is simple, yet surprisingly tasty.

It makes a quickly prepared meal.

Pan-Fried Swordfish Steaks

Simply dust the steaks in plain flour, dried thyme, salt and pepper by putting it all in a plastic bag and giving it a shake. Sizzle in hot olive oil on the barby.

This is one of the best ways to cook any fish fillets for that matter!

You've got kangaroos in the top paddock if you don't think this is good, healthy food.

Serve with one of the sauces below.

> **BARBECUE FRIENDLY**

Lemon Caper Sauce

Ingredients

1 brown onion, peeled and finely chopped
1tsp minced garlic
1Tbsp butter
½ cup dry white wine
juice of 1 lemon
1Tbsp capers
1tsp chopped parsley
sprinkle of sea salt and white pepper

Method

Sauté the onion and garlic in the butter in a saucepan until it is soft.

Add the rest of the ingredients and simmer until the sauce has thickened a little.

Ginger Coriander Sauce

Ingredients

1 brown onion, peeled and finely chopped
1tsp minced garlic
1Tbsp butter
½ cup dry white wine
½ cup fish or chicken stock
1tsp minced ginger (available in a jar)
1tsp ground coriander seed
1tsp chopped parsley
a sprinkle of sea salt and white pepper

Method

Sauté the onion and garlic in the butter in a saucepan until it is soft.

Add the rest of the ingredients and simmer until the sauce has thickened a little.

Pan-fried Tuna Steaks (Greece)

Ingredients

Tuna steaks seasoned with salt and pepper

Method

Put the steaks onto a hot, oiled, barbecue plate, or use a frypan instead.
Cook them to your liking, or about 2 minutes each side. Serve with some grilled haloumi cheese and pan-fried asparagus. Serve with one of the fish sauces in this section.

Lemon Artichoke Sauce

Ingredients

BARBECUE FRIENDLY

1 brown onion, peeled and finely chopped
1tsp minced garlic
1Tbsp butter
½ cup dry white wine
juice of 1 lemon
2 artichoke hearts, chopped (available from the supermarket in a jar)
1tsp dried thyme
1tsp chopped parsley
sprinkle of sea salt and white pepper

Method

Sauté the onion and garlic in the butter in a saucepan until it is soft.
Add the rest of the ingredients and simmer until the sauce has thickened a little.

Grilled Tuna Steaks with Pan-Fried Vegetables (Italy)

Ingredients

tuna steaks seasoned with salt and pepper
an onion and a clove of garlic, finely chopped, with olive oil for frying
300gm cherry tomatoes, halved
3 anchovy fillets
½ cup pitted kalamata olives
fresh basil leaves

Method

Put the steaks onto a hot, oiled, barbecue plate, or use a frying pan instead.
Note: When used, a char grill gives the tuna a nice, smoky flavour.
Cook them to your liking, or about 2 minutes each side.
Fry the onion and garlic lightly in the oil in a frying pan.
Add the tomatoes to fry along with the onions.
Add the anchovies and olives to cook quickly.
Add the basil leaves right at the end of cooking.
Serve with the tuna laid on top of the sauce.

Fish Provençal (France)

This dish is from Provence, a region of southern France, which exalts the flavours of capsicums, tomatoes, onions, garlic, olives, capers, fresh herbs, and wine (of course). Their food is all about fresh produce. There are many ways to make it, but I like the idea of cooking the fresh herbed fish separately and then laying it over the top.

Ingredients

2 red potatoes, peeled and sliced to 2mm thickness
good quality extra virgin olive oil for frying
1 red capsicum (red bell pepper), sliced to 2mm thickness
150gm baby spinach leaves
1tsp minced garlic
1 brown onion, finely chopped
1tsp minced garlic (fresh or bottled)
3 Roma tomatoes, or other tomatoes, sliced into about 6 pieces
12 pitted kalamata olives
2tsp capers
a few sprigs of fresh flat-leafed parsley
2Tbsp dry white wine
sea salt and freshly ground black pepper
400gm boneless fish fillets
1 egg, whisked with a dash of milk
½ cup breadcrumbs
sea salt and freshly ground black pepper
1tsp dried thyme
½tsp ground fennel

Method

This dish is made in two frying pans. In the first pan, get the potatoes frying on high heat till cooked through and slightly browned. Remove from the pan to a plate at the side of your cooking area.

Then, fry the sliced capsicum in a little more oil if necessary until starting to colour, both sides, and remove from the pan to the plate.

Meanwhile, in the second pan, fry the spinach leaves in a little oil with the garlic till wilted and tender, but do not overcook. Remove from the pan. This dish is served warm, so don't panic about keeping it hot. Put it on the plate at the side of your cooking area. Fry the onions and garlic in the same pan with a little more oil if necessary, until they are just starting to colour. Then add the tomatoes, olives, capers, fresh herbs, wine, salt and pepper. Cook this until reduced a little.

Toss the fish in the egg and then breadcrumbs seasoned with salt, pepper, dried thyme and a little ground fennel. Fry this in the first pan in a little oil till cooked and golden brown on both sides.

Arrange the individual components decoratively on plates and serve.

MARINATED RAW FISH

'Ota 'ika' (Samoa) - Samoan Raw Fish

My old friend, Fred, who has spent half of his life in the Pacific islands, and really appreciates good food, put me onto the next two marinated raw fish dishes and helped to simplify them a little for me. They are very different from each other.
If you have never tried good raw tuna, now may be the time. It is a taste sensation.

Ingredients

500gm sashimi-grade yellow fin tuna cut into 2cm cubes
1tsp sea salt flakes
½ cup Tahitian lime juice
1 French shallot, very finely sliced
1 very small carrot, very finely sliced
small 200ml can coconut cream

Method

Sprinkle the tuna with the salt, and then the lime juice.
Cover the mixture with cling wrap and chill it overnight in the refrigerator until the fish whitens, stirring it occasionally. The next day, add in the onion, carrot, and coconut cream. Serve it chilled.

Hawaiian 'Poke' (Hawaii) – Sliced Raw Fish

This one is similar in some ways to sashimi. It comes from the strong Japanese influence in Hawaiian culture.

Ingredients

500gm sashimi-grade yellow fin tuna cut into 2cm cubes
¼ cup soy sauce
1Tbsp sesame oil
1tsp sea salt flakes
1tsp sambal oelek, or bottled minced red chilli, or dried chilli flakes
1tsp bottled minced ginger root
1 green shallot, very finely sliced on the diagonal for appearance
1 French shallot, very finely sliced (or Maui onion, if it is available)
1 sheet nori (seaweed), very finely shredded
1Tbsp lightly dry-fried sesame seeds to use as a garnish

Method

In a ceramic or glass bowl, mix the ingredients together.
Cover the mixture with cling wrap and allow it to marinate for an hour before serving. Garnish with the toasted sesame seeds. Serve with some fresh lettuce leaves.
Note: You can also obtain Wasabi Furikake from supermarkets to use as a seasoning (this is sushi rice seasoning, and the Japanese equivalent of salt and pepper). It contains seaweed, and also sesame seeds. Aloha Fred!

OTHER FISH RECIPES

Tuna Casserole (Australia)

This is my Mum's recipe, and was a favourite of mine when I was growing up.

Ingredients

large can tuna, drained
small can corn kernels
the juice of 1 lemon
½ cup breadcrumbs
1 onion, finely chopped
1 green shallot, finely chopped
1 stalk celery, finely chopped
1 egg
1tsp dried thyme
1tsp sea salt and 1tsp freshly ground black pepper

ONE POT MEAL

Method

Mix all of the ingredients together and place in a casserole dish.
Cook in the oven at 180°C for 1 hour. This is really great nosh!

Tuna Rissoles (Australia)

Ingredients

400gm can tuna, drained (or as an option, use flaked, cooked white fish fillets instead)
¾ cup rice, cooked and drained
1 onion, finely chopped
2 eggs
the juice of 1 lemon
1Tbsp plain flour
1tsp sugar, 1tsp salt, 1tsp pepper

BARBECUE FRIENDLY

Method

Mix all of the ingredients together, form into patties, and fry in extra virgin olive oil.

Salmon Patties

Ingredients

200gm can red salmon
2 cups mashed potatoes
1 egg
1Tbsp capers and a few sprigs of fresh chopped dill
1tsp sea salt and 1tsp freshly ground black pepper

BARBECUE FRIENDLY

Method

Form into patties, roll in breadcrumbs, and fry in some olive oil in a frying pan.

PRAWNS

The prawns mostly enjoyed in Australia, such as the Eastern King Prawn and the Brown Tiger Prawn, are of the genus Penaeus, as is the Giant Tiger Prawn, the most important species of farmed crustacean in the world. They are most often eaten simply quickly boiled, and are very good done in that way.

Many more people are using green (raw) peeled prawns now in their seafood recipes.

Watch when you buy prawns that they are firm and fresh-looking, that the colour is good with no black bits on them, and that they are curled rather than straight.

To peel and eat cooked (pink) prawns, break off the head, peel off the shell along with the legs, and pinch off the tail. Then, add a little squeeze of lemon, and down the hatch!

I remember once netting a large bucket-full of prawns right at our camp site by the ocean at a place called Mallacoota, and then spending a very enjoyable evening with family and friends cooking, peeling, and eating them; and washing them down with some ice-cold beer. Life can be hard sometimes!

Prawn Cocktail

This is one of the simplest and most popular ways of eating prawns as an entrée.

Ingredients

800gm or so of cooked and peeled king prawns, or large shrimp
an iceberg lettuce

Method

Tear up the washed lettuce leaves and place them in cocktail glasses.
Halve most of the prawns and put them in the glasses, leaving about 4 nice ones to decorate each glass by hanging them over the edge of the rim.
Drizzle some seafood sauce over the top, as shown below, and serve immediately, garnished with some very finely chopped flat-leafed parsley.

Seafood Sauce

Mix together in a bowl:
1 cup good quality egg mayonnaise
1Tbsp tomato sauce (ketchup)
the juice of 1 lemon
1tsp Worcestershire sauce
1tsp minced chilli
1tsp sea salt
1tsp white pepper

Serve any remaining sauce on the side in a jug, or you may have to go and get some more of those yummy prawns in order to use it all up.

Special Entrée Garlic Prawns (Australia)

Ingredients

½ Kg frozen green prawns, thawed
400ml good quality extra virgin olive oil
3 cloves fresh garlic, chopped
60gm butter
sea salt flakes and freshly ground black pepper
parsley to garnish

Method

Marinate peeled green prawns with tails intact in extra virgin olive oil and crushed garlic for an hour or so if possible.
Put 6 prawns into each of six medium sized ramekins or ovenproof dishes with the extra virgin olive oil and garlic. Add a dollop of butter, salt and pepper, to each dish.
Cook them for about 10 minutes in a hot oven, until the prawns have changed colour.
Garnish them with a little chopped parsley.
Serve them to the table in the ramekins (be careful, as they are very hot!)
Soak up the oil and butter with some fresh sourdough bread.
Get 'em into ya!

Tempura Prawns in Honey and Sesame (Japan)

Ingredients

1Kg large green peeled king prawns
tempura batter: 1 egg, ½ cup cornflour, ½ cup plain flour, ½tsp salt and ¾ cup cold water
honey
toasted sesame seeds

Method

If you are using frozen prawns, simply soak them in water for a few minutes first to defrost them, and drain them.
Lightly whisk the batter; it should be a little lumpy.
Dip the prawns in the batter and fry them for about 1 minute each side in a frying pan in some hot, light olive oil in several batches so as not to overcrowd the pan.
Drain them on absorbent paper. Drizzle over the top some honey that has been heated for about 5 seconds in the microwave to make it runny.
Sprinkle on top some sesame seeds that have been lightly toasted in a dry frying pan.

Marinated King Prawns

Marinate some green (raw) peeled king prawns in some dry white wine, lemon juice, a little minced chilli, some crushed garlic, salt and pepper, for about half an hour.

BARBECUE FRIENDLY

Throw them on a hot barbecue plate or into a frypan with a little olive oil until they turn pink. Serve them with some fresh bread and butter, and cold beer.

OYSTERS

The Sydney Rock Oyster (saccostrea glomerata) is native to Australia and the variety that is mostly consumed there. It is a real delicacy, and very high in the mineral zinc. The other native variety (ostrea angasi) is known as the mud oyster. It too has been consumed for a long time, and grows around the southern coast of New South Wales. I have seen Australian aboriginal middens of shells 2 metres high. The oysters were consumed while waiting for the tides to come in and out in operating the fish traps, which were built across the mouths of small estuaries. A hard life indeed!

Pacific oysters (crassostrea gigas), also known as Coffin Bay oysters, are a variety introduced from Japan in the 1930s. Developed as triploid spawnless oysters to retain quality, they are increasing in production numbers in Australia and are very good.

Oysters Kilpatrick

Top some raw oysters with finely chopped lean bacon, and sprinkle with equal quantities of soy sauce and Worcestershire sauce. Grill till the bacon is sizzling. The soy sauce is a slight variation but makes them taste so much better. Thanks Justin.

Oysters Russian

Top raw oysters with a dollop of light sour cream mixed with lemon juice and Tabasco sauce and then put a spoonful of caviar on top.

Oysters Supreme

Grill the oysters and then top firstly with a sauce made of light sour cream, lemon juice, fresh chopped basil and ground chilli, and then secondly with breadcrumbs and garlic that have been fried together in a little butter.

Sake Oyster Shooters (Japan)

Place a washed oyster in each shooter glass, and add a couple of drops of soy sauce. Top it up with sake. The oyster should float. Top with a couple of slices of pickled ginger and a tiny bit of wasabi paste.

Bloody Mary Oyster Shooters

Place a washed oyster in each shooter glass, and add a drop of Tabasco sauce. Add 1tsp Worcestershire sauce, a sprinkle of salt and pepper, 10ml chilled Vodka, and top it up with some chilled tomato juice.

Horseradish Shooters

Place a washed oyster in each shooter glass, and add a grind of black pepper and sea salt. Add ¼tsp minced horseradish and a squeeze of lemon juice, along with 10ml chilled Vodka, and top it up with some chilled tomato juice.

SCALLOPS

Scallops are a bivalve mollusc, related to the oyster. They are migratory, and can swim by opening and closing their shell rapidly, making an audible whistling sound. They can live up to 18 years, and are able to change their sex. The white meat is the adductor muscle, and the orange part is the roe, all of which can be used. Be wary of buying scallops with the roe off, as it could be stingray, or almost anything else!

Scallops in Garlic Butter

Ingredients

2 Tbsp plain flour, seasoned with salt and pepper
400gm good quality frozen scallops, thawed
30gm butter
2 cloves garlic, finely chopped
1 Tbsp flat-leafed parsley, finely chopped
the juice of ½ lemon

BARBECUE FRIENDLY

Method

Toss the scallops in the flour, salt and pepper to coat.
Fry them lightly in the butter and garlic in a frying pan, turning them until golden, about 4 minutes. Or, cook them on the barby.
Sprinkle with the parsley and the lemon juice.

Scallops in Beer Batter

Dust the scallops in flour, and then in a beer batter made by whisking together ¾ cup flat beer, ¾ cup plain flour, ¼ tsp salt, 1 egg, and 2 tsp melted butter.
Fry quickly in some hot light olive oil both sides in a frying pan.

Sesame Scallops in Prosciutto

Wrap your scallops in half slices of prosciutto and secure them with a toothpick.
Fry them in hot oil, about 1 minute per side, along with some crushed garlic, and a small dash of soy sauce right at the end. Do not overcook them. Sprinkle some lightly toasted sesame seeds on top. These are great served on a bed of potato or parsnip mash.

Scallops with a Creamed Leek Sauce

Sauté a clove of minced garlic with a finely chopped leek in butter, in a saucepan.
When soft, add some white wine, an anchovy fillet, salt and pepper.
Add a 300ml carton of cream and simmer to reduce the sauce a little.
In a frying pan, fry some scallops in butter for about 3 minutes only, until cooked, and stir them into the sauce. Serve over some boiled rice.

LOBSTER

Australia's spiny lobsters, langouste, or crayfish (of the family palinuradae), are the Southern, Eastern and Western rock lobsters. The Southern lobster, mostly orange coloured through to purple is very closely related to the Eastern lobster, which is an olive green colour turning to bright orange when cooked. They have two long spiny antennae on top, can grow to around 5Kg, and can live for about 20 years.

Of a very different family (nephropidae), the American lobster, and the closely related European lobster, is a true lobster with very large front claws. They are the heaviest marine crustaceans in the world, weighing up to 20Kg and growing to around 1 metre. These recipes showcase the variety of ways that you can cook lobster, one of the very finest types of seafood available.

Boiled or Steamed Lobster Tails

Fill a large saucepan with water and add 1 teaspoon of salt for each litre of water.
Bring the water to the boil and drop the lobster tails into the pan.
Boil the tails for 8 minutes per 500gms of total weight.
You can also cook them in a prawn stock with some white wine added.
To steam them, pour 1 cup of water (or beer) into a saucepan, add salt, and bring the water to the boil. Insert a wooden skewer down the length of each lobster tail next to the shell. This will prevent them from curling up when steaming. Place the tails in a bamboo steamer on top of the pan, and steam for about 8 minutes before draining.

Fried Lobster Tails

Steam them as described above, but for 4 minutes only.
Cut the soft under shell of the tail lengthways down the middle, leaving the hard shell intact. Pour some melted butter and lemon juice over the meat of the tails, sprinkle with salt and pepper, and place shell side up into a hot frying pan.
Fry for approximately 8 minutes until the meat is opaque and firm to the touch.
If you wish, you may turn the tails over half way through cooking.

Barbecued Lobster Tails

This method uses the open grill on the barbecue to impart a slightly char grilled, smoky flavour to the lobster, due to the conduction of hot air from underneath.
Use kitchen scissors to cut down lengthways either side of each lobster tail on the underside and then gently pull away the soft, flexible shell.
This will expose the meat, which will remain in the body shell.
Combine a little extra virgin olive oil, lime juice, minced garlic,

BARBECUE FRIENDLY

minced ginger, salt and white pepper in a small bowl or jug and mix well together.
Drizzle this on the underside of the lobster.
Place the lobster tails, shell-side down, onto the open cast-iron grill plate.
Barbecue for 4 minutes, and turn them to cook for about 5 minutes on the other side.

Baked Lobster Tails

Preheat the oven to 200°C (400°F).
Split the soft shell of the lobster tails in half lengthways with a sturdy knife.
Place the lobster tails on a baking tray, shell side down, and brush them with a mixture of melted butter, lemon juice, salt and white pepper.
Bake them in the oven at 180°C for about 10 minutes, till cooked. Serve with vegetables.

Grilled (Broiled) Orange Mustard Lobster Tails

Ingredients (serves 4)

4 (about 150gm each) green (uncooked) frozen lobster tails, thawed
60gm (3Tbsp) butter, melted
1 orange, rind finely grated, juiced
1tsp wholegrain mustard
2tsp chopped fresh dill

Method

Preheat grill on medium-high. Line a grill tray with foil.
Use kitchen scissors to cut down lengthways either side of each lobster tail on the underside and then gently pull away the soft, flexible shell.
This will expose the meat, which will remain in the body shell.
Combine the butter, orange rind, 2Tbsp of the orange juice, mustard and dill in a small bowl or jug and mix well. Place the lobster tails, shell-side up, onto the lined tray. Place under the preheated grill and broil for about 5 minutes or until the shells turn orange. Turn the lobster tails over, brush well with the butter mixture and cook for a further 6 minutes, brushing liberally with the butter mixture frequently or until the flesh is no longer translucent. Serve immediately, perhaps with boiled or roasted potatoes, a green salad and wedges of lime.

Herbs and Butter Grilled (Broiled) Lobster Tails

Ingredients (serves 4)

4 (about 150gm each) green (uncooked) frozen lobster tails, thawed
60gm (3Tbsp) butter, melted
juice of one lemon
1Tbsp chopped fresh basil
2tsp chopped fresh dill
2tsp chopped fresh thyme

Method

Preheat grill on medium-high. Line a grill tray with foil.
Use kitchen scissors to cut down lengthways either side of each lobster tail on the underside and then gently pull away the soft, flexible shell.
Brush the tails with a mixture of the ingredients above, and grill (broil) using the above method.

Lobster Tails Thermidor

This recipe is involved, but worth the effort. Expensive lobster tails deserve respect. This recipe uses the grilling (broiling) method.

Ingredients

2 lobster tails defrosted overnight in the refrigerator (or you could use ½ lobsters)
1 L prawn stock (using the heads of cooked, peeled prawns that you eat whilst cooking)
1 cup dry white wine
1 bay leaf

Béchamel Sauce

50gm plain flour
50gm butter
1 cup milk
½ cup cream
2 small shallots, peeled and finely chopped
50ml Cointreau liqueur
1 cup of the stock used to poach the lobster
1Tbsp chopped flat-leaf parsley
2tsp English mustard
½ cup Gruyere cheese (or tasty cheese), grated
2tsp lemon juice
sea salt and freshly ground black pepper
½ cup grated parmesan cheese
½ cup breadcrumbs

Method Lobster

Bring the prawn stock, white wine, and bay leaf to the boil, and blanch the lobster tails for about five minutes. Remove the flesh, cut it into medallions, and reserve the shells intact.

Method Béchamel Sauce

Heat the butter in a frying pan till foaming, whisk in the flour, and cook till golden, about 2 minutes.

Whisk in the milk bit by bit till a smooth slightly thick sauce forms, and cook for 5 minutes. Add the cream to the sauce.

Put the shallots in a hot saucepan with a little butter and lightly cook. Add the Cointreau, burn off the alcohol, then add the stock and reduce this a little.

Add this to the béchamel, with the parsley, mustard, cheese, lemon juice, salt and pepper. Mix in the lobster meat to heat through.

Distribute the lobster and sauce between the 2 shells, and sprinkle with a mixture of the parmesan and breadcrumbs. Cook under a hot grill (broiler) for about 5-10 minutes until golden.

LANGOUSTINES

Langoustines (nephrops norvegicus), a delicious white shellfish closely related to the lobster, are caught in the north-east Atlantic and parts of the Mediterranean.

Usually larger and more expensive than King prawns, the flesh is very sweet.

They are also known as Norway Lobster, Dublin Bay Prawns, and Scampi.

When cooked whole they do not change colour as do prawns, but remain pink and become opaque where the flesh can be seen on the underside of the tail. Peel them by pulling off the upper body, and then by squeezing the sides of the tail the shell can be removed. Finally pinch off the tail. They are delicious just like this, perhaps served with a butter sauce.

If you cook them whole, do not discard the heads, shells and claws, but use them to make a stock for delicious bisque (see Prawn Bisque).

They are often sold frozen and raw, pre-prepared with the shell removed.

Langoustines in Champagne Tempura Batter

Ingredients

about 12 langoustines, frozen raw, then defrosted before cooking

cornflour for dusting the langoustines

light olive oil for frying

For the Batter

1 egg

½ cup plain flour

½ cup cornflour

½ tsp sea salt

pinch of chopped parsley

¾ cup Champagne (or sparkling Sauvignon Blanc, or sparkling Chardonnay)

Method

Dust the langoustines in cornflour.

Mix the batter with a whisk. Whisk only lightly, as it needs to be a little lumpy.

Dip the langoustines in the batter and then put them straight into hot oil a few at a time. You can use about 1cm oil in a frying pan.

Cook them for about 1 minute on each side, and remove them to drain on absorbent paper.

Serve with a wedge of lemon.

CALAMARI

The Southern Calamari, one of the best of all the squids, is a true delicacy, and found right around southern Australia. I have enjoyed many a late evening session on the jetty with mates catching calamari, and then an even later session afterwards, cooking and eating them while very fresh in a mate's kitchen (to his sleeping wife's disgust).
It is easy fishing and no bait is used. A simple squid jig, at the right time and tide, is gently moved up and down in the water. The squid, which have very big eyes and good vision, are attracted to it, thinking it to be a prawn. I'm not sure which of these tastes better. You little beauty!
As with most seafood, a very quick cooking time is used; or a very long cooking time in the oven can be used when it will become tender again.

BARBECUE FRIENDLY

Calamari Rings in Breadcrumbs

Slice each squid 'tube', 'hood', or 'sock' crossways to make rings about 1cm thick. Marinate the calamari rings in milk (the lactic acid helps to tenderise them) for half an hour; if you can wait that long. Dip them in plain flour, egg, and then breadcrumbs. Cook them for only about 1 minute on each side in a mixture of hot light olive oil and butter in a frypan. Do not overcook calamari or it will become rubbery and inedible.

Calamari Rings in Batter

Slice each squid 'tube', 'hood', or 'sock' crossways to make rings about 1cm thick. Marinate the calamari rings in milk (the lactic acid helps to tenderise them) for half an hour; again, if you can wait that long. Dip them in plain flour, and then the batter, made by whisking together ½ cup water, ½ cup plain flour, ½ cup S.R. Flour, 1tsp salt and a lightly beaten egg. Cook them for only about 1 minute on each side in hot light olive oil.

Chilli Calamari

Slice each squid 'tube', 'hood', or 'sock' crossways to make rings about 1cm thick. Marinate calamari rings for 4 hours or longer in chilli paste, soy sauce, minced garlic, white wine and a dash of sesame oil. Cook in a pan or on a barbecue in very hot oil until just cooked, about 1 minute on each side. Do not overcook it or it will be very chewy.

Stuffed Calamari

Make a stuffing mixture by first frying in some oil a chopped onion, one clove of garlic, one chopped stick of celery, 2 anchovy fillets, and 2 chopped slices of prosciutto. Mix into this ¾ cup of bread crumbs, ½ cup grated Parmesan cheese, an egg, some chopped parsley, salt and pepper.
Stuff this mixture into 4 cleaned calamari tubes, and put toothpicks through the ends to hold them together. In a baking tray, fry them in a little oil and garlic to sear them both sides, place them side by side and then pour over a 700ml bottle of Italian tomato pasta sauce. Bake them in the oven at about $140^{0}C$ for thirty minutes, slice them in half and serve them on plates with the sauce.

ABALONE

Several species of abalone are endemic to southern parts of Australia, where they are also called muttonfish. Blacklip, brownlip, redlip and greenlip abalone are found in southern regions. Tasmania, a southern State of Australia, is the world's largest supplier of wild abalone.

Abalone is also known as 'ormer' in the English Channel, 'awabi' in Japan, and 'pāua' in New Zealand. Its iridescent shell is a source of mother-of-pearl, and is so strong that researchers are studying its structure to improve the construction of body armour. They are a univalve mollusc with a flat, rough shell, reddish brown to reddish green in colour, containing a large muscular foot with a dark frill or lip.

Wild Abalone is commercially harvested by divers off shallow rocky reefs up to 40m deep. Greenlip and blacklip abalone are farmed, taking 3 years to grow to 'cocktail' market size.

They are great fun to catch just by using a face mask and snorkel, and a flat piece of steel or a screwdriver to quickly lever them off the rocks before they have a chance to hold on fast. Once they do, you can't get the little suckers off.

Always drown the abalone in cold fresh water. This leaves the meat tender and not tight. De-shell them straight after drowning, and clean away viscera. Then slice them in half to make two steaks. Cover them with cling-wrap and pound them several times with a meat mallet. This will shock the muscle into relaxing. It should now feel relaxed to the touch; otherwise it will be very tough when cooked, and will resemble the sole of a shoe. The flavour of abalone is something to be savoured and not overpowered with complex sauces. You must cook abalone very quickly or it will become very tough, around 45 seconds per side in very hot oil is plenty. Here's a good tip: If you are cooking a lot of abalone in the same pan, wipe the pan with paper towel every few times. The abalone bleeds a creamy white substance that will burn and change the flavour of the abalone.

Simple Sautéed Abalone with Salad

This is absolutely the best way to enjoy them.
Fry in hot light olive oil with a little butter added for flavour for about 45 seconds per side in a frypan or on the barby. You beauty! Serve with a Caesar salad or some vegetables on the side.

BARBECUE FRIENDLY

Breaded abalone

Place 2 eggs in a bowl and beat well. In another bowl, lightly season some bread crumbs with a little plain flour, a dash of lemon pepper, a dash of ground allspice, and a little onion powder (the abalone's greatest complement). Dip the abalone first in the egg mixture, and then in the seasoning mixture.

Place the seasoned abalone in a very hot sauté pan with plenty of melted butter to cook. Do not overcrowd the pan.

Cook for 45 seconds on each side. Season them with salt.

OCTOPUS

Char-grilled Baby Octopus in Red Wine

Red Wine Marinade

½ cup dry red wine
¼ cup extra virgin olive oil
1tsp balsamic vinegar
1tsp soy sauce
1tsp crushed garlic
1tsp crushed red chilli
1tsp freshly ground black pepper

BARBECUE FRIENDLY

Method

Get about 1kg good quality baby octopus, wash them well, cut each in half, and discard the head and beak.
Marinate the octopus for about 3 hours, or overnight, in the marinade.
Discard the marinade, and cook the octopus on a hot char grill or barbecue plate until they are tender; about 5 minutes.
Turn them and don't overcrowd them. They need to really sizzle, not stew.
Cook them in batches if necessary.

Char-grilled Baby Octopus in White Wine

White wine Marinade

½ cup dry white wine
¼ cup extra virgin olive oil
the juice of 1 lemon
1tsp crushed garlic
1tsp crushed red chilli
1tsp dried mixed herbs
1tsp freshly ground black pepper

BARBECUE FRIENDLY

Method

Get about 1kg good quality baby octopus, wash them well, cut each in half, and discard the head and beak.
Marinate the octopus for about 3 hours, or overnight, in the marinade.
Discard the marinade, and cook the octopus on a hot char grill or barbecue plate until they are tender; about 5 minutes.
Turn them and don't overcrowd them. They need to really sizzle, not stew.
Cook them in batches if necessary.

LAMB

ROAST LAMB

Greek-Style Roast Lamb (Greece)

Place a leg of lamb in a roasting tray, rub it all over with olive oil, and grind some fresh black pepper over the top. Place some sprigs of fresh rosemary, oregano and thyme across the top. In the tray put about ½ cup of white wine, a sliced tomato, a sliced lemon, and about three whole cloves of garlic. Cover the tray with foil and bake in a moderate oven for three hours. For the last hour remove the foil to brown the top and reduce the liquid a little. Strain the juices to make a light, pouring gravy.

This method was shown to me by our friend Helen from Greece. Serve this with the Greek-style Lemonades Patates, which are to die for (see Vegetables). Serve a mint sauce as well, that can be made according to the recipe below, if you like.

At times, I cook this in my large stainless-steel covered dish. At other times I use an electric kettle barbecue, which probably doesn't exceed 140^0C, for 4hrs slow-roasting. I have also used oven bags to roast lamb successfully for 3½hrs at 180^0C.

Mint Sauce

½ cup white wine vinegar
½ cup caster sugar
¼ cup water
½ cup mint, finely chopped

Place vinegar, sugar and water in a small saucepan. Cook, stirring over low heat until sugar dissolves. Cool slightly before stirring through the mint.

> These recipes are mostly of Greek origin; where lamb is a specialty. The other place, in my experience, where you will find outstanding lamb dishes is New Zealand.

Roast Lemon Lamb (Greece)

Boil 2 small lamb legs in water for ½ hour to lose some of the fat. Rub them with lemon juice, brush with olive oil and sprinkle on rosemary and oregano leaves and freshly ground black pepper. Pierce in several places and insert small slivers of fresh garlic. Roast the lamb in a moderate oven for about 2½ hours or until the meat is cooked to your liking. Baste with the pan juices and squeeze on some more lemon juice about half way through the cooking. Unbelievable flavour and really tender!

Marinated Lamb (Greece)

Marinate some small cuts of lamb for 3 hours in lemon juice, garlic and fresh chopped oregano, and then roll them up tightly in foil. Boil them in water for about an hour and then let them cool a little. Unwrap the lamb pieces and roast them in the oven for about another hour or until golden brown. My son Justin, who is a chef, showed me this technique. It is effectively a slow-roasting method, as the water never exceeds 100^0C.

Lamb Leg Pot Roast

Ingredients

2.5Kg leg of lamb
2Tbsp olive oil for frying
2 brown onions, roughly chopped
2 cloves garlic, roughly chopped
1 large carrot, finely chopped
1 stalk celery, finely chopped
1 cup dry red wine
1 cup water
1 anchovy fillet
400gm tin chopped tomatoes
1Tbsp concentrated tomato paste
2tsp dark soy sauce
2 bay leaves
1tsp dried mixed herbs (or fresh if available)
1tsp sea salt
1tsp freshly ground black pepper

> I commented to a Māori from New Zealand about the delicious lamb available there. He said, "We don't eat lamb; we eat sheep. They're bigger; feed the whole family."

ONE POT MEAL

Method

Brown the leg of lamb well on all sides in the oil in a large ovenproof pot for about 10 minutes, and remove it from the pan.

Then fry the chopped onions, garlic, carrot and celery in the pan juices till nicely browned.

Return the lamb to the pot.

Add the red wine, water, anchovy, tomatoes, tomato paste, soy sauce, bay leaves, herbs, salt and pepper.

Cover, and cook for $2\frac{1}{2}$ hours in the oven, turning and basting after 1 hour.

At this point, after 1 hour of cooking time, add the potatoes and sweet potato to cook in the sauce.

When cooked, remove the lamb to rest for a while, and then carve it.

Remove the potatoes and sweet potato to keep warm in the oven.

Using a stick blender, blend the sauce in the pot till smooth.

Serve the meat and vegetables with the sauce over the top.

You may want to cook some green vegies of some sort as well, to serve on the side.

Optional

After browning the meat and onions, you may want to put everything in a slow cooker to chug away all day. This is very efficient and will be a wonderfully delicious meal.

Get outside of that!

Rack of Lamb (France) with Potato Stacks - Racks 'n Stacks

Ingredients

2 French-trimmed racks of lamb, with 8 bones each
¼ cup olive oil for rubbing and cooking
sea salt and freshly ground black pepper for the rub
½ cup breadcrumbs
1 Tbsp flat-leafed Italian parsley, finely chopped
1 tsp fresh rosemary leaves
1 tsp fresh thyme leaves
1 finely grated lemon zest
1 tsp crushed garlic
1 tsp olive oil
extra salt and pepper to season

ONE POT MEAL

Method

Preheat the oven to 180°C (350°F).

Rub a little extra olive oil over the lamb racks, and season liberally with salt and pepper.

Heat a large heavy baking dish and cook the racks fat-side down on high for 2 minutes to brown them a little.

Place them fat-side up and spread on a mixture of the breadcrumbs, herbs, zest, garlic, olive oil, salt and pepper.

Cook them for about 30 minutes, or until the lamb is cooked to your liking.

Remove the lamb from the oven, and rest it loosely covered with foil for 5 minutes.

Cut each rack in half and serve the two pieces upright and facing each other.

Serve with the Potato Stacks and perhaps some green peas.

Potato Stacks

Method

4 peeled, washed, and sliced potatoes (a mandolin is great for this job)
2 tsp olive oil
½ cup cream
½ cup grated Parmesan cheese
1 tsp crushed garlic
sea salt and black pepper

Method

Mix well all of the ingredients together in a bowl.

Simply stack the slices into four mounds in the baking dish with the lamb.

Sprinkle a little extra Parmesan on the top of the stacks. Very munchable.

BRAISED LAMB

Lamb Shanks in a Red Wine Jus (France)

Ingredients (Serves 4)

8 small lamb shanks
olive oil for frying
a large brown onion, chopped
a chopped carrot
a chopped stick of celery
3 cloves crushed garlic
1tsp sugar
500ml (2/3 bottle) good quality dry red wine, shiraz, cabernet, or similar
500ml lamb or beef stock
2 bay leaves
a sprig of fresh rosemary or oregano
2Tbsp tomato paste
sea salt and freshly ground black pepper

ONE POT MEAL

Method

Brown the lamb shanks all over in a frypan in olive oil. Remove them from the pan and place them in a large covered casserole dish. Fry a large chopped onion, a chopped carrot and a chopped stick of celery in oil in the frypan, and put these into the oven dish with the meat.

The mixture of onion, carrot and celery is called in French cooking a 'mirepoix' (pronounced mihr-pwah), after the guy who invented it. The Italian version of the same thing is called a 'soffritto'.

Add the garlic to fry for a minute without burning it, and then add the sugar for a minute. Deglaze the pan by adding the red wine to simmer for a minute. Pour the whole thing over the shanks in the casserole dish.

Then add to the dish the stock, bay leaves, the sprig of fresh rosemary or oregano, the tomato paste, and a good grinding of sea salt and freshly ground black pepper.

The liquid should just cover the shanks. If not, top it up with a little water. Cook the shanks covered, in a moderate oven of 180°C, for about 2½ hours.

When cooked, with the shanks starting to fall apart, remove the shanks from the dish, strain the remaining gravy into a saucepan, and return the shanks to the casserole dish in the oven just to keep them warm.

To make the 'jus', make up the liquid in the saucepan to about 600ml by adding a little extra red wine if necessary, and simmer the liquid in the saucepan on the top of the stove till it reduces by about a half. To serve, place the shanks on a bed of mashed potatoes, and pour over the red wine jus.

This is definitely, IMHO, one of the top ten meat dishes of all time!

Lamb Shanks in a Chardonnay Jus (France)

Lamb shanks used to be a cheap cut of meat, but not anymore, it seems. There are so many gourmet recipes similar to this one appearing in restaurants and in recipe books that demand seems to have driven up the price of this cut of meat. They are well worth the money though, as they are an extremely flavoursome and versatile cut of lamb. Wrap your laughing gear around a couple of these!

Ingredients (Serves 4)

8 lamb shanks, French-trimmed
olive oil for frying
a chopped large onion
a leek, washed well and sliced
a chopped stick of celery
3 cloves crushed garlic
1tsp sugar
1 bottle of good quality Chardonnay (or Sauvignon Blanc, or other dry white wine)
1 cup water
3 bay leaves
a few sprigs of fresh thyme
1tsp sea salt and 1tsp cracked black pepper

ONE POT MEAL

Method

Brown the lamb shanks all over in a frypan in olive oil.

Remove them from the pan and place them in a large covered casserole dish.

Fry a large chopped onion, a leek, and a chopped stick of celery in oil in the frypan.

Add the garlic to fry for a minute, and then add the sugar for a minute. Deglaze the pan by adding the white wine to simmer for a minute. Pour the whole mixture over the shanks in the casserole dish.

Add to the dish the water, bay leaves, thyme, and a good grinding of salt and freshly ground black pepper. The liquid should just cover the shanks. If not, top it up with a little more water.

Cook the shanks covered, in a moderate 180°C oven, for about 2½ hours.

When cooked, with the shanks starting to fall apart, remove the shanks from the dish, strain the remaining gravy into a saucepan, and return the shanks to the casserole dish to keep warm.

Drain any excess fat off the liquid and then reduce it to about half its volume to use as gravy.

Serve with vegetables of your choice, but consider perhaps some grilled asparagus with this one.

Lamb Shanks in Tomato Sauce (Italy)

This is perhaps the most commonly encountered method that you will see in recipes for cooking lamb shanks, and it certainly is very good. Have a Captain Cook at this!

Ingredients (serves 4)

4-6 lamb shanks
plain flour, for dusting
sea salt and cracked black pepper
1 large carrot, coarsely chopped
1 large celery stick, coarsely chopped
6 pickling onions, peeled and halved (see note)
400gm can crushed tomatoes
2 anchovy fillets, chopped
3 cups (750ml) beef stock
3 sprigs rosemary
3 sprigs thyme
150gm baby spinach leaves
pasta, to serve, if desired

ONE POT MEAL

Method

Dust the lamb shanks in the flour, salt and pepper, and shake off excess.

Heat a little olive oil in a large deep saucepan over medium-high heat.

Cook the lamb shanks, in batches, for 3-4 minutes or until browned.

Reduce the heat to low and return all the lamb shanks to the pan.

Add the carrot, celery, and onion and cook for 3-4 minutes.

Add the tomatoes, anchovy fillets, beef stock, rosemary and thyme.

Cover the pan with a lid and cook for 1 hour.

Uncover, and continue cooking, stirring regularly, for another 30 minutes or until the shanks are very tender.

Stir through the baby spinach leaves and cook for another 3-4 minutes or until wilted.

Serve with some pasta, if desired.

Maybe sprinkle a little parsley over the top. Or you could serve it with some Herb Dressing on the side.

Herb Dressing

Blend some white wine vinegar, chopped basil, chopped flat-leafed parsley, chopped chives, chopped shallots, chopped capers, chopped garlic, chopped anchovies, some olive oil, salt and black pepper.

Navarin of Lamb (France)

The most likely explanation for the name seems to derive from the French word for turnip, which is 'navet'. It is a wholesome, full-flavoured braised lamb dish, using a collection of winter vegetables and herbs.

Ingredients

800gm lamb fillet (from shoulder or leg) cut into 2cm pieces
½ cup olive oil for frying
1 onion, chopped
1 small leek, chopped
1 garlic clove, crushed
1 carrot, chopped
1 stalk celery, chopped
250ml (1 cup) dry white wine
250ml (1 cup) water
6 chat (baby Coliban) potatoes, halved
1 swede (or turnip), cubed
1 parsnip, cubed
1 spring onion, chopped
200gm green beans, topped and halved
1tsp dried mixed herbs
1 dried bay leaf
1 anchovy fillet (or 1tsp Worcestershire sauce)
sea salt and freshly ground black pepper
fresh mint leaves to garnish

ONE POT MEAL

Method

Heat some oil in a large frypan and fry the lamb on top of the stove in batches until brown, and remove from the pan. (If you have a stainless steel covered oven dish, even better.)

Fry the onion, leek, garlic, carrot, and celery in a little oil in the pan until fragrant.

Add the wine to deglaze the pan, and then the water.

Put this mixture, along with the meat, in an oven-proof dish.

Add the rest of the ingredients, cover the dish, and cook in the oven on moderate heat of 180^0C for 2 hours.

Stir it a bit half-way through cooking time.

Serve with some fresh crusty bread if desired.

Mashed potatoes also go well with this dish.

Garnish with some mint leaves.

LAMB STEW

Irish Stew (Ireland, of course)

The authentic method of cooking Irish stew is to throw everything into a pot with some water, without browning any ingredients. In lean times it usually meant using the cheapest cuts of mutton, or whatever was available. No butcher will admit to selling mutton (older lamb) these days. In any case, the cheaper cuts of meat are usually the most flavoursome, given plenty of cooking time.

The method used, in that the meat or onions are not browned first, and that white pepper is used instead of black, gives this dish a unique taste.

The smell of this dish cooking is glorious, and takes me right back to the kitchen of my childhood days.

This dish was referred to by the early Irish immigrants of America as 'Mulligan Stew', and a hobo who cooked it up for his mates using whatever was available was known as 'The Mulligan Mixer'.

Ingredients

1Kg lamb leg, or mutton shoulder, or chump or leg chops (about 10), cut into large pieces
1Kg potatoes, chopped
2 large onions, chopped
2 large carrots, chopped
1 large parsnip, chopped
1 swede, chopped
1 leek, chopped
1 stalk celery, chopped
1tsp sea salt
1tsp ground white pepper
1Tbsp fresh flat-leaf parsley, or other herbs, chopped
1 litre water

ONE POT MEAL

Method

Put the meat, vegetables, seasoning, and water in a heavy pot on top of the stove.

Put the lid on and simmer it on the stove, stirring occasionally, for about $2\frac{1}{2}$ hours or until the meat is very tender and the liquid has reduced a little.

This dish is not thickened, as the potatoes will help to thicken the gravy naturally.

Serve in bowls with some of the chopped parsley sprinkled on top.

Sop up the gravy with pieces of fresh bread for an authentic experience.

LAMB CHOPS AND FILLETS

Marinated Lamb Loin Chops (an old family favourite)

Marinate some lamb loin chops in soy sauce, Worcestershire sauce, honey, red wine, minced garlic, salt and pepper for about 1 hour. Roughly drain and bake in the oven for 1 hour until well cooked. This is a favourite of my daughter Letitia.

Barbecued Lamb Fillets

Marinate some lamb back strap or lamb rump fillets in some honey, dark soy sauce, Worcestershire sauce, crushed garlic, black pepper, mixed herbs, a splash of olive oil, and a little red wine, for an hour or so if possible. Cook on the barbecue grill until done to your liking.

BARBECUE FRIENDLY

Lamb Noisettes (France)

This is similar to beef fillet mignon. Cut the T-bone out of some lamb loin chops, and roll them up with some bacon on the outside. Secure them with toothpicks. Spread some crushed garlic over the top and sprinkle on a little Worcestershire sauce, soy sauce, and ground black pepper. Cook with a little oil and butter in a hot frying pan to your liking.

Guinness Chops (Ireland)

Brown some nice lamb loin chops in a little oil and remove from the pan. Brown some onions in the pan, add a little sugar and a can of Guinness. Reduce the sauce a little without the lid, and then thicken it with a little cornflour and water mixed together. Put the whole lot in a covered casserole and cook for about $1\frac{1}{2}$ hours in the oven.

Rosemary Lamb Fillets (Greece)

Fry garlic in a little oil and butter and remove. Add lamb fillets and rosemary and brown until cooked to your liking. Remove and keep warm. Add white wine, salt and pepper to the pan and reduce the liquid a little. Return the lamb and garlic to the pan to coat.

Crusty Cumin Lamb Fillets with Yoghurt Sauce

Coat lamb fillet with cumin and ground black pepper. Brown it in olive oil until cooked. When it has rested, slice the fillet diagonally. Serve it with a yoghurt sauce made from plain yoghurt, garlic, chilli, and lime juice, along with steamed beans tossed in a little sesame oil.

Lamb Fillet with Mustard and Basil

Coat lamb fillet with olive oil, garlic, black pepper, chopped basil and Dijon mustard. Cook in a pan or on the barbecue until cooked to your liking. Serve with steamed or barbecued zucchini topped with tomato salsa and capers.

MINCED LAMB

This is a reasonably economical way to buy lamb; and there is an amazing variety of things you can do with it! As usual, the Greeks excel in this area!

'Moussaka' (Greece)

This recipe uses lamb mince, but you can also use chopped leftover roasted lamb. Similar dishes are made right around the Mediterranean region.
The name comes from an Arabic word meaning 'chilled', as it was originally eaten cold.

Ingredients

2 eggplants, sliced to 1cm thickness
2Tbsp extra virgin olive oil for frying
2 brown onions, sliced thinly
2 cloves garlic, sliced thinly
extra oil for frying
500gm lamb mince, or leftover roasted lamb
400gm can of chopped tomatoes
1tsp dried oregano, or fresh if available
1tsp chopped parsley
1tsp sea salt
1tsp freshly ground black pepper
a knob of butter
2Tbsp plain flour
1 cup milk
1tsp sea salt and 1tsp freshly ground black pepper
1tsp ground nutmeg
1 egg
½ cup grated tasty cheese

Method

Sprinkle eggplant slices both sides with salt and put them in a colander to drain for ½ hour, removing some moisture and bitterness. Rinse and dry them.
Fry them both sides in the oil. Don't use too much oil, as they are greedy for it, and will soak up as much as you give them. Remove them to the side.
Fry the onions and garlic in olive oil till translucent, and stir in the lamb mince, or leftover lamb, to fry a little.
Add the tomatoes, a little oregano, some finely chopped parsley, salt and pepper, and cook for a few minutes.
For the sauce, melt a little butter in a saucepan; add some plain flour to cook for a minute, and add a cup or so of milk and bring it to the boil, stirring it until the sauce is thickened and smooth. Then add some salt, pepper, a little ground nutmeg, and when it is cooled a bit, beat in an egg and the grated cheese.
Layer the eggplant, meat mixture and cheese sauce and bake for about ¾ hour at 180^0C.

'Keftethes' (Greece) - Lamb Patties with Pine Nuts

Ingredients

50gm pine nuts, dry toasted in a frying pan (with no oil)
500gm lamb mince
1 brown onion, finely chopped
2 slices of bread, soaked in water, and squeezed out
juice of half a lemon, and a little grated lemon zest
1 egg
1tsp dried oregano, or dried mixed herbs
1tsp parsley flakes
1tsp sea salt
1tsp freshly ground black pepper

BARBECUE FRIENDLY

Method

Dry toast the pine nuts and remove them from the pan to a bowl. Do not burn them.
Mix in the rest of the ingredients.
Roll the mixture into small meatballs, and coat them in plain flour.
Fry them in the olive oil in a frying pan or on a barbecue hotplate.
Serve them with lemon wedges and some fresh Greek-style plain yoghurt.
Note: Toasting the pine nuts in a dry frying pan provides an amazing flavour to the dish.

Shepherd's Pie (England)

This is an old English favourite, a similar dish to Cottage Pie, which is made with beef mince. You can also use chopped leftover roasted lamb for this dish.

Ingredients

1 brown onion and 1 clove garlic, both finely chopped
1 carrot and 1 stalk celery, finely diced
1Tbsp extra virgin olive oil
500gm lamb mince, or you can use chopped leftover roasted lamb
1 cup beer
a dash of Worcestershire sauce and a dash of soy sauce
1Tbsp plain flour
1tsp sea salt and 1tsp freshly ground black pepper
1 cup frozen peas and 1Tbsp tomato paste

Method

Fry the onion, garlic, carrot and celery in the oil in a frying pan (hence its name) till it is fragrant, and then add the lamb mince to brown a little.
Add the beer and sauces, a sprinkling of plain flour, salt and pepper.
Stir it, cover it, and simmer it for about ½ hour, adding a little more water if necessary.
Stir in the peas and tomato, put the mixture into a casserole dish and spread mashed potatoes all over the top (see Vegetables). Bake this uncovered in the oven for ½ hour.

OTHER LAMB DISHES

Lamb's Fry and Bacon (Australia)

Ingredients

1 young lamb's liver (this will be a little smaller and lighter in colour)
½ cup plain flour
1tsp sea salt
1tsp freshly ground black pepper
4 rashers middle bacon, rind removed, cut into 5cm pieces
1Tbsp olive oil for frying
1 large brown onion, sliced into rings
4 fresh sage leaves
a knob of butter
chopped parsley to garnish

Method

Soak lamb's fry in salted water for half an hour to clean it.

Rinse, drain, remove the skin, and slice the liver into 1cm slices.

Dredge the liver slices in the flour seasoned with salt and pepper.

In a large frypan, fry the bacon in the oil till sizzled and slightly browned, but not overcooked and hard, and remove it from pan.

Now fry the liver slices in the oil that is left in the pan, adding a little more if needed. You may need to cook it in two batches. Make sure that it is nicely browned on the outside, but still a little pink on the inside.

Make sure not to overcook the liver or it will toughen.

Remove the liver slices from the pan.

Now cook the onions and sage leaves, adding the butter to the same pan, until the onions are caramelised a little.

Add the plain flour to cook a little along with the onions, and then enough hot water to make some gravy, stirring until smooth.

Return the lamb's fry and bacon to the pan, and simmer, covered, for about 10 minutes.

Serve topped with some chopped parsley, perhaps along with some sourdough toast.

If serving this as a main meal, you may want to serve some mash and greens with it. It is also a great breakfast dish.

Some like to add some tomato sauce (ketchup) over the top.

Note: The bacon used in Australia is usually smoked middle bacon with the round loin attached, a combination of side and back bacon, which is sometimes called 'Canadian bacon'. The loin part, often sold rindless on its own, is usually called short cut bacon. In the USA, the most common bacon used is from the pork belly, sometimes called 'streaky bacon' or 'belly bacon' in other places, and is usually served very well cooked.

NOODLES

INFO ABOUT NOODLES

Cellophane or Mung Bean Noodles (Jelly Noodles)

These are usually sold dried, and need to be cooked for about 3 minutes in boiling water, unless you are using them in a soup.

Thin Egg Noodles

These are thin egg noodles, made from rice. They are available fresh (best) or dried. Cook them very quickly in boiling water. They come in both white and yellow (often food colouring has been added).

Rice Ribbon Noodles

Sold fresh (best) or dried, they are also available in sheets (from the fridge in the Asian grocery store). They are usually added at the very end of a soup, or stir fry, to avoid having them break up.

Stick Noodles or Rice Vermicelli

These look similar to mung bean noodles, and are made from ground rice. Just pour boiling water over them to soften them.

Soba Noodles

Beige in colour, these Japanese noodles are made from buckwheat flour. The dried noodles are cooked in the same way as pasta.

Udon Noodles

These are thicker white Japanese noodles made from wheat. The dried noodles are also cooked like pasta, for about 6 minutes. Used in stir fries and soups.

Hokkien Noodles

These are fat round egg noodles as above, made from wheat. They take about 3 minutes to cook in boiling water.

Singapore Noodles (Malaysia)

You can find this dish everywhere but Singapore. There are many variations that combine aspects of Asian, Indian and Western cuisine. It's a pretty good stand-by dish.

Ingredients

1 pkt Hokkien noodles
2 eggs
olive oil for frying
1 chicken breast, finely sliced
1 onion, finely chopped
2 cloves garlic, finely chopped
about a 2cm piece of grated fresh ginger, or use minced ginger
1 red capsicum (bell pepper), finely sliced
1 long red chilli, finely chopped
12 peeled green King prawns
1 Tbsp soy sauce
1 tsp sesame oil
1 tsp ground cumin
1 tsp ground coriander
1 tsp ground turmeric
1 tsp sea salt
1 tsp freshly ground black pepper
2 green shallots, finely sliced
2 shitake mushrooms, or other mushrooms, sliced
50gm bean sprouts
½ cup roasted peanuts

Method

Prepare some Singapore or Hokkien noodles as per the packet instructions, drain them and set them aside.
In a wok or frypan, make a simple two egg omelette with a little oil, remove it, slice it, and set it aside.
In some hot olive oil, fry in the wok the sliced chicken breast until it is cooked and golden, and remove it from the wok and set it aside.
Next, in the wok, fry the onion, garlic, and ginger, until the onions are just starting to change colour.
Add to the wok to fry for about two minutes the red capsicum and red chilli.
Then add the prawns, soy sauce, sesame oil, and spices.
Add the green shallots and mushrooms.
Return the pre-prepared noodles, the sliced omelette, and the cooked chicken to the wok, and the whole thing will be ready to serve in about one minute.
Top with some bean sprouts, and some roasted peanuts. Delicious!
Note: Instead of the cooked chicken, you could use some sliced Chinese Char Sui barbecued pork if you wish. Also, you could serve the noodles separately if you wish to conserve room in the wok.

PASTA

INFO ABOUT PASTA

Most dried pasta types are made from durum wheat, a unique ancient species of easily digested hard wheat grown for this purpose. It is high in protein and has a yellow endosperm, which gives pasta its colour. When the wheat is milled, the endosperm of the grain is ground into semolina (in a similar way to how grits is made from maize).

Pasta is usually just wheat and water, however some types contain eggs. Otherwise, it's all pretty much the same stuff, just in different shapes for different purposes. The small or very fine types might be used in soups for example, long thin ones could be used with various sauces, hollow ones may be stuffed, or you might roll up flat pasta to contain fillings.

In Italy, spaghetti, the most common pasta, is the usual choice for plain tomato sauces. A meat sauce, or ragù, such as Bolognese, would more likely accompany ribbon pasta such as tagliatelle, papardelle, or fettuccine, as they hold onto the meat a little better.

PASTA COOKING TIPS

Boil the pasta of your choice in water that is already boiling, and to which you have added a little salt to make it tastier. Stir it every now and then to stop it sticking together.

It should be cooked 'al dente', meaning 'to the bite'. This means that it should be cooked thoroughly, but still offer a little resistance to the bite.

Some people will tell you to add a little oil to the pasta pot to stop it sticking together; whereas others will say that it only makes the sauce slide off the pasta.

Allow about 120gm of pasta per person, unless you like to make extra for leftovers.

ABOUT CURED MEATS

Various types of cured meats are used in pasta and other Italian dishes.

Pancetta is pork belly meat that is fully salt cured and seasoned with spices such as chillies, peppercorns, garlic, and fennel, and dried for at least three months.

Some types of pancetta from Italy have Protected Geographical Status in Europe, in the same way as some wines and cheeses.

It is sometimes rolled and sometimes left in a slab that can be sliced thinly or cut into cubes for frying.

Prosciutto, a specialty of Parma, is similar, but is made from whole pork leg, and takes about twelve months, sometimes longer, to prepare. It is usually more expensive.

Salamis are similar, but are made from ground pork that is uncooked, but fermented and cured, and air-dried. My son Justin seems to have learned this art well from Italian friends.

TRADITIONAL PASTA RECIPES

Classic Pasta 'Bolognese' (Italy) - aka 'spag bol' (slang)

This is meant to be predominantly a meat sauce, or 'ragù' in Italian, not a tomato sauce. This recipe contains a few unusual, but very authentic, tricks that work well.

Ingredients

500gm packet fettuccine (or other flat pasta such as papardelle, or tagliatelle)
2 Tbsp olive oil
1 brown onion, 1 small carrot, and 1 stick celery, finely chopped (retain celery leaves)
800gm quality pork and veal mince (or you can simply use beef mince)
3 thin slices of pancetta (or 1 rasher of bacon), finely chopped
½ cup cream
½ cup (125ml) Chianti (or good dry red wine from Australia, or elsewhwere)
400gm can Italian diced tomatoes (or use bottled tomato passata)
1 clove garlic, finely chopped or minced
1 anchovy fillet, chopped
1tsp minced chilli
1tsp sugar
a few leaves of fresh basil or oregano, or some dried mixed herbs
½tsp sea salt
½tsp freshly ground black pepper
some celery leaves and continental (Italian) flat-leafed parsley
1 cup grated parmesan (Parmiagiano-Reggiano) cheese

Method

First, in a large frying pan on moderate heat, fry the onion, carrot and celery in the oil till the raw onion smell is gone, and remove from the pan. This is called a 'soffritto' which is Italian for 'sub-fried', and provides a good flavour base for the sauce.

Fry the mince and pancetta in the pan in a little more oil, breaking it up with a wooden spoon, and stir it around to brown a little, without letting it go hard.

Add the cream and stir it in. You will find that it helps to soften the meat. This is an authentic step, and makes a big difference to the flavour, as it protects the meat from the acidity of the wine and tomatoes. Return the soffritto to the pan, add the wine to deglaze the pan (lifting off the tasty stuff), and allow the mixture to reduce a little.

Add the tomatoes, garlic, anchovy, chilli, sugar (unless the tomatoes have added sugar, to balance the acidity), herbs, salt and pepper.

Simmer on low heat with the lid on for at least two or three hours, stirring occasionally. Take the lid off half way through cooking to allow it to reduce and thicken.

Ten minutes before serving, add some finely chopped celery leaves, about the same amount of finely chopped continental parsley, and a small swirl of cream or butter.

Serve over drained pasta and top it with the grated cheese. Molto bene!

'Lasagne al Forno' (Italy)

The name 'Lasagne' seems to come originally from the name of the dish in which it was cooked. 'Forno' means something that is baked in an oven.

Ingredients

a quantity of Bolognese sauce (see the previous recipe)
500gm packet pre-cooked instant Lasagne sheets
55gm (1/2 cup) grated Parmesan or Pecorino Romano cheese for the top

Cheese Sauce

3 cups milk
1 brown onion slice
8 fresh parsley stalks (keep the tops for a garnish)
8 whole black peppercorns
4 whole cloves
2 bay leaves
50gm butter
50gm (1/3 cup) plain flour
35gm (1/2 cup) finely grated parmesan
½tsp ground nutmeg
1tsp mustard
1tsp sea salt
1tsp white pepper

Method

Make the Bolognese ragù (meat sauce) as per the previous recipe.

Meanwhile, to make the cheese sauce, combine the milk, onion, parsley stalks, peppercorns, cloves and bay leaves in a medium saucepan and bring to a simmer over medium heat. Remove from heat and set aside for 15 minutes to infuse. Strain the milk mixture through a fine sieve to remove the solids.

Melt the butter in a large saucepan over medium-high heat until foaming. Add the flour and cook it, stirring for 1-2 minutes or until the mixture bubbles and starts to come away from the sides of the pan. Remove from the heat.

Gradually pour in half the milk, whisking constantly, until the mixture is smooth. Gradually add the remaining milk, whisking until the sauce is smooth.

Place saucepan over medium-high heat and bring to the boil, stirring constantly with a wooden spoon, for 5 minutes or until the sauce thickens and coats the back of the spoon. Remove from the heat. Add the parmesan, nutmeg, mustard, salt and pepper, and stir until the cheese melts.

Grease a rectangular ovenproof dish, and put down alternating layers of meat sauce, pasta sheets, and cheese sauce, and top it with the Parmesan cheese.

Bake in a preheated 180°C oven for 40 minutes. Cut the lasagne into portions and serve with a green salad or vegetables.

'Polpette di Carne al Sugo' (Italy) - Spaghetti with Meatballs

Meatballs Ingredients

2 Tbsp extra virgin olive oil for frying
1 Kg good quality beef mince
1 small finely chopped brown onion
½ cup breadcrumbs
2 eggs
1 Tbsp finely chopped Italian parsley
1 tsp sea salt
1 tsp freshly ground black pepper

Sauce Ingredients

1 Tbsp extra virgin olive oil for frying if needed
1 onion, finely chopped
2 cloves garlic, finely chopped
½ cup good quality dry red wine
700ml jar of Italian tomato cooking sauce (passata - passed through a sieve)
1 anchovy fillet, finely chopped
1 Tbsp finely chopped oregano
1 small sprig fresh rosemary
½ tsp sugar
1 tsp sea salt
1 tsp freshly ground black pepper

Other Ingredients

500gm packet good quality spaghetti, or similar
finely grated Parmesan cheese to serve

Method

Mix the meatball ingredients together, and roll it up into small balls, about 60 of 30mm.

Fry the polpette (meatballs) in a frying pan in two batches in the olive oil, and remove.

Drain off any fat in the pan and use a little more olive oil if needed for the sauce.

For the sauce, lightly fry the onion and garlic in oil in the frying pan.

Add the red wine and allow the mixture to reduce for a couple of minutes.

Add the rest of the ingredients and allow the sauce to simmer till the pasta is cooked.

While the sauce is cooking, cook the pasta in lightly salted boiling water in a large pot until it is cooked but still firm (al dente, 'to the tooth', in Italian) and thoroughly drain it using a colander.

Return the pasta to the pot along with the sauce and meatballs.

Serve the pasta with the grated Parmesan cheese on the top.

This makes a large quantity, for quite a few people, or with excellent leftovers for lunch the next day.

'Fettuccine alla Boscaiola' (Italy) - Woodman's Pasta

Ingredients

500gm egg fettuccine (or other pasta)
1 Tbsp extra virgin olive oil
150gm pancetta (or prosciutto, or bacon), chopped
1 leek, finely sliced
100gm sliced brown mushrooms or a small tin champignon mushrooms
several dried shitake or porcini mushrooms, re-hydrated in water
1 chopped spring onion
2 cloves chopped garlic
$\frac{1}{2}$ cup white wine
$\frac{1}{2}$ cup chopped flat-leafed (Italian) parsley
$\frac{1}{4}$ cup chopped sage leaves
salt and freshly ground black pepper
200ml cream
1 cup grated Parmesan cheese

Method

Put the pasta on to cook in a large pot of salted boiling water.

In a frying pan, fry the pancetta and leek in the oil till fragrant.

Add the mushrooms, spring onion, and garlic to cook for a further couple of minutes.

Add the white wine, parsley, sage, salt and pepper, and stir till it is just simmering.

Then add the cream and $\frac{1}{2}$ cup of the cheese, and stir till it is just simmering.

Serve the sauce over the drained pasta, topped with the rest of the cheese.

'Fettucine alla Boscaiola con Pollo' (Italy)

As a variation you might want to make Fettucine alla Boscaiola con Pollo that simply adds the bit on the end that means, 'with Chicken'.

Follow the recipe above, and add in at the end a finely sliced chicken breast that has been well browned and cooked through by frying the chicken pieces in some olive oil in a frying pan.

Add a little finely chopped flat-leafed parsley as a garnish.

'Linguine all'Amatriciana' (Italy)

This is an easy tomato-based pasta dish that you can throw together quickly for an easy and tasty meal.

It comes from the Lazio region around Rome, from the town of Amatrice, which was previously in the Abruzzo region.

Authentically, it is made with 'guanciale', bacon made from pork cheeks, but this can be substituted with other ingredients as shown in the recipe.

If using guanciale, you will not need much oil, as it is quite a fatty cut of meat in itself.

Ingredients

500gm linguine, or other pasta, cooked according to directions and drained
1Tbsp extra virgin olive oil
1 guanciale pork cheek (if available, or substitute 150gm pancetta, or 150gm prosciutto, or 3 rashers of quality middle bacon, chopped)
1 large brown onion, finely chopped
2 cloves fresh purple garlic, finely chopped
1 whole red chilli, chopped
½ cup pinot grigio white wine (or similar dry white wine)
400gm can quality crushed tomatoes
small handful of fresh basil
1 cup grated pecorino Romano cheese, or Parmesan cheese, to top
a small handful of fresh flat-leafed parsley, finely chopped, to garnish

Method

Put the pasta on to cook 'al dente' meaning 'to the tooth'.

Meanwhile, fry the pancetta, onion, garlic, and chilli in a little olive oil till lightly browned, but not burned.

Deglaze the pan with the white wine (to lift the tasty bits off the pan).

Add the can of tomatoes to the pan along with the basil.

Simmer the sauce for about 15 minutes until it has thickened a little.

Serve the sauce over the pasta.

Top with the cheese.

Garnish with the parsley.

'Fettucine alla Carbonara' (Italy) - Coalminer's Pasta

Authentically, it is made with 'guanciale' bacon, which is made from pork cheeks.

While cooking some pasta (ordinary pasta without eggs is fine as there are eggs in this recipe), follow the recipe for the sauce. It will be done by the time the pasta is cooked.

The authentic sauce does not use cream, but relies on the eggs to provide the sauce, which should not be too thick, and the heat from the cooked pasta to cook the eggs.

I guess you could then call it, 'Bacon and Egg Pasta'.

It is really easy, and one of the all-time greats!

Ingredients

1 packet fettucine, or other pasta, cooked according to the packet directions
1 guanciale pork cheek (if available, or substitute 3 rashers of quality bacon, chopped)
1 small onion, finely chopped
2 cloves fresh purple garlic, finely chopped
extra virgin olive oil for frying
3 fresh eggs
1 cup grated parmesan cheese
½ cup high quality extra virgin olive oil for the sauce
½ tsp sea salt
½ tsp freshly ground black pepper
parsley to use as a garnish, finely chopped

Method

Put the pasta on to cook 'al dente', meaning 'to the tooth'.

Sauté the chopped bacon, onion and garlic in a frying pan in a little olive oil.

Meanwhile, mix up the sauce by whisking together the eggs, half of the grated parmesan cheese, the olive oil, sea salt and freshly ground black pepper.

When the pasta is cooked, drain it and return it to the pot.

Add the bacon mixture.

Stir in the sauce, cooking for only one minute more, using the heat of the pasta.

The secret to this recipe is to not overcook it! The sauce should be creamy, not too thick and just heated through.

Top with rest of the parmesan cheese, and add an extra twist of black pepper.

Garnish with some finely-chopped flat-leafed parsley.

'Penne all'Arrabbiata' (Italy) - Angry Pasta

This is a traditional, simple tomato and chilli pasta.

It is red and volatile, just like an angry Sicilian, it seems.

You can use as many, or as few, chillies as you wish.

It is normally cooked using penne pasta and served without parmesan cheese.

It is usually topped instead with some chopped parsley.

As tomato is the dominant flavour you will need to use a good quality tomato puree.

Ingredients

500gm packet penne pasta, cooked according to packet directions
1Tbsp extra virgin olive oil
1 large brown onion, peeled and finely chopped
3 cloves garlic, finely chopped
3 hot red chillies, finely chopped
1 whole dried red chilli, crumbled (or 1tsp pepperoncino-dried chilli flakes)
700gm jar good quality Italian tomato cooking sauce (tomato puree)
1tsp sea salt
1tsp freshly ground black pepper
1 cup finely chopped flat-leafed (Italian) parsley to garnish

Method

Put the pasta on to cook according to packet directions.

Meanwhile, fry the onion and garlic lightly in the oil till the onion is transparent (do not burn the garlic as it will taste very bitter).

Add the chillies and dried chilli to fry for another minute.

Add the tomato puree, salt and pepper, and simmer for 15 minutes.

Serve the sauce over the pasta.

Garnish with the chopped parsley.

'Pasta all'Aglio e Olio' (Italy) Pasta with Garlic and Oil

This is a simple Roman variation of this dish where just the olive oil, onion, and garlic are used, with perhaps a little more olive oil as a dressing.

Make sure to use an excellent quality extra virgin olive oil.

Many Italians love the wonderful simplicity of the flavours of this dish.

This is a pasta 'in bianca', meaning that the sauce contains no tomatoes.

Some freshly grated pecorino Romano cheese over the top is appropriate for this dish.

'Penne alla Puttanesca' (Italy) - Whore's Pasta

This has all the basic Mediterranean flavours. The sugo, or sauce, is usually very quickly made using very fresh ingredients. This is important to the final result.

Ingredients

500gm packet penne pasta, cooked according to packet instructions and drained
1Tbsp extra virgin olive oil
1 large brown onion, peeled and finely chopped
2 cloves garlic, finely chopped
2 anchovy fillets, chopped
2 red chillies, finely chopped
6 thin slices prosciutto, chopped
½ cup Chianti (or other dry red wine)
12 kalamata olives, pitted
12 capers (available in a jar from supermarket)
4 fresh, excellent quality (important), vine-ripened tomatoes, coarsely chopped
small handful oregano leaves (or basil)
small handful flat-leafed parsley leaves
½ tsp sea salt
½ tsp freshly ground black pepper
grated Parmesan cheese to serve

Method

Cook the pasta according to directions.
Meanwhile, lightly fry the chopped onions, garlic, anchovies, and chillies in the olive oil.
Add the prosciutto to fry for a bit longer.
Deglaze the pan by adding the red wine.
Add the kalamata olives, capers, tomatoes, oregano or basil, parsley, salt and pepper. Simmer for about 10 minutes.
Serve the sauce over the freshly cooked pasta, and top it with the Parmesan cheese.

Potato Gnocchi (Italy)

Ingredients

2 cups mashed potato, seasoned
1 egg
1 cup plain flour, or a little more as required to make firm dough

Method

Mix the plain flour with the mashed potato and the egg until a firm dough forms.
Roll the dough into sausage shapes and slice into 2 cm lengths. Shape the gnocchi around a fork and drop them into salted boiling water, about 20 at a time.
Take them out when they float, and top them with a plain tomato pasta sauce, and some grated parmesan cheese. Sweet potato can also be used for this dish.

'Fusilli con Pollo e Pesto' (Italy) - Chicken and Pesto Pasta

The word pesto comes from pestare meaning 'to crush', and so describes the process of grinding up ingredients using a mortar and pestle (which comes from the same word).

It is similar to the French equivalent 'pistou'.

There are two main styles of pesto:

1. Pesto alla Genovese is a green pesto and made with Pecorino Romano cheese (a sheep's milk cheese, from the word 'pecora' meaning sheep).
2. Pesto alla Siciliana is a red pesto and made with Parmigiano-Reggiano cheese (a cow's milk cheese) and contains sun-dried tomatoes. You can try either style in this recipe, or you can try the Calabrese variation of the red pesto.

Both of the cheeses used are from very old recipes, have protected PDO status, and are really great with pasta dishes.

Method

Cook a 500gm packet fusilli (spiral) pasta (or other pasta if you wish) according to the packet directions, and drain it.

Brown the sliced chicken breasts in the oil in a frying pan, and cook them until done.

Using a mortar and pestle, grind up the pesto using the following ingredients and steps:

Pesto alla Genovese (Green)

1. 2 cloves garlic, and ½ cup dry toasted pine nuts (crush to a paste)
2. Add a handful fresh basil, 1tsp coarse sea salt, and ½tsp black pepper
3. Add ½ cup grated Pecorino Romano cheese and 1Tbsp extra virgin olive oil

Pesto alla Siciliana (Red)

1. 2 cloves garlic, and ½ cup dry toasted pine nuts (crush to a paste)
2. Add a handful fresh basil, 1tsp coarse sea salt, and ½tsp black pepper
3. Add ½ cup grated Parmigiano-Reggiano cheese and 1Tbsp extra virgin olive oil
4. Add 6 halves of pomodori secchi (European-style sun-dried tomatoes in oil)

Pesto alla Calabrese (Chilli Hot)

1. 2 cloves garlic, and ½ cup dry toasted pine nuts (crush to a paste)
2. Add a handful fresh basil, 1tsp coarse sea salt, and ½tsp black pepper
3. Add ½ cup grated Parmigiano-Reggiano cheese and 1Tbsp extra virgin olive oil
4. Add 6 halves of pomodori secchi (European-style sun-dried tomatoes in oil)
5. Add 1 grilled and peeled red capsicum
6. Add 2 chopped red chillies

Stir the pesto into the cooked pasta along with the cooked chicken pieces.

Top with some more grated Parmesan or pecorino Romano cheese, and serve.

Spinach and Ricotta 'Cannelloni' (Italy) - large reeds

You can make this using cannelloni tubes if you wish, but you have to then stuff the mixture into them, and this is time-consuming, fiddly, and quite annoying.

The easier way is to buy fresh lasagne or cannelloni sheets from the supermarket that you can roll up yourself with the mixture inside. You can then have the whole thing in the oven in less than twenty minutes.

Ingredients for the Tomato Sauce

1 brown onion, very finely chopped
2 cloves garlic, minced
1Tbsp extra virgin olive oil
700gm jar of Passata or Provvista Sugo Italian cooking sauce (available at supermarket)
1tsp sea salt (if there is none in the Sugo)
1tsp freshly ground black pepper
½tsp sugar
a few leaves of finely chopped flat-leafed parsley
a few leaves of finely chopped fresh oregano

Ingredients for the Filling

1/3 cup pine nuts (about 50gm), lightly toasted in a dry saucepan (using no oil)
1/3 cup grated parmesan cheese
500gm fresh ricotta cheese
200gm baby spinach leaves, roughly chopped

Ingredients for Assembly

8 (375gm) fresh lasagne sheets, cut in half to make 16 tubes (depending on dish size)
½ cup grated mozzarella cheese
½ cup grated tasty cheese
½ cup grated parmesan cheese
a few fresh basil leaves to sprinkle on top as a garnish, if you have them available.

Method

In a saucepan, first lightly toast the pine nuts till they start to colour, and remove them. You can then use the saucepan to make the sauce (that makes sense doesn't it!)

For the sauce, in the same saucepan, lightly fry the onion and garlic in the oil. Then add the rest of the sauce ingredients to cook on top of the stove for about 10 minutes.

Mix all of the filling ingredients together in a bowl, and spoon the mixture equally down the centre of the eight pieces of the lasagne sheets. Turn the long edges over to make the cannelloni tubes.

Pour a little of your tomato sauce mixture into the bottom of a large oven dish, arrange the tubes on top, and pour the rest of the sauce over the top of the cannelloni to cover them. Then sprinkle over the Mozzarella, Tasty, and Parmesan cheeses (a great combo).

Cook in the oven at 180^0C for about 15 minutes.

Sprinkle over the basil leaves and serve.

Salmon Pasta with Capers and Dill

Ingredients

500gm pappardelle pasta
1Tbsp extra virgin olive oil for frying
2 French shallots, or 1 onion, very finely chopped
1 clove garlic, very finely chopped
1tsp minced chilli (optional)
a splash of dry white wine
200gm can red salmon, drained and mashed
small carton light sour cream
1Tbsp horseradish cream
2tsp capers
1 sprig fresh dill
1tsp sea salt
1tsp freshly ground black pepper
grated Parmesan cheese to top and chopped parsley to garnish

Method

Put the pasta on to cook according to packet directions.
Meanwhile, in a frying pan, fry the onion, garlic, and chilli lightly in the oil till the onion is transparent (do not burn the garlic as it will taste very bitter).
Add the wine, salmon, creams, capers, dill, salt and pepper, and simmer for 10 minutes.
Serve the sauce over the pasta.
Top with the Parmesan cheese, and garnish with the chopped parsley.

Macaroni Cheese (Italy)

Ingredients

500gm packet macaroni pasta
50gm butter
1 onion, very finely chopped
2Tbsp plain flour
2 cups milk
1 cup grated Gruyere cheese
1 cup grated vintage cheddar cheese
½ cup grated parmesan cheese

Method

Cook the macaroni in a large pot according to packet directions, and drain.
In another pot, fry the onion in the butter till it is translucent, add the flour to cook a little, and then add the milk, stirring until the sauce is smooth and simmering.
Stir in the Gruyere and cheddar cheese till combined, about 2 minutes.
Stir the sauce into the pasta, and serve topped with the parmesan cheese.

PORK

ROAST PORK

'Lechon Asada' (Cuba) - Shredded Roast Pork

As with many Cuban dishes, the idea is simple slow cooking with basic ingredients. Lechon Asada means 'roast suckling pig', so you could do it whole if you like.
Use at least a 2.5Kg pork shoulder or leg marinated overnight in this tasty greenish Chimichurri marinade.

Chimichurri Marinade Ingredients

½ cup extra virgin olive oil
½ cup orange juice (preferably Seville bitter orange juice)
½ cup lime juice
½ cup red wine
½ cup chopped flat leafed parsley
2Tbsp chopped jalapeno chilli peppers
4 cloves chopped garlic
1tsp sea salt
1tsp freshly ground black pepper

BARBECUE FRIENDLY

Method

Cook in the oven at 180°C for 2½ hours covered, and 1 hour uncovered, until the meat will shred easily. This is commonly served on fresh crusty bread, or you can serve it with a Mojo Criollo sauce on the side if you wish (see the recipe below).

'Mojo Criollo' Sauce (Creole)

This is a popular pinkish Creole garlic sauce used for many dishes (originating from 'mojado' meaning 'wet', and pronounced 'mo-ho-cree-yo-yo').
Marinate 2 finely sliced brown (yellow) onions for 30 minutes in a bowl in the following, making sure that the onions are pressed down into the liquid:
1 cup orange juice (preferably Seville bitter orange juice)
½ cup lime juice
½ cup red wine
Then fry in a little olive oil for about half a minute the following:
4 cloves crushed garlic
1tsp rosemary
1tsp dried oregano
1tsp ground cumin seed
1tsp sea salt
Then stir in the onion mixture to cook a little (be very careful of the vicious spatter). Serve it on the side with the pork and perhaps some rice and black beans.

'Jerk' Pork (Jamaica) - Spicy Marinated Pork

This is the most famous dish in Jamaican cuisine. It is authentically cooked over pimento wood coals for a smoky flavour. The term 'jerk' is said to come from the Spanish word 'charqui', for jerked or dried meat, which then became 'jerky' in English.

The term now refers more to the method of marinating the meat, using the main ingredients of pimento (allspice), native to the Caribbean, and very hot red chillies.

The same recipe can be used with chicken and fish.

Jerk Paste Ingredients

the juice of a Tahitian lime
1 green shallot, finely chopped
1 green jalapeno chilli, finely chopped
1Tbsp extra virgin olive oil
1Tbsp balsamic vinegar
1Tbsp rum
2tsp crushed hot chilli (available in a jar)
2tsp crushed garlic
2tsp crushed ginger
2tsp honey
2tsp ground allspice (pimento)
1tsp freshly ground black pepper
1tsp ground cinnamon
1tsp ground nutmeg
1tsp sugar
1tsp dried thyme

BARBECUE FRIENDLY

Ingredients

Leg of pork, with the rind cut in a criss-cross pattern

Method

Mix all of the jerk paste ingredients together.

Rub the pork all over with the paste using disposable gloves (it is a vicious brew), put it in a baking dish, cover it with cling-film, and allow it to marinate for as long as possible, preferably overnight. Take off the cling-film.

Slow cook it in the oven or in a covered barbecue for 4 hours at about 150^0C, or until it starts to fall apart, and then turn up the heat to about 200^0C for a while till the skin is nice and crispy.

Baby Back Pork Ribs (United States)

The eating and cooking of ribs in the USA is not just popular, but almost an obsession. Those who like them seem to like them a lot, and there are as many different ways of cooking them as there are experts. If you really insist on ruining your health, give them a go. I have tried to make them as healthy as possible; so please don't blame me.

'Baby back ribs' or 'loin ribs' are taken from the top of the pig's rib cage below the spine and the 'spare ribs', or 'side ribs', are taken from the belly side of the rib cage below the section of back ribs and above the breast bone. 'Baby' indicates a market weight pig. It's amazing; almost everything is used on a pig except the squeal.

Ingredients

2.5Kg baby back pork ribs

Ingredients for the Marinade and Basting Sauce

1Tbsp olive oil
1 small brown onion, very finely chopped
3 cloves fresh garlic, very finely chopped
1Tbsp crushed chilli
1Tbsp honey
1Tbsp dark soy sauce
1Tbsp Worcestershire sauce
1Tbsp concentrated tomato paste
1Tbsp red balsamic vinegar
1Tbsp mixed dried herbs
1 cup red wine
1tsp sea salt
1tsp cracked black pepper
1tsp raw sugar

BARBECUE FRIENDLY

Method

Peel the thin membrane off the inside of the ribs, if that is not already done, and boil the ribs in water for about 15 minutes to remove the excess fat. Drain off the water.

Meanwhile, lightly fry the onion and garlic in oil in a saucepan, add the rest of the marinade ingredients, and simmer for about 20 minutes until the sauce thickens slightly.

Put the ribs in a large roasting tray, and pour about half of the sauce over the ribs to thoroughly coat. Keep the rest to pour over the ribs half way through the cooking time.

Bake them on low heat in the oven or a closed barbecue at about $140^{\circ}C$ for 4 hours, until they are starting to fall apart.

You can crank the heat up to about $200^{\circ}C$ for the last twenty minutes if they look like they need a good sizzle. Or, you could finish them off on the barbecue grill.

Put them in the centre of the table and stand back from the stampede!

Glazed Leg of Ham

I like to serve this as a delicious breakfast centrepiece for family and friends that is a bit more upmarket than just serving up bacon and eggs. It also has the advantage that it will comfortably serve quite a number of people.

The food is cooked indoors easily, and is, I think, a good breakfast alternative to eating around a smoky barbecue at that time of the day.

Serve it on a table outdoors if you can, as food tastes so much better in the open air. You will find that a meal like this at breakfast time is often enjoyed much more than an evening meal by many people.

Ingredients

2.5Kg smoked leg ham on the bone
1 cup breakfast marmalade
1tsp ground cloves
½tsp ground cinnamon
½tsp ground nutmeg
½tsp ground cardamom
½tsp fine sea salt
½tsp freshly ground black pepper

Method

Peel the skin from the ham, being careful to leave the fat layer in place. Now score the fat in a criss-cross pattern to make diamond shapes in it.

Mix up the spices in a cup, and sprinkle them all over the surface of the fat.

Spread plenty of marmalade over the top and sides of the leg so that most of it stays in place. The pattern in the fat will help to hold it there.

Put it on a rack in a baking tray in a moderate $180^{0}C$ oven, pour a cup of water in the bottom to stop any residue from burning on the bottom, and bake it for about 1 hour until the fat is golden and crunchy.

Take it to the table, and carve the meat vertically (across the grain) down to the bone.

Breakfast Suggestions

Perhaps serve bowls of fresh fruit as a starter, along with some toasted muesli, and some plain Greek-style yoghurt.

A plate of scrambled or fried eggs can be cooked indoors in a frying pan.

Maybe have some halved tomatoes fried in a pan and sprinkled with some fresh herbs.

For the potato lovers, some potato pancakes are just great.

And, of course, serve plenty of fresh sourdough bread as an accompaniment.

For the sweet-toothed people, perhaps some nice banana muffins or some pancakes would go down well.

A glass of champagne (or sparkling chardonnay, or sparkling sauvignon blanc, or similar) is always a nice accompaniment to a relaxed breakfast, too.

BRAISED PORK

Braised Pork in Apple Cider with Sage Scones

This is very similar to my recipe called 'Braised Beef with Dumplings'.

Ingredients

½ cup extra virgin olive oil for frying
800gm pork shoulder or leg, cubed
1 rasher of bacon, rind removed, and finely chopped (or use pancetta)
1 large onion, finely chopped
1 stick of celery, finely chopped
1 clove garlic, finely chopped (or 1tspn crushed garlic)
1tsp ground cumin seed
1 bulb fennel, thinly sliced
½ cup plain flour
1½ cups apple cider (1 small bottle) and 1 cup of water
a few sprigs fresh sage)
1 bay leaf, dried or fresh
1 small tin of whole champignons
8 small whole pickling onions (small brown onions, peeled)
50gm green beans, peeled and halved
½tsp salt and ½tsp white pepper

ONE POT MEAL

Method

Brown the pork in a little olive oil in an oven-proof dish in batches, and remove it from the pan. Then fry the bacon, onion, celery, garlic, cumin, and fennel in the same dish in a little oil for a few minutes until the onion becomes transparent.
Sprinkle over the flour, and stir the mixture until the flour starts to cook.
Deglaze the pan with the apple cider and water (this lifts the tasty bits off the pan). Add the herbs, champignons, pickling onions, beans, salt and pepper, and return the pork to the pot. Cover the pan, and cook it in the oven at 180°C for 1½ hours.

The Sage Scones

2 cups self-raising flour, plus extra for kneading
1Tbsp finely chopped fresh sage
½tsp fine sea salt
60gm cold butter
1 cup full cream milk

Mix the flour, sage, and salt together in a large bowl. Rub the butter into the flour with your fingers until it resembles fine breadcrumbs. Make a well in the centre, mix in enough milk, till you have firm dough, and then knead the dough on a lightly floured surface until smooth. Roll it out to 2½cm thickness, and use a glass to stamp out rounds of dough. Place these on top of the braised pork, leaving a little space between each one to allow for expansion, and cook uncovered for the last 25 minutes of the cooking time, or until the dumplings are browned on top. Garnish with some flat-leafed parsley.

Pork Chops in Apricot Sauce

Ingredients (Serves 4)

1.2Kg pork loin chops
1Tbsp olive oil for frying
1/3 cup dry white wine
1/3 cup orange juice
1tsp ground coriander
½tsp salt
½tsp white pepper
1 onion, finely chopped
1 clove garlic, finely chopped
small can apricot puree
1tsp minced ginger
1tsp ground coriander
1Tbsp chopped parsley
1tsp sea salt
1tsp white pepper

Method

Marinate the pork chops for 2 hours or more in the wine, orange juice, coriander, salt and pepper. Remove from the marinade and keep what is left of the marinade.

Pan-fry the pork chops on the stovetop or barbecue till cooked and remove from the pan to keep warm.

To the pan drippings add the finely chopped onion and the chopped garlic to brown just a little.

Add the small can of apricot puree, minced ginger, ground coriander, some chopped parsley, salt and white pepper, and any leftover marinade.

Simmer for 10 minutes until slightly reduced and thickened.

Return the chops to heat through in the sauce and serve.

Perhaps serve with mashed potatoes and spinach.

PORK STEW

Dublin Coddle (Ireland)

This is an old-fashioned (at least 200 years old) classic dish that was commonly consumed in Ireland; and anywhere else that Irish people happened to go after that.

It is very similar to Irish Stew, which was usually made of the lesser cuts of lamb.

The name 'coddle' refers to being cooked in water below boiling point, in a kind of similar way to Coddled Eggs.

It is said that this dish was popular in Ireland because the wife could go to bed, leaving it cooking slowly on the stove till hubby came home late from the pub.

Ingredients

250gm thick-cut smoked bacon, rind removed (you can sometimes get bacon off-cuts)
500gm good quality pork sausages
2 large brown onions, peeled and thickly sliced
1 large carrot, peeled and chopped coarsely
1 stalk celery, chopped
4 large potatoes, peeled and sliced to about 3mm thickness
2tsp sea salt
2tsp ground white pepper
½ cup chopped parsley
some vegetable or chicken stock or water

ONE POT MEAL

Method

In about 1 litre of water in a large cooking pot, boil the bacon and sausages for about 10 minutes. Remove them, cut them into large chunks, and return them to the pot, retaining the water.

Add the onions over the top in a layer, then the carrot and celery, and then the potatoes, adding a little sea salt and ground white pepper with each layer.

Sprinkle the chopped parsley over the top.

Add some stock or water to bring the level about half way up the contents of the pot, cover, and cook on top of the stove at a slow simmer for at least two hours.

Check the level of liquid occasionally so that it doesn't get too low, and top it up a bit if necessary with water.

The potatoes will naturally thicken the dish a little.

This dish was traditionally served with Irish Soda Bread and Guinness. Not too shabby!

You could also cook this in a slow cooker with good results.

Note: This dish provides a tasty alternative to plain sausages, which are sometimes referred to in Australia as snags, bangers, or mystery bags.

PORK MINCE

Chinese Dumplings (China) 'Jiaozi'

Jiaozi (Mandarin) are also known as Gow Gee (Cantonese romanisation), or 'Potstickers' as a rough English translation. Their equivalent in Japan is Gyoza. In Nepal and Tibet they are known as Momo. They can be steamed, boiled, or the traditional method is to fry them on the bottom first and then steam them. Gow Gee wrappers and Gyoza wrappers can be obtained ready-made from the supermarket. Shao mai are similar, with the difference that they are formed into a cup shape with the filling visible at the top.

Ingredients for the Dough

2 cups plain flour
1 cup boiling water (for greater dough elasticity)
1 Tbsp extra virgin olive oil for frying the dumplings

Ingredients for the Dipping sauce

2 Tbsp dark soy sauce
1 Tbsp Shaoxing rice cooking wine
½ tsp sesame oil

Ingredients for the Filling

250gm pork mince
5 dried shitake mushrooms, re-hydrated in water
1 green shallot, finely sliced
1 Tbsp finely chopped coriander leaf
2 tsp dark soy sauce
1 tsp minced ginger
1 tsp minced red chilli
1 tsp minced garlic
1 tsp five spice powder
1 tsp sea salt and 1 tsp ground white pepper

Method

For the Dough, mix the flour and water together in a bowl and knead it on a floured surface for 5 minutes until smooth. Roll into a 3cm diameter log and set it aside.
For the Dipping sauce, mix the ingredients in a small bowl and set it aside for later.
For the Filling, in a bowl, mix together all of the ingredients well.
Now cut off 1cm slices of dough, and roll the pieces into 9cm diameter rounds.
Place a heaped teaspoonful of mixture in the centre of the circles of dough, wet the edges of the dough with your finger, lift the edge of the dough circle and fold it over.
Pleat the dumplings to form a crescent shape, pinching the edges together to seal.
Fry the dumplings in hot oil in a pan for 2 minutes, or until the bottoms are golden.
Then add ½ cup water, cover the pan, and allow the dumplings to steam for about 5 minutes, until the water is absorbed. Do the frying and steaming in two batches.
As an option, you could replace half the pork with peeled and chopped green prawns.

'Lumpiang Sariwa' (Phillipines) - Fresh Spring Rolls

This is my simplified version of the fresh and crunchy un-fried spring rolls that originally come from China, but are common throughout Asia. They are made with a basic stir-fry mixture wrapped in lettuce leaves and some plain homemade egg crepes.

Ingredients

1Tbsp peanut oil
1 brown onion, finely chopped
1 clove garlic, finely chopped
300gm pork mince (or pork and veal)
1 small carrot, julienned
1 stalk celery, julienned
1 green shallot, finely chopped
1tsp minced red chilli
1tsp sea salt and 1tsp white pepper
½ cup frozen chopped green beans
1 cup small frozen green prawns, thawed
(optional) finely sliced bamboo shoots, boiled twice in water (only some types of shoots), iceberg or other lettuce leaves for assembling the rolls

Method

Fry the onion and garlic lightly in the oil, and then add the mince to fry till the pork is cooked through. Add the rest of the ingredients and fry for a further 4 minutes, adding some water if necessary. The mixture should be fairly dry.

Crepes

1 cup plain flour
2 cups milk
3 eggs
butter for cooking

Mix the flour, milk and eggs in a bowl, whisking until well combined.
Heat a medium size, non-stick frying pan over medium-low heat. Grease with a small amount of oil or butter. Pour a ladle of batter into the pan, swirling it to cover the base with a very thin layer. Cook the crepes for 1 minute on each side until just cooked. Transfer to a plate and cover to keep warm. Repeat with the remaining batter.
To assemble, place lettuce leaves on top of the crepes, spoon on the mixture, and roll them up. Drizzle some of the peanut sauce along the top of the rolls.

Peanut Soy sauce

2tsp peanut oil
½ cup roasted peanuts, crushed
1tsp minced garlic and ½tsp minced red chilli
1 cup water with 2tsp cornflour mixed into it
¼ cup dark soy sauce and ½tsp sugar

Fry the peanuts, garlic, and chilli in the oil in a small saucepan for a minute or so, then add the rest of the ingredients to simmer for a few minutes until slightly thickened.

RICE

Risotto with Pancetta (Italy)

Risotto is a well-known and respected dish around the world. In Italy, it is often served as a first course, and sometimes together with Osso Bucco. It is a little fiddly to make correctly, but provides a delicate meal along with an education for you as you make it.

Ingredients

1 litre chicken stock, heated (this gives a ratio of 4:1 of stock to rice)
1Tbsp extra virgin olive oil
100gm pancetta, finely chopped
1 large brown onion, peeled and finely chopped
2 cloves fresh garlic, peeled and finely chopped
250gm packet Arborio rice (or other risotto rice)
1tsp sea salt and 1tspn freshly ground black pepper
½ cup pinot grigio dry white wine (or other dry white)
a small handful of thyme leaves
1 small knob of butter
1 cup grated parmesan cheese

See Chicken Noodle Soup recipe for the stock preparation

ONE POT MEAL

Method

Put the chicken stock in a saucepan to heat up to a simmer.
Meanwhile, fry the pancetta, onion, and garlic slowly in the oil in a large pot until the onion is translucent or glassy. There should be enough oil with fat from the pancetta.
Stir in the rice, salt and pepper, and continue stirring for a couple of minutes until the rice is translucent. This is important to avoid ending up with 'gluggy' risotto.
Pour in the wine and add the thyme. Stir for about 1 minute until the liquid is absorbed.
Now comes the part with the hot chicken stock. - A half a cup at a time, stir in the stock with a flat-ended plastic spatula, until the liquid is absorbed each time. This will take about twenty minutes of constant stirring (now, where is that sauvignon blanc?) so that when the stock is used up, the risotto will be soft but with a slight bite (al dente). If you think you need a little more liquid, use boiling water.
Switch off the heat, add the butter and half of the parmesan cheese, stir them in well, and put the lid on. This makes the risotto extra creamy.
Serve as soon as possible, as it continues to cook in its own heat, topped with the rest of the parmesan.

Variations

You can add other ingredients. Cook them separately and add them in at the end.
- Sliced and cooked chicken breast
- Sun dried tomatoes or cherry tomatoes
- Mushrooms or champignons
- Red salmon and capers
- King prawns, peeled and lightly-fried

Chicken, Chorizo and Prawn Paella (Spain)

This dish is very similar to the Creole or Cajun Jambalaya that has Spanish and French influences. Paella is the national dish of Spain originating in Valencia. Early recipes used marsh rat, rabbit, and even snails. Many types of paella are popular today, with the coastal seafood versions being the most famous. The word 'paella' means 'pan', and special very large flat frying pans can be purchased for cooking it.

Chorizo (pronounced chor-eetho), originally from Spain and Portugal, is now popular in Mexico. All are made with minced pork. The Spanish variety are flavoured with smoked paprika. The cheaper Latin American and Mexican Chorizo are made using chillies instead. There are two main types, an air-dried fermented sausage that can be sliced and eaten like salami, and smaller fresh sausages that must be cooked before eating.

Ingredients

200gm chicken breast fillet, sliced fairly thinly
1 Spanish chorizo sausage, sliced to about 1cm
½ cup good quality extra virgin olive oil
1 onion, finely sliced
2 cloves garlic, finely sliced
1 Chipotle chilli, finely sliced
1 green Jalapeño chilli, finely sliced
1tsp ground turmeric
¾ cup medium-grain rice
400gm can chopped tomatoes
1 cup chicken stock
¾ cup Rioja (Spanish dry red wine) if available, or similar wine
1tsp sea salt and 1tsp freshly ground black pepper
12 frozen peeled green prawns, thawed
some chopped flat-leafed parsley to garnish
lemon wedges to garnish

ONE POT MEAL

Method

Brown the chicken along with the chorizo in a little olive oil in a large frying pan until it is cooked through and the sausage is starting to lose its fat. Remove it from the pan.
Add the onion, garlic, chipotle, jalapeño, turmeric, and extra oil if necessary, to soften.
Add the rice, tomatoes, chicken stock, wine, salt and pepper, and cook for a few minutes till it is hot. Then turn it down to a low heat and cook it for about 20 minutes, until the rice is cooked and the mixture is reasonably thick. Stir the mixture occasionally so that it doesn't stick and add a little water if it looks too dry.
Return the chicken and chorizo to the pan to heat through.
Add the green prawns to cook for about 4 minutes.
Do not stir in these last stages as the sign of a good traditional paella is when the bottom of the food starts to catch on the pan and fry in the oil that appears, going a little bit crunchy This is the best bit.
Serve with chopped flat-leafed parsley and lemon wedges to garnish.

Sushi (Japan)

Seasoned rice vinegar (awasezu) is used for making sushi, and there are many types. It is made by adding saki, salt, and sugar to rice vinegar (komezu). It is different to rice wine, such as the Chinese Shaoxing rice wine. The easiest way to buy it is from the Asian section of the supermarket where it is often sold simply as Sushi vinegar.

Ingredients

2 cups sushi rice, or use Calrose short-grain rice
2 cups water
1/3 cup sushi vinegar (or mix 1/3 cup plain rice vinegar, 3tsp sugar, and 1/2tsp salt)
nori sheets (dried seaweed)
pickled ginger as an accompaniment (available in a jar)
wasabi paste (Japanese horseradish)
Japanese soy sauce

Filling Ingredients

Use your choice of any of the following in combination:
- canned tuna
- canned red salmon
- smoked salmon slices
- cooked prawns
- avocado slices (sprinkled with lemon juice)
- Lebanese cucumber
- asparagus
- sun-dried tomatoes

Method

Rinse the rice several times in water and drain in a colander for half an hour.
Bring the rice and water to the boil, put the lid on and simmer for about 12 minutes.
Turn off the heat and leave the lid on for another 10 minutes so that all the water is absorbed.
Gently stir the vinegar into the rice, fluffing it up, and allow it to cool to body temperature.
Using a bamboo rolling mat and a sheet of baking paper on top (to keep it clean), place a sheet of nori on top of the mat, and spread some rice over the top, leaving the end section clear.
Place your fillings across the sheet and roll up the sushi tightly, sealing the edge with a little water.
Cut each roll into about 4 pieces.
Eat immediately or refrigerate.
Serve with pickled ginger on the side in a bowl.
The wasabi paste and soy sauce are usually mixed together by the eater according to their own tolerance and taste.

SALADS

BEEF SALAD

Warm Beef Salad with Rice Noodles (Vietnam)

Ingredients

300gm beef fillet steak, finely sliced
2tsp Shaoxing rice cooking wine
2tsp peanut oil
2tsp dark soy sauce
1tsp minced garlic
1tsp minced red chilli
1tsp minced ginger root
1tsp sea salt and 1tsp cracked black pepper
peanut oil for frying
1 packet fresh rice noodles, cooked according to directions
lettuce leaves, oak or coral
2 green shallots, finely chopped
1 stalk celery, finely chopped
1 carrot very finely julienned (very thin strips)
a handful of bean sprouts
a few fresh coriander and mint leaves, chopped
pkt fried shallots (from an Asian food supplier)
½ cup roasted peanuts

Method

Marinate the steak in the wine, oil, soy, garlic, chilli, ginger, salt and pepper for an hour. Fry it in the oil till cooked to your liking and set it aside to be served warm.
Cook the rice noodles and set them aside to be served warm.
Toss together the salad ingredients of lettuce, shallots, celery, carrot, sprouts, and fresh leaves.
Serve in bowls with noodles on the bottom, then the salad, and the beef on the top.
Mix together the dressing ingredients, and then top the lot with some fried shallots and the peanuts.

Nuoc Cham Dressing (Vietnam)

½ cup hot water (using hot water helps to combine all of the flavours)
1tsp minced garlic
1tsp minced ginger root
1 long red chilli, deseeded and very finely sliced (or use 1tsp minced chilli)
¼ cup fish sauce (nuoc mam)
¼ cup lime juice (the juice of 2 Tahitian limes)
¼ cup brown sugar

Warm Beef Salad with Blue Cheese Dressing (Spain)

This also has Moroccan influence as displayed in the spices and the cous cous base.

Ingredients

2 scotch fillet beef steaks (nicely marbled with fat if possible)
extra virgin olive oil (EVOO) for coating the steak
Make up a dry Spanish spice rub in a cup with:
½tsp ground cumin
½tsp ground coriander
½tsp turmeric
½tsp ground chilli
½tsp smoked paprika
½tsp ground cinnamon
½tsp ground cloves
½tsp black pepper
1 cup cous cous
mixed lettuce leaves
baby spinach leaves
½ Spanish red onion, very finely shaved
1 red capsicum (bell pepper), finely sliced
1 long red chilli, deseeded and very finely sliced
1 green shallot, very finely sliced
½ cup sultanas
some flat-leafed parsley leaves
some fresh mint leaves
the juice of ½ a lemon
1tsp balsamic vinegar
½tsp sea salt and ½tsp freshly ground black pepper
½ cup dry toasted pine nuts as a garnish

Method

Rub the steaks all over with the oil on a plate.
Rub them both sides in the spice mixture.
Char grill the steaks to your liking on a barbecue grill, and set them aside to rest.
Cook the cous cous in boiling water according to the packet directions.
Assemble and toss the salad in a large bowl using the rest of the salad ingredients.
Finely slice the steak on a cutting board and lay the strips over the top of the salad.
Drizzle some of the dressing over the top and put the rest in a serving jug.
Sprinkle the toasted pine nuts over the top as a garnish.

Blue Cheese Dressing

Blend together 100gm plain yoghurt, 50gm blue cheese, 50ml milk, the juice of ½ a lemon, and a little sea salt and freshly ground black pepper.

LAMB SALAD

Lamb Salad with Yoghurt Dressing (Greece)

Ingredients

600gm lamb rump steaks, or lamb shoulder steak, cut into strips
the juice of ½ a lemon
1Tbsp olive oil
1tsp minced garlic
1tsp minced red chilli
1tsp finely chopped fresh sage leaves (or dried)
1tsp rosemary leaves
1tsp sea salt
1tsp freshly ground black pepper
extra virgin olive oil for frying
mixed salad leaves
rocket salad leaves
1 carrot, finely sliced
1 stalk celery, finely sliced
1 French shallot, very finely shaved
1 green shallot, finely sliced
1 cup cabbage, finely sliced
1 cup pitted kalamata olives
4 anchovy fillets, chopped
10 cherry tomatoes, halved
200gm Greek feta cheese, cubed

Method

Marinate the lamb in the juice, oil, garlic, chilli, leaves, salt and pepper for an hour.
Fry the meat in the oil in a frying pan until done to your liking, and put to one side.
In a bowl toss the rest of the salad ingredients together.
Drizzle over the dressing and serve the rest in a jug on the side.
Garnish the top with a little extra chopped parsley.

Yoghurt Dressing (Greece)

Make the dressing by mixing together:
1 cup plain Greek-style yoghurt
the juice of ½ a lemon
2 finely diced pickled dill cucumbers
1 green shallot, finely sliced
1 clove fresh garlic, finely chopped (or minced)
2tsp capers
2tsp flat-leafed parsley, finely chopped

CHICKEN SALAD

Chicken Salad with Peanut Sauce (Thailand)

Ingredients

500gm chicken breast fillets, sliced lengthways
1tsp dark soy sauce
1tsp minced garlic
1tsp minced ginger
1tsp Shaoxing rice cooking wine
1Tbsp peanut oil
1 pkt Hokkien noodles, or similar, cooked according to packet directions
lettuce leaves, oak or coral
2 green shallots, finely chopped
1 stalk celery, finely chopped
1 carrot, very finely julienned (very thin strips)
a handful of fresh bean sprouts
a few fresh coriander and mint leaves, chopped
pkt fried shallots (available from an Asian food supplier)

Method

Marinate the chicken in the soy, garlic, ginger, and wine for an hour.
Fry in the oil till cooked, and set aside to be served warm.
Cook the rice noodles and set aside to be served warm.
Toss together the salad ingredients of lettuce, shallots, celery, carrot, sprouts, and fresh leaves.
Serve in bowls with noodles on the bottom, then the salad, and the chicken on the top.
Top with some fried shallots and serve with the Peanut Sauce.
Option: Bring home a roasted chicken, tear it into pieces and serve it on plates with lettuce and tomato. Make the quick Peanut Sauce that will pour over the chicken and go just as deliciously well with the salad.

Peanut Sauce (Thailand)

Ingredients

1 small finely chopped brown onion, 1tsp minced garlic, and 1tsp minced red chilli
1tsp minced ginger, 1tsp chopped lemongrass, and 1 anchovy fillet
1tsp ground turmeric and 1tsp ground coriander seed
½ cup crushed roasted peanuts (or peanut butter)
180ml (small) can coconut milk
1Tbsp lemon juice, 1tsp dark soy sauce, and 1tsp sugar

Method for the Peanut Sauce

Fry the onion, garlic, and chilli in a little oil in a saucepan for 2 minutes, till starting to colour. Add the rest of the ingredients and simmer about 5 minutes till thickened.

Chicken and Mango Salad with Noodles (Malaysia)

500gm chicken breast fillets, coarsely sliced lengthways
1tsp dark soy sauce
1tsp minced garlic
1tsp minced ginger
1tsp Shaoxing rice cooking wine
1Tbsp peanut oil
1 pkt rice noodles, or similar, cooked according to packet directions
lettuce leaves, oak or coral
2 green shallots, finely chopped
1 long red chilli, deseeded and very finely sliced
1 ripe mango, cubed
1 stalk celery, finely chopped, including the fresh top leaves
a handful of fresh bean sprouts
a few fresh coriander and mint leaves, chopped
½tsp sea salt and ½tsp white pepper
1 avocado, cubed, and put into the dressing
½ cup desiccated coconut, lightly dry-fried in a dry frying pan
½ cup of fried shallots (available from an Asian food supplier)
½ cup of roasted cashew nuts

Method

Marinate the chicken in the soy, garlic, ginger, and wine for an hour if possible.
Fry the chicken in the peanut oil till cooked, and set aside to be served warm.
Cook the rice noodles and set them aside to be served warm.
Toss together the salad ingredients of lettuce, shallots, chilli, mango, celery, sprouts, fresh leaves, salt and pepper.
Put the avocado in the lime dressing to stop it turning brown.
Serve in some large bowls with noodles on the bottom, then the salad, then the avocado along with the dressing, and then the chicken on the top.
Top with the dry-fried coconut and the fried shallots.
Sprinkle over the cashew nuts.

Lime Dressing

Mix together in a bowl the following ingredients:
1tsp Shaoxing rice cooking wine
1tsp fish sauce
1tsp sugar
juice of 2 Tahitian limes

SEAFOOD SALAD

Prawn and Noodle Salad with Nam Pla Dressing (Thailand)

Ingredients

1 packet vermicelli rice noodles, cooked to directions
a few fresh lettuce leaves
a few baby spinach leaves
a handful of fresh bean sprouts
a few fresh mint leaves
a few fresh coriander leaves
1 small carrot, very finely sliced
1 Lebanese cucumber, very finely sliced
1 red capsicum (bell pepper), finely sliced
250gm green prawns, peeled
2 Tbsp peanut oil
50gm roasted cashew nuts

> **Nam Pla Dressing**
> Mix together in a cup:
> ½ cup hot water
> 1tsp minced garlic
> 1tsp minced red chilli
> juice of 1 Tahitian lime
> 1Tbsp fish sauce
> 1Tbsp rice wine vinegar
> 1Tbsp brown sugar

Method

Follow the packet instructions to prepare the noodles and set them aside.
Mix the noodles and vegetables together and divide among serving bowls.
Fry the prawns lightly in some oil for a few minutes till they are cooked pink and add the cashews to heat through. Do not overcook the prawns.
Distribute the warm prawns and cashews over the salad, and use the above Thai dressing over the top.

Options

You could add a few nice seedless grapes to the top of this dish if available.

You could substitute some fresh sea scallops for the prawns if you wish.
Simply dust the scallops in a little seasoned flour, and then fry them quickly in some peanut oil and a dash of sesame oil. Only cook them for a minute or so on each side.
You could also toast some sesame seeds a little in a dry pan for a little extra sesame flavour. Sprinkle them on the top.

You could substitute some calamari strips for the prawns if you wish.
Simply score the inside of some calamari tubes in a criss-cross pattern and then slice them into strips. Marinate them for ½ hour if possible in ½ cup lemon juice, 1tsp minced garlic, 1tsp minced red chilli, a little extra virgin olive oil, salt and pepper.
Fry them very quickly in oil both sides. They will usually curl up for a nice appearance when they hit the hot oil.

VEGETABLE SALAD

Potato Salad (Australia)

This is one of the best salads that you could serve. It could serve as a meal on its own.

Ingredients

1Kg Desiree potatoes, peeled, cut into 2cm cubes
4 eggs
½ cup mayonnaise
½ cup Greek-style plain yoghurt
1 small lemon, juiced
1 small red onion, finely chopped
1 shallot, finely chopped
2tsp Dijon mustard
salt and pepper
10gm butter
2 rashers bacon, finely chopped
¼ cup basil leaves, finely shredded
¼ cup parsley, finely chopped

Method

Place potatoes in a large saucepan. Cover with cold water. Bring to the boil over high heat. Reduce heat to medium and cook potatoes, uncovered, for 3 to 4 minutes or until tender when pierced with a skewer.

Drain the potatoes, and transfer them to a bowl.

Boil the eggs for about 7 minutes, run then under cold water to stop them cooking, shell them, and chop them into halves. Set them aside.

Combine the mayonnaise, yoghurt, lemon juice, onion, shallot, mustard, salt and pepper in a small bowl.

Pour this over the warm potatoes to absorb the flavours, and stir gently.

Cover the potatoes with plastic wrap and set them aside to cool a little.

Meanwhile cook the bacon in the butter in a frypan for about 3 minutes until golden.

Then stir it into the potato along with the basil and the parsley. Top with the eggs.

Waldorf Salad (United States)

Ingredients

2 Granny Smith apples, washed, cored and diced
the juice of ½ a lemon
1 stick celery, diced
2 cups seedless grapes, washed
½ cup egg mayonnaise
½ cup Greek-style natural yoghurt
a pinch of salt and pepper
1 cup walnut pieces
some Cos lettuce leaves

Method

Stir the lemon juice into the apple to coat thoroughly (to prevent it from going brown).
Add the celery, grapes, mayonnaise, yoghurt, salt and pepper, and stir together.
In a dry frypan, lightly toast the walnuts for a couple of minutes till fragrant.
Place 2 lettuce leaves onto each serving plate, spoon the salad mixture into the lettuce cups, and top with the walnuts. Serve immediately.

Caesar Salad

Ingredients

some Cos lettuce leaves
3 rashers bacon, chopped and fried in a little butter
croutons of toast or bread fried in the bacon fat
6 anchovy fillets (purchased from supermarket bottled in oil)
½ cup grated parmesan cheese

Method

Chop some of the Cos lettuce leaves and place them inside some whole leaves.
Drizzle the dressing below over the leaves. Then put on top the bacon pieces, toasted croutons, and the anchovy fillets. Sprinkle with the grated parmesan cheese.

Caesar Salad Dressing Ingredients

½ cup commercial mayonnaise
1 Tbsp extra virgin olive oil
1 Tbsp Dijon mustard
the juice of ½ a lemon
1 tsp minced garlic
1 very finely chopped anchovy fillet
sea salt and pepper to taste

Method

Mix all of the ingredients together well.
Note: I prefer to use mayonnaise in the dressing rather than raw egg yolks due to the possibility of contamination by salmonella bacteria.

Tomato and Bocconcini Salad (Italy)

Chop fresh tomatoes or cherry tomatoes and place in a bowl with chopped baby bocconcini cheese, baby spinach leaves, pitted black olives, and chopped fresh basil.

Serve with Balsamic Dressing

Mix together some extra virgin olive oil, red balsamic vinegar, garlic, salt and pepper, and a pinch of sugar.

Green Garden Salad (Italy)

In a bowl toss together some mixed lettuce leaves, endive, quartered Roma tomatoes, sliced green capsicum (bell pepper), and some pitted green olives.

Serve with Salad Vinaigrette

Mix together some extra virgin olive oil, white wine vinegar, lemon juice, crushed garlic, a pinch of sugar, salt and pepper. You could also add a little Dijon mustard if you wish.

Or, serve it with a Poppy Seed Dressing (See Dressings)

Asparagus and Rocket Salad

Char grill asparagus after marinating it in olive oil, lemon juice and salt. Place on top of a rocket leaf salad with shaved parmesan cheese, cherry tomatoes and a rocket pesto.

Serve with Rocket Pesto

Blend together some rocket leaves, a clove of garlic, some extra virgin olive oil, some toasted pine nuts, and some parmesan cheese.

Artichoke Salad

Top some mixed salad leaves with pickled artichoke hearts, pickled asparagus, pitted black olives, and chopped celery.

Serve with Dill Dressing

Combine plain yoghurt, chopped dill, seeded mustard, a little olive oil and some white wine vinegar.

Tabouleh Salad (Lebanon)

Combine soaked burghul, lemon juice, olive oil, salt and pepper. After standing for $\frac{1}{2}$ hour to develop flavour, add chopped shallots, mint, parsley and chopped tomatoes.

Coleslaw Salad

Slice half a Savoy cabbage very finely, and stir in a mixture, processed in a blender, of a chopped onion, a chopped carrot, a stalk of celery, two shallots, and the juice of a large lemon, along with a cup of whole-egg mayonnaise.

SAUCES AND DRESSINGS

There are hundreds of preparations known as sauces ('sauce' from the Latin 'salsus'- salted), often very different in their appearance, and also in method of preparation.

There are also many commercially available pre-prepared sauces from national cuisines, such as the English Worcestershire or Tomato or Mint, American Barbecue, Italian Balsamic, Mexican Mole or Tabasco, Chinese Soy, Hoisin, Blackbean, Oyster, Satay, Chilli and Fish Sauces, and others. These offer a huge range of quick possibilities for tasty dishes, and are added to prepared dishes or used cold.

CLASSIC SAUCES

The classic sauces are the product of well-tried French cooking methods, are most often cooked as needed, and are served hot, over or with, food.

They are extremely delicious, and add moisture and visual appeal to a dish.

It is well worth practising your use of these basic French sauces, as you will learn a lot about cooking as you do; so don't be frightened.

Some of these are referred to as 'mother' sauces, meaning that they are the starting point for the other variations.

Here are some of these:

- Béchamel sauce; milk-based, thickened with a white roux
- Espagnole sauce; brown stock based (usually veal), thickened with a brown roux
- Velouté sauce; white stock based, thickened with a blonde roux
- Allemande sauce; based on Velouté, thickened with egg yolks and heavy cream

Many of the classic sauces start with a roux, so we need to understand what this is.

Also, a little more information about the cooking and use of stock is called for.

These sauces and some of their variations are presented here and sometimes simplified, as the traditional French methods can sometimes be very involved, require a lot of separate steps, and actually take days in the preparation.

ROUX

A roux is a mixture of fat and flour, cooked in a saucepan (this is where the implement gets its name).

Butter is often used to cook the flour.

The longer it cooks the darker it gets. This is why you will sometimes see sauces simply described as a 'white sauce' or a 'brown sauce'. It depends on the colour of the roux and the colour of the stock, and other ingredients.

A roux must be cooked over a low heat for good consistency and delicate flavour, stirring constantly, and adding warm liquid until it is smooth.

It can then be heated until it boils and thickens, and then cooked a little more to develop flavour.

Cool stock is often added during the preparation of a sauce a couple of times to help the fat rise to the surface and clear the sauce.

It is best to use a wooden spatula for making sauces.

STOCK

Stock is the flavourful clear liquid obtained after cooking and straining vegetables, fish, veal, chicken, or beef.

Any fat is usually taken off the top.

Various types of stock can be bought ready-made, or you can make your own.

Vegetable stock can be made by frying a few vegetables, then cooking them in water, and then straining the resulting liquid.

Cooking chicken, veal, or beef bones will produce these stocks.

Leftover roasted chicken bones for example, will make a good chicken stock, or you can simply cook a couple of chicken carcasses in water for about three hours. These are available from the supermarket at a very reasonable price. I like to have homemade chicken stock on hand for making soup, or risotto, or for use as a general purpose stock. Two carcasses will usually provide two one-litre containers of stock that can be frozen for later use. This is a plain stock, which is quite OK because your recipe method will provide instructions for including whatever other flavourings or seasonings are needed in the dish.

White stock can be made by boiling up veal bones.

Brown stock can be made with about 2.5Kg beef soup bones (available from a butcher) and a little extra stewing beef. Oven-roast the bones and beef in a little oil till really well browned, along with a carrot and an onion.

Then put it all in a big pot with lots of water, after tipping off any fat and splashing some wine in the pan to loosen the tasty bits, and simmer this for about 5 hours. Finally, strain the liquid, after it is cooled, into containers.

'Béchamel' Sauce (White Sauce, or Coating Sauce)

Ingredients
2 cups milk
1 slice of onion
1 chopped small stick of celery
8 black peppercorns
1 bay leaf
a pinch of ground nutmeg
60gm butter
3 Tbsp flour
sea salt and ground white pepper

Method
Heat the milk, vegetables, and spices in a saucepan until it starts to bubble at the edges and remove from the heat. After letting it stand for 20 minutes, strain it.
Melt the butter in a saucepan, and stir in the flour over low heat for about 1 minute. Stir in the milk until smooth. Season the sauce with salt and pepper. Stir over medium heat until boiling. Simmer for a few more minutes over low heat to develop the flavour.

'Mornay' Sauce

To Béchamel sauce, add ¼ cup grated cheese, and 1tsp mustard, and pour over the dish. If browned on top, the dish is described as 'au gratin'.

Parsley Sauce

To Béchamel sauce, add 2 Tbsp chopped parsley, for potatoes, vegies, fish, or chicken.

Caper Sauce

To Béchamel sauce, add 2 Tbsp chopped capers, for potatoes, vegies, fish, or chicken.

'Velouté' Sauce

Make a Béchamel sauce, but cook the roux a little longer until it is straw-coloured. Use chicken, veal, or fish stock instead of the milk, according to the type of dish.

'Allemande' Sauce

This makes a thicker sauce. Beat 2 egg yolks with 2 Tbsp cream, and add some Velouté sauce. Stir it over low heat for a few minutes until glossy.

'Soubise' Sauce (Onion Sauce)

Make a Velouté sauce as above and stir in some lightly fried chopped onion.
This can be used on vegetables, veal, chicken, or eggs.

Simple Sauce 'Espagnole' (Brown Sauce)

In French cooking, the first three ingredients are called a 'mirepoix'.

Ingredients

3 Tbsp extra virgin olive oil for frying
1 small onion finely diced
1 small carrot finely diced
1 small stick of celery finely diced
2 chopped brown mushrooms
2 chopped rashers of bacon
1 Tbsp plain flour
½ cup tomato juice or crushed tomatoes
2 cups brown stock
some chopped fresh herbs such as parsley, thyme, sage, rosemary, oregano, or basil
½ tsp cracked black pepper
¼ cup dry red wine (or sherry)
sea salt and freshly ground black pepper

Method

In a saucepan, fry the vegetables and bacon in the oil until golden.

On medium heat, add the flour and stir until the flour is cooked and the roux is medium-brown.

Add the tomato juice and one cup of the stock, the herbs and cracked pepper and heat to the boil.

Simmer for 20 minutes.

Skim the surface to take off any scum and excess fat. Add the other cup of stock and the red wine and bring to the boil again.

Simmer for 20 minutes more. Skim the surface again, season it with salt and pepper to taste, strain it if desired, swirl in a small knob of butter on the top, and serve.

Pepper Sauce

Make a brown sauce as above and at the end of cooking add some green or black peppercorns to simmer for a few minutes.

Note: If added too early, the pepper takes on a bitter taste.

'Demi-Glace' (Rich Brown Sauce)

To the above strained Espagnole (brown sauce), add 1 litre of brown stock, and ½ cup red wine. Boil this down by two-thirds to get a thick, rich sauce.

EMULSIFIED SAUCES

Note: Be aware that when using raw eggs in recipes, there is always a small risk of contamination by salmonella bacteria. This applies to the two recipes below.

'Hollandaise' Sauce

Ingredients

200gm unsalted butter, melted and clarified (skim off the white solids)
3 egg yolks
3 Tbsp water
juice of half a lemon
sea salt and ground white pepper

Method

Melt the butter over low heat without stirring and skim off the solids floating on top. Fill a saucepan about half full of water and bring it to just below boiling point. Put the egg yolks in a Pyrex bowl that fits just inside the pan. Whisk in the water, and keep whisking for about 5 minutes until the egg yolks thicken and lighten.
Remove from the heat, and very gradually while whisking, pour in the clarified butter. Whisk in the lemon juice and salt and pepper to taste. If the sauce is too thick you can whisk in a little hot water. Serve immediately.

'Béarnaise' Sauce

This is a tarragon-flavoured variation on the Hollandaise recipe. Be careful here as not everybody likes the flavour of tarragon (including me). You could possibly substitute flat leafed Italian parsley.

Ingredients

200gm unsalted butter, melted and clarified (white solids skimmed off)
¼ cup very finely chopped shallots
2 Tbsp finely chopped fresh tarragon
¼ cup white wine vinegar
¼ cup white wine
3 egg yolks
sea salt and ground white pepper

Method

Place shallots, tarragon, vinegar and wine on medium heat and boil until reduced to about 2 Tbsp of liquid.
Set up a double boiler arrangement with a Pyrex bowl and a saucepan. Place the egg yolks in the bowl and whisk in the reduced vinegar. Keep whisking for about 5 minutes until the mixture thickens.
Remove from the heat and very slowly whisk in the clarified butter. Whisk in salt and pepper to taste.

'Beurre Blanc' (France) - White Wine Butter Sauce

Ingredients

1 shallot, very finely chopped
1 sprig thyme leaves
a few stalks flat-leaf parsley, very finely chopped
1 cup sauvignon blanc white wine (or similar)
½ cup heavy cream
100gm cold butter, cut into very small pieces
sea salt and ground white pepper (so that it doesn't colour the sauce)

Method

In a small saucepan cook the herbs in the wine on low heat until there is only two tablespoons of liquid.

Stir in the cream, bring it to a low boil, and reduce the liquid to two tablespoons.

On low heat, continually whisking, add the butter piece by piece to the reduced wine, incorporating each piece. Keep the sauce below boiling point.

Simple Brown Gravy

Common brown gravy is the simplest form of a pan sauce. Meat served with this sauce is called by the French, 'au jus'.

These sauces are usually prepared following the roasting or sautéing of a meat dish in a pan. The valuable flavours and juices in the pan are the starting point of the sauce. If there is a lot of pan juice, you may want to use mostly these flavours for excellent thin gravy.

Firstly, pour off any excess fat.

'Deglaze' the pan with about 1 cup of hot water (you could use the leftover water available after cooking vegetables, some white or red wine, or stock) to lift the flavours off the bottom of the pan.

It's very handy to have wine available for these pan sauces, as it gives you something to drink while you stir the gravy!

Boil and stir continually with a wooden spoon to lift the flavours from the bottom of the pan for about 5 minutes, adding any meat juices that are left after the carving of the meat. Season with salt and pepper, and strain the gravy if you wish.

Or, for a thicker gravy, starting with the pan juices, and a little of the leftover fat, you can add about 1Tbsp plain flour to make a roux, stirring until the flour is cooked, and then continue with the deglazing as above. This will make thick gravy and is the more commonly used method.

You may also choose to add some additional herbs, or spices, or a small dash of some prepared sauce such as Worcestershire sauce, or soy sauce.

Bazza's Barbecue Sauce

Ingredients

2 cups red wine
¼ cup balsamic vinegar
¼ cup honey
1 anchovy fillet, chopped
1 Tbsp soy sauce
1 Tbsp sugar
a pinch of salt and pepper

Method

Simmer all ingredients in a saucepan until reduced to about half the quantity. Use with meat dishes and barbecued meat.

Bazza's Chilli Sauce

Ingredients

½ cup olive oil
2 chopped onions
4 cloves chopped garlic
8 chopped hot red chillies
1 chopped red capsicum
1 chopped tomato
1 anchovy fillet
the juice of 1 lemon
1 sprig of thyme
2 tsp sugar
3 Kaffir lime leaves
sea salt and black pepper

Method

Fry the onions, and garlic in oil until the onion starts to brown. Add the chillies and capsicum for a minute. Add the rest of the ingredients and simmer for ½ hour. Strain the mixture to serve. This will keep for a few days in the fridge.

Bazza's Special Sauce

This is made using pretty much all of the usual ingredients of commercial sauces.

Fry some finely chopped onions and garlic in oil until slightly browned. Add some red wine, tomato puree, honey, and soy sauce. Then add a little tamarind paste, chopped anchovy, chopped dates, chopped prunes, grated ginger, mustard, ground chilli, salt and pepper. Cook for about 15 minutes. Adjust the flavours and seasoning to your taste.

This sauce can be added to any cooked or browned meat dish to complete the cooking for an excellent casserole. It will keep in the fridge for a few days if necessary.

DRESSINGS

Dressings are preparations usually served cold and made from raw ingredients. They are used with salads mainly, but may be suitable for use with other meals or for snacks.

Note: Health authorities warn against using raw eggs in dressings due to the risk of salmonella bacteria being present in eggs. Some use pasteurized eggs for this reason.

Mayonnaise

1 egg yolk
1tsp prepared mustard
1tsp white wine vinegar
¼tsp sea salt
a pinch of ground white pepper
1 cup extra virgin olive oil

In a food processor, put the room temperature egg yolk, mustard, vinegar, salt and pepper, and mix for about ½ minute until the mixture lightens and thickens slightly. Very, very slowly, add the oil to the mixture. It should emulsify.

Garlic Aioli

2tsp crushed garlic
1 egg yolk
1Tbsp lemon juice
¼tsp sea salt
a pinch of ground white pepper
1 cup extra virgin olive oil

In a food processor, put the room temperature garlic, egg yolk, lemon juice, salt and pepper, and mix for about ½ minute until the mixture lightens and thickens slightly. Very, very slowly, add the oil to the mixture. It should emulsify.

Bazza's Special Poppy Seed Salad Dressing

Ingredients (Serves four)

1/3 cup mayonnaise
1/3 cup lemon juice
2tsp mustard
2tsp honey
2tsp poppy seeds
1tsp salt

Method

Mix all of the ingredients together in a cup and Bob's your uncle! This is great for livening up a boring old salad.

Store this in the fridge until ready to use. It should keep for a few days.

SOUPS

BEEF SOUP

'Pho' (Vietnam) - pron. 'fur'. Noodle Soup

Pho (as it is written in English) is a famous Vietnamese noodle soup with Chinese and French influences. It is made with beef or chicken and is very popular worldwide. This is my simplified healthy beef version which takes less than an hour to prepare.

Ingredients (Serves 4)

800gm good quality rump steak
1Tbsp olive oil
1 brown onion, finely sliced
1 clove garlic, finely sliced
1tsp ground chilli
1tsp ground ginger
1 anchovy fillet, chopped
½tsp ground coriander seed
½tsp ground cardamom
½tsp ground fennel seed
½tsp sugar
½tsp sea salt and ½tsp ground black pepper
1¼ litres of water
1tsp lemon grass, chopped (bottled is OK as well)
1 bay leaf
1 kaffir lime leaf
1 stalk of fresh coriander leaves (cilantro), chopped, including the washed root
1 packet of thin rice noodles

ONE POT MEAL

Method

Trim the rump steak, slice it thinly, and put it aside for later addition. Put the steak trimmings (about 200gm) in a large soup pot with the oil and onion and fry them until golden brown. This provides the colour and flavour from the sugars that are created. Add the garlic, chilli, ginger and anchovy to fry for a minute. Garlic should not be fried for a long time as it will give it a bitter taste. I prefer anchovy fillets to fish sauce. Then add all the spices to fry for another minute to refresh all of the flavours.
Add the water, lemon grass and leaves, and cook the dish covered for half an hour. Add the sliced steak to cook (for about 10 minutes). I prefer this to totally raw beef. At about the same time, add the noodles to cook according to the time on the packet. Serve in large soup bowls. Garnish the soup with fresh chopped spring onions or fresh bean sprouts. Serve with pickled onions, and finely sliced red chillies on the side. Soy sauce and Chilli Paste (I like Pun Chun brand) are also optional condiments.

LAMB SOUP

'Köfteli Ayran Çorbasi' (Turkey) - Meatballs in Yoghurt Soup

This recipe is similar to many found in the Middle Eastern region.

Ingredients for Meatballs

500gm lamb mince (or chicken, or pork, if you wish)
1 small onion, finely chopped
2 eggs
1Tbsp chopped fresh mint
1Tbsp chopped flat-leafed parsley
1Tbsp breadcrumbs
1Tbsp flour
sea salt and freshly ground black pepper

Ingredients for Soup

750mls chicken stock (homemade preferably)
¼ cup white rice
2 cups Greek-style yoghurt (or goat's milk yoghurt)
1 egg yolk
1 cup chopped baby spinach leaves
1tsp sweet paprika
1tsp sea salt (no salt if you are using commercial stock)
1tsp ground black pepper
2 spring onions, finely chopped

ONE POT MEAL

Method

Mix together the meatball ingredients and make small round balls.

Put the stock in a large pot or frying pan and when it is simmering, add the rice and the meatballs to cook for about 20 minutes.

Remove the meatballs and keep them warm.

Allow the stock to cool slightly, as otherwise the yoghurt may curdle (interestingly, goat's milk yoghurt does not separate on boiling as does cow's milk).

Whisk the egg yolk and yoghurt combined, and gradually add this to the stock mixture.

Add the spinach leaves, paprika, salt and pepper to taste, and return the meatballs to the pot.

Bring to a simmer, and serve topped with the chopped spring onions.

CHICKEN SOUP

'Tom Yum Gai' (Thailand) - Chicken Noodle Soup

Ingredients (serves 4)

1 Tbsp vegetable oil
2 garlic cloves, thinly sliced lengthways
2 fresh red birds eye chillies, deseeded, finely chopped
1 stem lemon grass, pale section only, bruised
1 litre (4 cups) chicken stock
2 (total about 500gm) single chicken breast fillets
400gm packet fresh thin rice noodles (or other dried noodles)
80ml (1/3 cup) fresh lime juice and a little of the rind
1½ Tbsp fish sauce
150gm packet baby spinach leaves
½ cup loosely packed fresh coriander leaves, to garnish. Lime wedges, to serve

ONE POT MEAL

Method

Heat the oil in a large saucepan over medium-high heat. Add the garlic, chilli and lemon grass, and cook, stirring, for 2 minutes or until fragrant. Add stock. Cover and bring to the boil. Reduce heat to low. Add chicken and simmer, covered, for 15 minutes or until cooked through. Use a slotted spoon to transfer chicken to a plate. Set aside for 5 minutes to cool slightly. Coarsely shred chicken.

Add the noodles to the stock. Bring to the boil and cook for 2 minutes or until noodles are tender. Add the lime juice and rind, fish sauce and chicken, and cook for a further 1 minute or until heated through.

Meanwhile, bring a large saucepan of water to the boil over high heat. Add the spinach and remove it from heat. Refresh this under cold running water. Drain well.

Ladle the soup among serving bowls. Top with spinach and coriander. Serve immediately with lime wedges, if desired.

Chicken Stock

This is easily made in advance. Buy two very cheap chicken carcasses from the supermarket. Put them in a large pot on the top of the stove in about 3 litres of water, and cook them for 2 hours.

Let the pot cool down and store it overnight in the refrigerator. The next day, skim off the fat, and strain the liquid into some plastic containers. I use two 1 litre plastic containers with screw-top lids for this purpose (you will lose some of the total liquid).

I sometimes use one litre for whatever dish I am cooking, and freeze the other one for later use in a risotto, paella, laksa or other recipe.

I do not use additional flavourings or seasonings when making the stock, as these can be added later according to the requirements of the recipe.

Chicken Laksa (Malaysia)

Ingredients (Serves 4)

500gm chicken thigh fillets, chopped into bite-sized pieces
olive oil for frying
1 onion, finely chopped
1 sweet red capsicum (bell pepper), sliced
1tsp minced garlic, or 1 clove finely chopped
1tsp minced red chilli, or 1 fresh red chilli finely chopped
1tsp dried chilli flakes (these provide a different flavor)
1tsp minced ginger, or 1cm fresh ginger root
1tsp chopped lemongrass (bottled), or 1 stalk fresh lemongrass
1tsp ground coriander seed
1tsp ground turmeric
1tsp cracked black pepper
1 anchovy fillet
1 litre chicken stock (see previous recipe)
2tsp light soy sauce
1tsp fish sauce
1tsp sugar
1tsp good quality sea salt
2 fresh whole kaffir lime leaves (if available)
small 200ml can coconut cream
1 Tahitian lime, finely sliced into rounds (or other lime)
1 stalk fresh coriander leaves
1 green shallot, finely sliced
1 bunch baby bok choy, chopped (or other Asian greens)
1 packet thick rice noodles

ONE POT MEAL

Method

Fry the chicken pieces in oil till browned all over and almost cooked through.

Add the next group of ingredients down to the anchovy fillet and allow to fry a little till fragrant (you may need an extra dash of oil).

Add the chicken stock, allow it to heat through, and simmer for about 10 minutes.

Add the next group of ingredients down to the coconut cream and simmer for about a further 5 minutes.

Finally, add the lime, coriander, shallot, and bok choy. These don't really need to cook, and can be added just before serving.

While the laksa is cooking, heat the packet of noodles according to the packet instructions, and place the noodles in the serving bowls. The laksa can then be poured over the top, with the lime slices placed on top for decoration.

HAM SOUP

Pea and Ham Soup (England) – aka 'pig an' peas'

Ingredients

1Tbsp olive oil for frying
1 carrot, finely diced
1 brown onion, finely diced
1 stalk celery, finely diced
2 litres water
2tsp chicken flavour booster
600gm smoked bacon hock
250gm dried green split peas
1 clove minced garlic
1tsp sea salt
1tsp freshly ground black pepper
1tsp ground coriander seed
1tsp dried mixed herbs
2 potatoes, finely diced
2 green shallots, finely chopped

ONE POT MEAL

Method

In a large soup pot, lightly fry the onion, carrot, and celery in a little olive oil, as a flavour base.

Add the water, chicken booster, bacon hock, split peas, garlic, salt and pepper, coriander, mixed herbs, potatoes and green shallots.

Cook everything up together for about 1 1/2 hours on the stovetop.

Then take out the hock, cut off all the meat and dice it finely, discard the bones, skin and fat, and return the meat to the pot.

Serve with toast, crumpets, or fresh sourdough bread and parsley butter.

If you want to dress it up to impress, you could fry up a few small pieces of prosciutto to serve on the top as a garnish.

This is a great dish for wintertime that doubles as a hand warmer if you eat it on your lap in front of the telly.

FISH AND SEAFOOD SOUP

Chicken and Prawn Wonton Soup (China)

Wontons are Chinese dumplings made with pre-pared wrappers usually found in the refrigerated section of the supermarket. They are made by spreading a wrapper flat in the palm of your hand, placing a small amount of filling in the centre, wetting the edges, and sealing them together with your fingers. Fold one corner over to make a triangle, and then fold in the sides over the top, sealing them together. 'Burp' out any extra air so that they don't explode when cooked.

Soup Ingredients

1½ litres chicken stock (made from 2 inexpensive chicken carcasses obtained from the supermarket, as previously described in Chicken Noodle Soup)
1 onion, finely chopped
1 small carrot, finely sliced
1 stick celery, finely sliced
1 bunch baby bok choy, or choy sum, finely sliced
1 spring onion, roughly chopped
1 small anchovy fillet, finely chopped
1tsp oyster sauce
1tsp sea salt flakes
1tsp ground white pepper

Wonton Ingredients

20 wonton wrappers
12 peeled green prawns, chopped into small pieces
1 spring onion, finely chopped
2tsp soy sauce
2tsp Shaoxing rice cooking wine, or dry sherry
2tsp cornflour
1tsp crushed garlic
½tsp crushed chilli
½tsp crushed ginger root
½tsp sugar

ONE POT MEAL

Method

Boil up the chicken carcasses first for about an hour in approximately 2 litres of water to make the stock.
In your soup pot, fry in a little oil the onion, carrot and celery until light brown.
Strain the chicken stock into the pot, and add the rest of the soup ingredients to cook for 20 minutes while assembling the wontons.
Mix the wonton ingredients together, and assemble as above.
Put them into the soup for about 5 minutes till cooked, when they will rise to the surface. Serve the soup and wontons in large bowls.

'Tom Yum Thale' (Thailand) - Spicy Seafood Soup

Various types of Tom Yum soup are common in Thailand.
'Tom' means 'boiled' and thus soup, and 'Yum' means 'hot and sour' and so it means spicy.
This one is called 'Thale' (pron. 'tar-lay'), which means that it contains mixed seafood.
'Tom Yum Goong' uses prawns only.
There are many variations in ingredients and also cooking methods in different regions.
And there are also a multitude of Westernised versions.

Ingredients (Serves 4)

1½ litres of fish stock
1tsp minced garlic
1tsp lemongrass, bottled (or 1 stalk fresh if available)
1tsp minced red chilli
1tsp minced ginger root
1tsp galangal powder (if available)
1tsp dried red chilli flakes
1tsp brown sugar
1 small can button mushrooms, drained
2 fresh kaffir lime leaves (if available)
1 anchovy fillet
1 red capsicum (bell pepper), sliced thinly
1Tbsp fish sauce
16 green prawns, peeled (frozen is OK)
8 calamari rings (frozen is OK)
4 sea scallops, roe on (frozen is OK)
1 white fish fillet, cut into small cubes, and checked for bones (frozen is OK)
some stalks of fresh coriander leaves
1 green shallot, thinly sliced
1 lime thinly sliced

ONE POT MEAL

Method

First make some seafood stock by cooking up some fish pieces and a few prawns in about 2 litres of water with some sea salt and white pepper, a chopped onion and a small chopped carrot (you don't need high quality seafood for this).

Simmer for about an hour and then strain the liquid into a soup pot, discarding the rest.

Add the rest of the ingredients to the stock down to the fish sauce, and simmer for about 15 minutes.

Add the seafood and cook for 5 minutes more.

Add the coriander, shallot, and lime slices, and serve.

'Bouillabaisse' (France) - Fish Soup

This is an easy version of the traditional French dish that started as a humble lunchtime meal cooked on board ship, using a variety of bony fish that the fishermen would not be able to later sell at the market. Today, it is considered to be a delicacy right through the whole Mediterranean region.

Quite a few types of fish were mixed together, but added one type at a time. The word 'Bouillabaisse' refers to the boiling and simmering as the heat was raised and lowered. 'Caldeirada' is a similar typical Portuguese fish soup-stew, 'Suquet de Peix' is a similar Spanish fish stew, Greece has a similar dish called 'Kakavia', and Italy has its 'Zuppa di Pesce'. Variations are very common, some including potatoes and other vegetables.

Ingredients (Serves 4)

1½ litres fish stock
olive oil for frying
1 onion, finely chopped
1 clove garlic, finely chopped
1 stalk celery, finely chopped
1 small carrot, finely chopped
1 cup dry white wine
1tsp minced red chilli
1tsp dried thyme (or fresh thyme)
1tsp ground turmeric
1tsp ground fennel seed
2 bay leaves
200gm can chopped tomatoes
2 boneless fish fillets of different sorts, cubed
8 calamari rings or pieces
16 green prawns, peeled
4 scallops, roe on

ONE POT MEAL

Method

Make a fish stock first by cooking up some leftover fish pieces of any sort along with the bones, some prawns or prawn heads and shells as well, a chopped onion and a chopped carrot, 1tsp sea salt and 1tsp white pepper, in about 2 litres of water for about an hour or so. Then strain the liquid to use in the recipe, discarding the rest.

Meanwhile, fry the chopped onion, garlic, celery and carrot in a little olive oil until just starting to colour.

Add the dry white wine, red chilli, thyme, turmeric, fennel, bay leaves, and tomatoes. Now add in the fish stock. Cook the mixture for about 15 minutes.

Add the diced white fish, calamari, prawns, and scallops.

Simmer for about 5 minutes only, finally adding salt to taste and some chopped parsley.

Serve immediately with garlic bread or some soft, fresh, French crusty bread.

I like to top this with some good feta cheese crumbled over the top in Greek style.

SEAFOOD BISQUE

Lobster 'Bisque' (France)

Cook a lobster in water and white wine with carrots, onion, celery, parsley, thyme and black pepper for about 5 minutes.

Remove the tail meat and main flesh from legs of the lobster and set it aside.

Cook the rest of the carcass for about an hour until the liquid is reduced by about half.

Strain off the liquid to use as stock.

Then make a roux with some plain flour and butter by cooking the flour in the butter in a frying pan.

Gradually add the stock, stirring until the mixture is smooth.

Add the chopped lobster meat and some cream and reheat. Voila!

Prawn and Seafood 'Bisque' (France)

Make a seafood stock by frying some onions in butter in a pot and adding a chopped carrot, some chopped celery, some dried mixed herbs, salt and pepper, water, and some prawn shells and heads, after peeling some green king prawns.

Cook this for about an hour and then strain it, reserving the reduced liquid as stock.

Make a roux in a separate pan by frying some plain flour in butter, and then add the stock slowly. Stir the mixture until smooth.

Then put in the chopped prawn meat, chopped scallops, chopped calamari, and chopped boneless fish to cook for about 3 minutes only, or it will go chewy.

Stir in a small carton of pure cream to heat through and serve with some chopped green shallots on top. One of the best!

Oyster 'Bisque' (France)

Fry a chopped onion and a stick of celery in a little oil until the onion is transparent.

Add a cup of vegetable stock, ½ cup of white wine, 2 large chopped potatoes, a stalk of fresh thyme, salt and pepper, and cook for about 30 minutes. The potatoes will help to thicken the bisque.

Add ½ cup milk, and 16 oysters. Cook for about 2 minutes and then blend the mixture.

Add the remaining 8 oysters (of the 2 dozen you have likely purchased), heat through, and serve immediately topped with a little finely chopped parsley.

Serve with some fresh crusty French bread and butter.

VEGETABLE SOUP

Leek and Vegetable Soup with Pork Wontons (China)

This is my version of a classic Chinese dish, made easily and quickly. Wontons are Chinese dumplings, and the wrappers come pre-made in refrigerated packs. Use them straight away as they are quite thin and will dry out after opening.

Soup Ingredients

1 finely diced brown onion
1 finely sliced leek (without the dark leaves)
1 finely chopped clove garlic (or 1tsp minced garlic)
1 finely chopped red chilli (or 1tsp sambal oelek or minced chilli)
½ finely sliced red capsicum (bell pepper)
375ml (1½ cups) chicken stock
1 litre (4 cups) boiling water
1Tbsp sliced dried shitake mushrooms (after soaking in water)
1tsp dark soy sauce or kecap manis
1tsp chopped lemon grass
1tsp finely sliced fresh ginger
1 chopped anchovy fillet
1 cup finely sliced bok choy (or cabbage)
2 finely chopped shallots
1 small packet or brick of vermicelli rice noodles
1tsp sea salt
½tsp ground white pepper

Wontons — 'swallowing clouds' in Cantonese

1 packet ready made fresh wonton wrappers
300gm pork mince
1 egg
1 finely chopped shallot
1tsp kecap manis
1tsp minced garlic
½tsp ground white pepper

Method

Fry the onion and leek in a little olive oil in a large saucepan until they are lightly cooked, and add the garlic, chilli, and red capsicum to fry just a little. Add the chicken stock and water, mushrooms, soy sauce, lemon grass, ginger, anchovy, bok choy, shallots, noodles, salt and pepper. Cook for about 15 minutes.

Mix together the wonton filling ingredients and place about 2tsp in each wonton wrapper. Fold into a triangle, sealing the edges with water, and fold the 2 wings over the top again to make small parcels. Drop these into the soup to cook for about 5 minutes in two batches. Serve the soup in bowls with the wontons.

'Zuppa di Farro' (Italy) - Wheat Soup

'Farro' is the Italian name for emmer wheat (triticum dicoccum) used as a whole grain in this traditional soup from Tuscany. It was the staple crop of ancient Egypt, fed the Roman legions, and fed the Roman poor for centuries. Sometimes spelt wheat is sold as farro, although it is softer, does not need soaking as emmer usually does, and is not as firm when used in this dish.

Ingredients

extra virgin olive oil
1 onion, finely chopped
1 clove garlic, finely chopped
1 stick celery, finely chopped
1 carrot, finely chopped
1 large waxy potato, diced
1 red chilli, finely chopped
1 large tomato, diced
100gm pancetta, finely chopped
a few stalks of sage, torn
a few stalks flat leafed parsley, torn
400gm dried borlotti beans, soaked overnight
100gm farro (emmer wheat) from specialty shops
1tsp sea salt
1tsp freshly ground black pepper

ONE POT MEAL

Method

Fry the onion, garlic, celery and carrot in some olive oil till fragrant.
Add the potato, chilli, tomato, pancetta, and herbs, and cook till softened.
Add the beans, farro, salt and pepper, and enough water to cover.
Cook for about 1 hour.

'Soupe à l'oignon gratinée' (France) - French Onion Soup

Originally a food for poor people, it is today a classic dish. Fry lots of sliced brown onions slowly in butter with about 1tsp sugar until they are golden brown. Stir in half a cup of flour and brown it. Add as much water as you think you need, sea salt and black pepper, a dash of Worcestershire sauce, and cook it for about half an hour or more. Serve topped with sliced French baguette grilled with grated Gruyère cheese on top.

'Vichyssoise' (France) - Leek and Potato Soup

Fry some chopped onions and chopped leek and a few stalks of chopped celery in plenty of butter. Add some chopped potatoes, water, salt and white pepper, and some chicken stock. When the potatoes are cooked, process the lot till smooth. Add a carton of cream heat through.
Serve topped with chopped chives and parsley, or maybe some fried croutons.

'Minestrone' (Italy) - Thick Soup

Fry onions and garlic. Add carrots, celery, shallots, zucchini and green beans and cook a bit. Add a can of cooked beans of some sort, a small tin of tomatoes, bay leaves, mixed herbs, salt and pepper, pasta and water. After about an hour, stir in some fresh basil and parsley leaves and serve.

Tomato Bouillon (France) - Tomato Broth

Process some good quality vine-ripened tomatoes with some water, a little beef booster, a pinch of sugar, sea salt and freshly ground black pepper. Dilute to the desired consistency and cook for about 10 minutes. This makes a delicious luncheon soup with fresh bread.
This is very simple and quick, but also very nice.

Pumpkin and Cumin Soup

Put some chopped pumpkin (Queensland Blue pumpkin works well) into a soup pot along with some chopped onion, chicken stock, ground cumin, pepper and salt and water and cook for about ½ hour.
Blend and add a little cream if desired.

Mushroom Soup (France)

Brown some chopped onions and garlic in a little butter in a pot. Add some chopped brown mushrooms to cook for a few minutes. Then add some white wine, beef stock, freshly ground black pepper, a little soy sauce, and some water.
Cook this for about a quarter of an hour.

Cream of Cauliflower Soup

Boil small cauliflower florets in water until tender. In a soup pot sauté some finely chopped onion in about 50gm butter and when soft add some plain flour to slightly cook in the butter about 1 minute. Add about 2 cups of milk and stir until smooth (This makes a basic white onion sauce). Return the cauliflower and the water it was cooked in to the pot to cook a little. Add some salt and pepper, a little chicken stock and a carton of cream to heat through, and serve.

Sweet Potato and Chick Pea Soup

Fry a little chopped onion and then add a chopped tomato, chopped sweet potato, some chopped garlic, grated ginger, a drained can of cooked chick peas, a little ground chilli, some ground cumin and ground coriander, salt and pepper, and some chicken stock.
When the sweet potato is cooked, blend the whole mixture. The chick peas give it a nice texture.
Coconut cream or cream may also be added if desired.

STIR-FRIES

All of the recipes that follow use a simple four-step process to stir-fry tasty meals. A barbecue or stove-top gas-fired wok burner is best, as you need to get plenty of heat into the food; but you can use a large heavy-based saucepan if you need to.

BEEF

Beef with Black Bean Sauce (China)

Step 1 - The Meat

Start with about 500gm finely sliced rump or topside beef, and marinate it for about an hour if possible to tenderise it in the following:
2Tbsp soy sauce
2Tbsp white wine
Brown the meat in hot peanut oil, to which has been added 1tsp sesame oil, and remove it from the pan. Do this in small batches if necessary, so that you do not stew it.

Step 2 - The Aromatics

Fry in oil a finely chopped or sliced large brown onion until it is transparent, and add the following ingredients, available in jars, to stir fry for one minute only:
1tsp minced garlic
1tsp minced ginger
1tsp minced red chilli

Step 3 - Add the Liquid

Prior to cooking, make a stir fry liquid by stirring into ½ cup water the following:
1Tbsp soy sauce (light or dark, or kecap manis)
1Tbsp Shaoxing rice cooking wine, or dry sherry
1tsp sea salt
1tsp ground white pepper
1tsp sugar
1tsp cornflour mixed in ¼ cup water as a thickener

Step 4 - Add the Vegetables and the Cooked Meat

The vegetables are added last along with the meat already cooked, to reheat.
Chop up very finely (so that they will cook quickly), and add:
1 carrot, 1 stick of celery, 1 green capsicum (bell pepper), and 1 bunch of fresh asparagus cut into 3cm pieces.
Also add about ½ cup of black bean sauce (from the supermarket) at this point.
Put the lid on it now if you have one, to help steam the vegetables quickly.
Cook for a few minutes.
Serve with fresh rice noodles (see Noodles), and top with some crunchy bean sprouts and some toasted sesame seeds (dry fried in a dry pan with no oil).

'Sate Daging' (Indonesia) - Sate Beef

This is my version of this spectacular national dish, made here with all natural and readily available ingredients. You could absolutely live on this tasterrific stuff!

Step 1 - The Meat

Start with about 500gm finely sliced rump or topside beef, and marinate it for about an hour if possible to tenderise it in the following:

2 Tbsp kecap manis, which is Indonesian-style soy sauce (or use dark soy sauce)
2 Tbsp white wine

Brown the meat in hot oil in the pan and remove it to a bowl.
Do it in small batches if necessary, so as not to stew it in its own liquid.

Step 2 - The Aromatics

Finely slice one large brown onion, and fry it in a little more oil until it is transparent, and then add the following to stir fry for about one minute only:

2 tsp minced garlic
2 tsp minced chilli (or Sambal Oelek, Indonesian-style chilli paste from supermarket)
1 tsp minced ginger
1 tsp chopped lemongrass
1 cup roasted peanuts blended in 1 cup hot water
1 tsp ground cumin
1 tsp ground coriander
1 tsp turmeric
$\frac{1}{2}$ tsp ground white pepper
$\frac{1}{2}$ tsp sea salt
1 anchovy fillet

Step 3 - Add the Liquid

400ml can coconut milk
2 Tbsp kecap manis
2 tsp sugar
the juice of $\frac{1}{2}$ a Tahitian lime

Step 4 - Add the Vegetables and the Cooked Meat

The vegetables are added last along with the meat already cooked to reheat.
Add a finely sliced red capsicum (bell pepper). Put the lid on.
At the end after the mixture has cooked for a few minutes, add some snow peas, or sugar snap peas, and a chopped shallot.
Serve with pre-prepared Hokkien noodles, or similar, or some plain rice.
The flavour blend is magic!

LAMB

Mongolian Lamb (China)

Step 1 - The Meat

Start with about 500gm finely sliced lamb back strap, rump, or shoulder, and marinate it for about an hour if possible to tenderise it, in the following:

2Tbsp dark soy sauce
2Tbsp white wine

Brown the meat in hot peanut or extra virgin olive oil, to which has been added about 1tsp sesame oil, and remove it from the pan.
Do this in small batches if necessary, so as not to stew it, which might toughen it.

Step 2 - The Aromatics

Finely chop or slice one large brown (yellow) onion and three green shallots.
Fry these in a little more oil until the onion is transparent and add the following to stir fry for about one minute only:

2tsp minced garlic
1tsp minced ginger
2tsp minced red chilli

Step 3 - Add the Liquid

Prior to cooking, make a stir fry liquid by stirring into ½ cup water the following:

1Tbsp dark soy sauce
1Tbsp Shaoxing rice cooking wine, or dry sherry
1tsp sea salt
1tsp ground white pepper
1tsp sugar
1tsp cornflour mixed in a little water as a thickener

Step 4 - Add the Vegetables and the Cooked Meat

The vegetables are added last along with the meat already cooked, to reheat.
Chop up very finely (so that they will cook quickly), and add:
1 carrot, ½ green capsicum, ½ red capsicum (bell pepper), and 1 bunch of fresh broccolini cut into about 3cm pieces.
Also now add about 1Tbsp oyster sauce (from the supermarket).
Put the lid on at this point to help steam the vegetables quickly.
Cook for a few minutes, and add some snow peas just at the end.
Serve with steamed or boiled rice.

PORK

Sweet and Sour Pork (China)

Step 1-The Meat

Start with about 700gm of good quality cubed pork loin, leg, or shoulder. Marinate the pork in the following:
2Tbsp soy sauce (or kecap manis)
2Tbsp white wine
1 egg yolk
Drain the meat and toss it in some cornflour.
Cook this in peanut oil in the wok or pan till the pork is cooked through and remove it from the pan.

Step 2-The Aromatics

Add the following to the pan with a little oil:
1 small onion, finely chopped
3 shallots, chopped roughly
1tsp minced garlic
1tsp minced ginger
1tsp minced chilli (or sambal oelek)

Step 3-Add the Liquid

Prior to cooking, make a stir fry liquid by stirring into ½ cup water the following:
2Tbsp tomato sauce
1Tbsp soy sauce (light or dark, or kecap manis)
1Tbsp Shaoxing rice cooking wine, or dry sherry, or white wine
1tsp sea salt
1tsp ground white pepper
1tsp sugar
1tsp cornflour mixed into a little water as a thickening ingredient

Step 4-Add the Vegetables and the Cooked Meat

The vegetables are added last to the mixture, along with the cooked meat.
Put the lid on at this point to help steam the vegetables quickly.
Chop up very finely, and add:
half a red capsicum (bell pepper)
half a green capsicum (bell pepper)
1 small tin champignons (button mushrooms)
half a tin of diced pineapple, drained
Serve with rice.
You can also top this with some snow peas and nice crunchy bean sprouts if you wish.

San Choy Bow (China)

Step 1 - The Meat

Start with about 500gm of good quality pork mince.

Fry the meat in hot oil in a wok or large frying pan, to which has been added 1tsp sesame oil, until the meat is cooked through.

Step 2 - The Aromatics

Add the following to fry with the meat for a couple of minutes:

1 small onion, finely chopped

3 green shallots, chopped roughly

1tsp minced garlic

1tsp minced ginger

1tsp minced chilli (or sambal oelek)

Step 3 - Add the Liquid

Prior to cooking, make a stir fry liquid by stirring into ½ cup water the following:

1Tbsp soy sauce (light or dark, or kecap manis)

1Tbsp Shaoxing rice cooking wine or dry sherry or white wine

1tsp Chinese five spice

1tsp sea salt

1tsp ground white pepper

1tsp sugar

1tsp cornflour mixed into a little water as a thickening ingredient

Step 4 - Add the Vegetables

The vegetables are added last to the mixture.

Put the lid on at this point to help steam the vegetables quickly.

Chop up very finely and add:

half a red capsicum (red bell pepper)

half a green capsicum (green bell pepper)

1 small tin sliced water chestnuts

Serve with washed iceberg lettuce leaf cups into which you serve several spoonfuls of the mixture.

You can also top these with sugar snap peas and crunchy bean sprouts if you wish.

Use your hands to roll them up and eat them.

They are a taste sensation!

CHICKEN

Honey Chicken (China)

Step 1 - The Meat

Start with about 700gm of good quality chicken breast fillets, cut into bite-sized pieces.

Dip the chicken in a batter made by whisking together:

½ cup water
½ tsp sea salt
½ tsp white pepper
1 egg
½ cup S. R. Flour
½ cup cornflour (made from corn, not wheat)

Cook this in peanut oil in the wok or pan till the chicken is sizzled, and cooked through. Remove it from the pan to a plate.

Step 2 - The Aromatics

Add the following to the pan with a little oil to cook for a few seconds:

1tsp minced garlic
1tsp minced ginger
1tsp minced chilli (or sambal oelek)

Step 3 - Add the Liquid

Prior to cooking, make a stir fry liquid by stirring into ½ cup water the following:

½ cup honey
1tsp soy sauce (light or dark, or kecap manis)
1tsp Shaoxing rice cooking wine or dry sherry
1tsp sea salt
1tsp cornflour mixed into a little water as a thickening ingredient

Add the liquid

Step 4 - Add the Vegetables and the Cooked Meat

The vegetables are added last to the mixture, along with the already cooked meat.
Put the lid on at this point to help steam the vegetables quickly:

1 small onion, chopped coarsely
1 green shallot, chopped finely
half a red capsicum (bell pepper), chopped into squares

Sprinkle over some sesame seeds.
Serve with rice.
You can also top this with snow peas and crunchy bean sprouts if you wish.

Lemon Chicken (China)

Step 1 - The Meat

Start with about 700gm of good quality chicken breast fillets, cut into bite-sized pieces.

Dip the chicken in a batter made by whisking together:

½ cup water
½ tsp sea salt
½ tsp white pepper
1 egg
½ cup S. R. Flour
½ cup cornflour (the type made from corn, not wheat)

Cook this in peanut oil in the wok or pan till the chicken is cooked through and remove it from the pan to a plate.

Step 2 - The Aromatics

Add the following to the pan with a little oil to cook for a few seconds:

1 tsp minced garlic
1 tsp minced ginger
1 tsp minced red chilli (or sambal oelek)

Step 3 - Add the Liquid

Prior to cooking, make a stir fry liquid by stirring into ½ cup water the following:

½ cup lemon juice
1 Tbsp honey
1 tsp soy sauce (light or dark, or kecap manis)
1 tsp Shaoxing rice cooking wine or dry sherry
1 tsp sea salt
1 tsp cornflour mixed into a little water as a thickening ingredient

Add the liquid.

Step 4 - Add the Vegetables and the Cooked Meat

The vegetables are added last to the mixture, along with the already cooked meat.
Put the lid on at this point, if you have one, to help steam the vegetables quickly:

1 small brown (yellow) onion, chopped coarsely
1 green shallot, chopped finely
half a red capsicum (red bell pepper), chopped into squares

Serve with rice.
You can also top this with snow peas and crunchy bean sprouts if you wish.

'Mie Goreng' (Indonesia) - Fried Noodles

In preparation, soak some Hokkien noodles in hot water to separate them.
You buy them from the supermarket in sealed packets (see Noodles).
Beat 4 eggs lightly and make two thin omelettes in the wok using a little peanut oil.
Remove them from the pan, slice them, and keep them warm on a plate.

Step 1 - The Meat

Start with about 500gm finely sliced chicken fillets, and marinate it for about an hour if possible to tenderise it in the following:
2Tbsp soy sauce (or kecap manis)
2Tbsp white wine
Brown the meat in hot oil in the pan and remove it to a plate.
Do it in small batches if necessary, so as not to stew it.

Step 2 - The Aromatics

Finely chop or slice one large brown (yellow) onion.
Fry it in a little more oil until it is transparent, and add the following to stir fry for one minute only:
1tsp minced garlic
1tsp minced ginger
1tsp minced red chilli (or sambal oelek)

Step 3 - Add the Liquid

Prior to cooking, make a stir fry liquid by stirring into $\frac{1}{2}$ cup water the following:
1Tbsp soy sauce (light or dark, or kecap manis)
1Tbsp Shaoxing rice cooking wine, or white wine vinegar
1tsp sea salt
1tsp ground white pepper
1tsp sugar
1tsp cornflour mixed in water as a thickener

Step 4 - Add the Vegetables and the Cooked Meat

The vegetables are added last along with the meat already cooked to reheat.
Add the Hokkien noodles and a handful of peanuts to fry for a minute or two.
Return the chicken to the pan.
Then add a finely chopped carrot, a finely sliced red capsicum, a cup of finely sliced won bok cabbage, and a chopped bok choy.
Put the lid on at this point to help steam the vegetables quickly.
Serve this topped with the egg omelette slices.

PRAWNS

'Nasi Goreng' (Indonesia) - Prawn Fried Rice

This is a great breakfast dish, made using cooked rice, or you can make it using leftover cooked rice. This is what I would call, 'Bacon and Eggs, Indonesian-Style'.

Beat 4 eggs lightly and make two thin omelettes in the wok using a little peanut oil. Remove them from the pan, slice them up, and keep them warm on a plate.
Boil or steam about 1 cup rice, or cook it just covered with water in the microwave for about 6 minutes till it has absorbed the water.

Step 1 - The Meat

Get 500gm raw peeled king prawns, and marinate them for a few minutes in:
1 Tbsp soy sauce (or kecap manis)
1 Tbsp white wine
Cook them in hot oil in the pan till they just change colour and remove them.
Do them in batches if necessary, so as not to stew them.

Step 2 - The Aromatics

Finely chop or slice one large brown (yellow) onion and 3 chopped rashers of bacon and fry them in a little more oil until the onion is transparent and the bacon is cooked, and add the following to stir fry for one minute only:
1 tsp minced garlic
1 tsp minced ginger
1 tsp minced red chilli (or sambal oelek)

Step 3 - Add the Liquid

Add in the cooked rice to fry a little along with the aromatics, maybe 2 minutes.
Meanwhile, make a stir fry liquid by stirring into ½ cup water the following:
1 Tbsp soy sauce (light or dark, or kecap manis)
1 Tbsp Shaoxing rice cooking wine or white wine vinegar
1 tsp sea salt
1 tsp ground white pepper
1 tsp sugar
Add some of the liquid gradually till the stir fry has good consistency.

Step 4 - Add the Vegetables and the Cooked Meat

Add a ½ of a very finely chopped carrot, and ½ of a very finely sliced red capsicum (red bell pepper), along with a chopped green shallot.
Add the cooked prawns to the top to reheat a little.
Serve the rice topped with the sliced eggs.

SWEETS AND DESSERTS

SWEET CLASSICS

Chocolate 'Panacotta' (Italy) – Cooked Cream

Panacotta is an Italian expression which means 'cooked cream'. It is most often made these days using dariole moulds, the word 'dariole' coming from an Old French word that means a small, filled pastry. These moulds are now used more for panacotta, crème caramel, mousse, and castle pudding.

Unlike custard, no eggs are used to thicken panacotta. Gelatine is used instead.

Early panacotta recipes used boiled fish bones instead of gelatine.

Ingredients

300ml thick double cream (48% milk fat)
300ml milk (or cream)
½ cup caster sugar
1tsp vanilla extract (or a scraped out vanilla bean; the bean is removed afterward)
3tsp gelatine powder
100gm good-quality dark (70% cocoa) or white chocolate
fresh strawberries or raspberries

Method

Heat the cream, milk, sugar and vanilla in a saucepan until the mixture is quite warm and the sugar is dissolved.

Add the gelatine that has been fully dissolved in about ½ cup warm water and stir it in well.

Add the chocolate and stir until it is dissolved.

Pour the mixture into 4 dariole moulds, ramekins, or suitably shaped cups that have been lightly greased with butter and refrigerate them for at least 4 hours.

To serve, break the seal by inserting a small knife around the mould, turn them onto serving plates, and gently shake to release them.

If they are difficult to remove, dip the bottoms of the moulds briefly into warm water.

Serve with fresh berries on the side, and decorate with a mint leaf.

'Pâte à choux' (France) Profiteroles with Chocolate Ganache

Profiteroles are made from a light French pastry dough called pâte à choux, choux meaning 'cabbage' because of its appearance, and filled with whipped cream or crème pâtissière (French pastry cream). See the recipe for Crème Pâtissière.

The dough is also used to make éclairs, croquembouches, and other delicacies.

In Australia, profiteroles are known simply as 'Cream Puffs'.

Ingredients for the Cream Puffs

1 cup (250ml) water
100gm butter
1tsp castor sugar
1 cup plain flour
4 eggs

Whipped Cream

300ml carton of cream
1tsp vanilla essence
½ cup castor sugar

Ingredients for the Chocolate Ganache

100gm good quality dark chocolate
½ cup cream

Method

Preheat the oven to 200°C.

Put the water, butter, and sugar into a large saucepan to heat to a rolling boil.

Switch off the heat, add the flour, and mix with a wooden spoon until the mixture becomes a paste and starts to come away from the sides of the saucepan.

Tip the mixture into a mixing bowl to cool for about 10 minutes.

Add the eggs one at a time, mixing well each time until you have a smooth, glossy, soft dropping mixture.

Using a dessertspoon, drop spoonfuls of mixture in rows onto two baking trays that you have covered with baking paper.

Bake for about 25 minutes or until puffed and golden brown.

When cooled, cut them in half and fill with the beaten whipped cream.

Pour over the chocolate Ganache that you have made by melting the chocolate with the cream in a bowl over a saucepan of simmering water.

It is best to wait till the sauce has cooled a little and is thick enough for pouring over the top of the cream puffs so that it partially sets.

CUSTARDS

While 'custard' may refer to a wide variety of thickened dishes, in French cookery the word custard (crème moulée) refers only to egg-thickened custard.

When starch is added, the result is French pastry cream, 'Crème Pâtissière', which is made with milk or cream, egg yolks, sugar, flour or cornflour, and usually flavourings such as vanilla, chocolate, or lemon. Crème pâtissière is a key ingredient in many French desserts including Millefeuille (or, Napoleons) and filled tarts. It also used in Italian pastry and in the Boston cream pie. In Australia, the 'Vanilla Slice' (not-so-nice slang, 'snot block') is similar (see the following recipe).

With heavy cream, it is known as 'crème mousseline'.

When starch alone is used as a thickener (without eggs), it is 'blancmange'.

Commercially available custard powder is cornflour-based, and thickens to form a custard-like sauce, without using eggs, when mixed with milk and heated. I grew up on this stuff, and quite liked it. Instead of using that, I suggest that you try your hand at making the real thing, which is so much better.

Some brands of custard powder contain hydrogenated vegetable oil, a product now banned in some countries due to health fears relating to heart disease.

Crème caramel, or caramel custard is a rich custard dessert with a layer of soft caramel on top, as opposed to crème brûlée, which is custard with a hard caramel top. It is a variant of plain custard (crème) where some sugar syrup, cooked to caramel stage, is poured into the mould before adding the custard base. It is usually cooked in a bain-marie in the oven, and is turned out with the caramel sauce appearing on top.

Crème brûlée, French for 'burnt cream', is a dessert consisting of a rich custard base topped with a contrasting layer of hard caramel. It is served cold, or with the custard cold and the caramel warm. The custard base is normally flavoured with vanilla, lemon, chocolate, fruit, or liqueur. A thin coating of granulated white sugar on the top of each brûlée is carefully melted with a propane blow-torch to form a solid caramel sheet.

Crème brûlée flambée is where a very thin layer of liqueur is poured on top and set alight.

Zabaglione, 'zabaione' in Italy, 'sabayon' in France, and 'sambayón' in South America, is an Italian dessert, traditionally served with fresh figs, made with egg yolks, sugar, a sweet wine such as Marsala wine or Prosecco, and sometimes cream, mascarpone, or whole eggs. It is a very light custard, which has been whipped to incorporate a large amount of air.

Custards are a culinary area that is very interesting, one where you will learn a lot while experimenting, and one where the fruits of your labour are very deliciously rewarding.

'Crème Pâtissière' (France) - French Pastry Cream

Ingredients

3 cups (750ml) full cream milk
1 vanilla bean or 1tsp vanilla essence
½ cup plain flour
1 cup caster sugar
a pinch of salt
8 egg yolks

Method

Heat the milk along with the vanilla bean with its seeds scraped into the milk. When the milk starts to simmer, take it off the heat to cool a little. Add the essence now if you are using it instead of the bean.

In a large bowl, mix together the flour, sugar and salt.

Add the egg yolks, and whip them until smooth with a balloon whisk.

Pour in a little of the milk, whisking the mixture, and gradually add the rest of the milk.

Return the mixture to the saucepan; simmer it for a few minutes, stirring with a wooden spoon until it thickens. Then return it again to the bowl, stirring it occasionally with the whisk as it cools.

Vanilla Slices (using the recipe for French pastry cream)

In a preheated 200^0C oven, bake two 25cm square sheets of puff pastry on baking paper on oven sheets for 20 minutes until the pastry puffs and browns. Remove from the oven and using a clean tea towel, gently press down on the sheets to flatten them, and then allow them to cool.

Lightly grease a 23cm square dish with butter, line it with baking paper, and place one pastry sheet, flat face down, in the bottom. Pour in the warm custard. Place the other sheet, flat face up, on the top.

Refrigerate for a couple of hours to set the custard.

Ice the top of the slices with the mixture below and cut into squares.

Icing Mixture

2 cups of icing sugar
2tsp butter, softened
2Tbsp milk
½tsp vanilla essence

Mix together well the ingredients in a bowl sitting in hot water in the kitchen sink. Ice the slices when it is spreadable. If it is too thick add a touch more milk, if it is too thin add a little more icing sugar. As a traditional option, you can add 2Tbsp passionfruit pulp to the mixture.

Crème Caramel (France) – Caramel Custard

For the Caramel

½ cup water
1 cup sugar

For the Custard

300ml carton of double cream
1 cup milk
3 eggs and 2 egg yolks
½ cup sugar
1tsp vanilla essence

Method

Put the sugar and water in a saucepan to make the caramel. Melt it on low heat until the mixture is a golden colour, taking care not to burn it. Pour it into the base of 4 ramekins or dariole moulds (of approximately 150ml each) that have been very lightly greased with butter.

Heat the cream and milk together till simmering, and then turn it off and let it cool a bit.

Place the eggs, sugar and vanilla essence in a bowl and mix well with a fork, taking care not to produce bubbles as these will appear in the custard. Do this just before adding the cream and milk mixture as the eggs can react with the sugar and form lumpy bits.

Stir the cream and milk mixture very gradually into the egg mixture to avoid curdling, until well combined. Strain the custard into a jug for a smooth texture.

Pour the custard mixture slowly on top of the caramel in the moulds.

Place the moulds into a baking tray, with something in the bottom of it to keep them just off the bottom (so the caramel doesn't overheat), and carefully pour boiling water into the tray till it comes half way up the moulds (this method provides an even cooking temperature).

Place the baking tray on the middle rack of the oven and bake the creme caramel for about 45 minutes at $140^{\circ}C$ (long cooking time at a low temperature is one of the secrets of this dish).

Do not allow the water to boil as this can produce a coarse texture.

Refrigerate the moulds for at least 4 hours.

To serve, run a small sharp knife around the edge of each mould, place the serving dish upside down over the mould, invert them, give them a shake while holding them firmly together and lift off the mould.

The caramel sauce will run down the outside of the custard.

'Crème Brûlée' (France) – Burnt Cream

Make the custard as in the previous recipe, and pour it straight into the greased ramekins.

Refrigerate it for four hours.

Sprinkle a little sugar on the top and use a domestic blow torch to caramelise the sugar.

To do crème brûlée flambée instead, pour 2tsp Grand Marnier liqueur over the sugar and carefully light it with a match.

The flame will go out when the alcohol burns off.

'Crème Anglaise' (England) - Custard Sauce

Ingredients (for 4)

3 cups (750ml) full cream milk
1 vanilla pod (or 2tsp vanilla essence)
8 egg yolks
½ cup sugar

Method

Keep back ½ cup of the milk and put the rest into a saucepan with the vanilla pod that has been sliced down the middle and the seeds that have been scraped out with a small spoon.

Bring the milk almost to the boil and then take it off the heat to cool for about 15 minutes, to give the vanilla time to infuse into the milk.

Put the egg yolks and sugar into a bowl with the reserved milk and mix them together until creamy.

If using vanilla essence, add this now.

Take out the vanilla pod.

Gradually add the warm milk to the egg mixture and stir.

Put the mixture back into the saucepan and cook it gently until it coats the back of a spoon and has the consistency of cream. Be careful not to overheat it at this stage or it may curdle.

Serve the custard over plum pudding, cake, fresh fruit, or other accompaniment.

Custard Tart (England)

Modern recipes use a blind baking method and baking beads placed inside the pastry to partially cook the pastry first and stop the pastry breaking or shrinking. I prefer my grandmother's old-fashioned method as it is much quicker and less fiddly to make. The custard is similar to the crème brûlée recipe.

Ingredients for simple Shortcrust Pastry

1½ cups plain flour
pinch of salt
60gm butter, chopped
½ cup sugar
½ cup milk
have on hand some ground nutmeg to sprinkle on top of the tart

Method

Put sifted flour and salt into a bowl and add the butter, crumbling it up with your fingers until you have a breadcrumb feel to it.

Stir in the sugar and then stir in enough of the milk to make firm dough. Wrap this in plastic wrap and put it in the fridge for a half an hour to rest. Then, roll out the pastry to about 5mm and place it on a 25cm pie plate, crimping the edges nicely.

Brush the pastry with some of the two spare egg whites that have been lightly beaten. This helps to seal off the pastry from the custard mixture.

Actually, my dear old grandma's custard tarts were to die for, and part of the taste and appeal was the very slightly soggy pastry.

Pour in the custard, sprinkle it with the ground nutmeg, and bake for about 45 minutes at $180^{\circ}C$, until the custard looks to be set in the middle. It will firm up more as it cools.

To me, this tastes exactly like my grandmother's custard tart. My brother Dennis said that hers were better than mine.

For the Custard

1 cup cream
1¼ cups milk
3 eggs and 2 egg yolks
½ cup sugar
1tsp vanilla essence

Method

Heat the cream and milk together till simmering, turn off the heat, and let it cool a bit.

Place the eggs, sugar and vanilla essence in a bowl and mix well with a whisk, to dissolve the sugar. Do this just before adding the cream and milk mixture as the eggs can react with the sugar and form lumpy bits.

Stir the cream and milk mixture very gradually into the egg mixture to avoid curdling, until well combined. Strain the custard into a jug if you wish, for a smooth texture.

Custard Pots

This recipe is somewhere between a Crème Anglaise and a Crème Pâtissière recipe, and is cooked in a saucepan on the stovetop.

I think this version of mine for custard tastes better than the baked version.

Ingredients

300ml carton of double cream
1 cup milk
6 large egg yolks
½ cup sugar
3tsp cornflour
1tsp natural vanilla extract

Method

In a large saucepan heat the cream and milk until it is just about to simmer. This is when the surface begins to gently roll but no bubbles have yet formed.

While that is heating, beat the egg yolks, sugar, vanilla, and cornflour together in a large bowl with a balloon whisk.

Carefully pour the hot liquid, a little at a time, into the egg mixture, whisking vigorously. Then pour the mixture back into the saucepan.

Heat just to a low simmer and stir constantly with a wooden spoon until the mixture is thick and creamy.

You can serve this warm as a sauce, or as a dessert with fruit. Or, pour the custard into 4 ramekins and cover them with plastic wrap to prevent a skin from forming, and chill them in the refrigerator, and perhaps finish them with a brûlée top.

Zabaglione (Italy)

Ingredients (for 4)

6 egg yolks
½ cup caster sugar
¾ cup Marsala, Madeira, Vermouth, or Sherry

Method

In a metal bowl suspended over simmering water, beat the egg yolks and sugar until thick and foamy. Beat in the wine. Continue whisking for about 5 minutes, making sure that the water doesn't touch the base of the bowl, until it makes thick creamy foam that coats the back of the spoon. Further whisking will thicken it more if desired.

The eggs need to be cooked gently so the mixture stays smooth, so make sure that it does not overheat while whisking. Remove it from the heat occasionally if necessary.

Serve immediately over fresh fruit, with biscotti. It can also be served chilled. In this case, beat the mixture when it is off the heat until it has cooled. Try folding in some mascarpone cheese (Italian light cream cheese from the Milan region) when cold. You can make your own very cheaply and easily with the following recipe.

Mascarpone Cream (Italy)

2 cups heavy cream (preferably organic)
1Tbsp lemon juice (originally the tartaric acid from wine sediment was used for this)

Method

In a double boiler or bowl over water as above, heat the cream until it reaches about 85^0C, then add the lemon juice and stir it with a balloon whisk. The mixture will begin to thicken as it curdles. Remove the bowl from the heat and let it cool down. Put it in the fridge overnight in a strainer or cheesecloth over a bowl to drain it, and it will then be ready to use.

'Tiramisu' (Italy) - pick-me-up

This is my version of the famous Italian dessert that can be made by using the previous recipes.

Ingredients

1 packet of Italian biscotti (finger biscuits) See Biscuit recipe to make them yourself
250gm homemade mascarpone cheese (or purchase some)
1 cup cold strong coffee
1tsp natural vanilla extract
½ cup homemade Irish Cream Liqueur (recipe below)
2 cups zabaglione, cold (recipe on previous page)
milk chocolate, grated

Method

Spread the mascarpone cheese over one side of enough biscuits to vertically line four tapered serving glasses (about 16 biscuits) with the cheese on the insides.

Mix together the coffee, vanilla, liqueur, and pour into each glass enough liquid to come about ¾ of the way up the glass (this will be absorbed into the biscuits).

Top up the glasses with zabaglione, and decorate the top with a little grated chocolate.

Refrigerate for an hour to serve cold.

Here is the recipe for the liqueur.

Homemade Irish Cream Liqueur

Mix the ingredients together in a jug, pour into a bottle, and refrigerate for one week.

350ml whisky (½ a bottle)
300ml cream
3 eggs
400gm tin sweetened condensed milk
½ cup cold strong espresso coffee
½ cup chocolate topping
½tsp coconut essence

Pavlova (Australia, New Zealand)

This recipe is ideal for using up the leftover egg whites when making French pastry cream as above. Few recipes use as many egg whites as this one.

I have put it here in this section for convenience.

Named after the Russian ballet dancer Anna Pavlova in connection with a tour of Australia and New Zealand; there is ongoing discussion about who actually invented it.

It is certainly a favourite national dish in both countries.

Ingredients

8 egg whites
2 cups caster sugar
4tsp corn flour
2tsp lemon juice (or you could use 2tsp white vinegar)
2tsp natural vanilla essence

For the Whipped Cream

300ml carton whipping cream
2Tbsp sugar
1tsp vanilla essence

Method

Preheat the oven to 140°C.

Beat the egg whites with an electric mixer until stiff peaks form.

Gradually add the sugar, mixing well, until the mixture is stiff and glossy.

Add the cornflour, lemon juice, and vanilla, and whisk until just combined.

Shape the mixture into a round on a baking tray lined with non-stick baking paper.

Bake it for $1\frac{1}{2}$ hours in the oven.

Turn the oven off and allow the pavlova to cool down in the oven with the door half open; otherwise it could deflate.

Top the pavlova with lots of whipped cream, and fruit such as banana slices, kiwi fruit slices, peach slices, mango pieces, chopped strawberries, and passionfruit pulp.

For the whipped cream, just beat the cold ingredients together with an electric beater.

As an option, you could also make four or six smaller pavlovas instead, and decorate them with whipped cream and fruit in a similar way.

If you are going to do this, you may find it helpful to draw some circles on the baking paper to help keep the size of the pavlovas uniform.

You will need to cut the cooking time back to about 1 hour for the smaller pavs.

Lemon Curd Tart

This tart is a delicious twist on the custard tart.

The filling is like custard, but without the cream.

It is otherwise similar to a custard tart, and this recipe also takes me right back to my childhood days, and grandma's own lemon tart.

Ingredients for the Shortcrust Pastry Case

1½ cups plain flour
a pinch of salt
60gm butter, chopped
½ cup sugar
½ cup milk

Ingredients for the Lemon Curd

1 cup caster sugar
2/3 cup Meyer lemon juice freshly squeezed and strained. Or, use other lemons
5 large eggs
125gm butter, softened
Note: Meyer lemons are a Chinese hybrid of lemons and oranges, and produce sweet juice without bitterness; and without having to use too much sugar in the recipe.

Method

For the pastry case, put the sifted flour and salt into a bowl and add the butter, crumbling it up with your fingers until you have a breadcrumb feel to it.

Stir in the sugar and then stir in enough of the milk to make firm dough. Wrap this in plastic wrap and put it in the fridge for a half an hour to rest.

Roll out the pastry to about 5mm between sheets of baking paper, and place it on a 25cm pie plate, crimping the edges nicely. The easiest way is to put the pie dish upside down on the pastry, turn the whole thing over, and peel off the top baking paper.

Bake it for about 30 minutes at 180^0C, until the crust looks to be set.

To make the curd, in a medium heatproof bowl over a saucepan of simmering water, combine the sugar, lemon juice, and eggs. Simmer for about 10 minutes or so, stirring constantly, without letting the bowl touch the water. This is to control the heat so that the eggs don't curdle. If the bowl is getting too hot, lift it off the water for a couple of minutes.

Thicken it by stirring till it coats the back of a spoon, remove the custard from the stove, and gradually whisk in the butter, adding a tablespoon at a time.

Then place the bowl in a sink of cold water and stir it to stop it cooking.

Cool the curd for 15 minutes before pouring it into the prepared pastry case.

Refrigerate for a few hours before serving.

Lemon Meringue Pie (United Kingdom)

Follow the previous recipe for making the pastry case and lemon curd filling, but with the following variations.

Bake the pastry for only 20 minutes at 180^0C, as it will be baked again after it is topped with the meringue.

Reserve the egg whites to make the meringue topping.

Allow the pastry and curd to cool down before filling the pie with the curd and the meringue. Use the back of a spoon to lift the meringue into decorative peaks.

Bake the filled pie at 200^0C for about 10 minutes till the peaks of the meringue start to lightly brown.

Method for the Meringue

Beat the 5 egg whites with an electric mixer until stiff peaks form.

Gradually add $1\frac{1}{4}$ cups caster sugar, mixing well, until the mixture is stiff and glossy.

Add 2tsp cornflour, 1tsp lemon juice, and 1tsp vanilla, and whisk until just combined.

Key Lime Pie (United States)

Also known as West Indian lime and Mexican lime, its name derives from Florida Keys. It has a smaller, stronger flavoured fruit than the Tahitian lime, and turns from green to a light yellow colour when fully ripe. Use either type of lime for this recipe.

As with the above recipe, bake the pastry case for only 20 minutes at 180^0C, as it will be baked again after it has been filled.

Ingredients for the Filling

4 egg yolks
400gm can sweetened condensed milk
$\frac{1}{2}$ cup lime juice
1Tbsp finely grated lime rind
whipped cream and finely grated lime rind, to serve

Method

Using an electric mixer, beat the egg yolks in a mixing bowl for 3 to 4 minutes or until they are light and fluffy.

Gradually beat in the condensed milk, lime juice, and lime rind.

Pour the mixture into the case, and bake for about 10 minutes or until the filling has just set. Remove it from the oven to cool.

Refrigerate for 3 hours or until chilled.

Serve it in wedges with whipped cream.

BAKED CHEESECAKE

Cheesecakes have been made for centuries, and possibly originated in Greece.
There are two main types of cheesecakes.
The first type is a baked cheesecake, popularised in the USA. There are also many similar European versions.
It is sort of like a cake, or maybe like a torte, but it is also like a custard in that it uses eggs. There is quite a bit of work involved in cooking these.
Here are two different baked cheesecakes.

Baked New York Cheesecake (United States)

Ingredients

250gm packet sweet plain biscuits
250gm slightly melted butter
500gm cream cheese
½ cup castor sugar
1Tbsp lemon juice
4 eggs
½ cup sour cream
2tsp lemon juice
1Tbsp castor sugar

Method

Make the base by crushing up the biscuits, mixing the butter in well, and pressing the mixture into the bottom and sides of a greased cake tin (you can use a glass for this).
Put it in the fridge for ½ hour to set the base a bit.
Beat up the cream cheese till smooth, add the sugar and lemon juice, and mix well.
Add the eggs, one at a time, and beat well.
Pour the mixture into the case and bake for ¾ hour at 180^0C.
Add a topping made by mixing together the sour cream, lemon juice and castor sugar, and bake for a further 5 minutes.
When it has cooled put it in the fridge. Decorate the top with whipped cream and fresh strawberries to serve.

Baked Ricotta and Honey Cheesecake (Italy)

Line a cake tin with ready-made shortcrust pastry, and add a filling made by mixing together 4 eggs, ¼ cup castor sugar, ½ cup plain flour, ½ cup honey, ½tsp ground cinnamon and 500gm Ricotta cheese.

Bake it in the oven at 180^0C until cooked, almost an hour.

NO-BAKE CHEESECAKE

The second type of cheesecake is a no-bake, or chilled cheesecake, more common in Australia and the UK. It is not baked, but made with cream cheese and set in the refrigerator with the help of gelatine. This uses a much easier method.

Personally, I prefer the taste and texture of this type of cheesecake.

I don't have a sweet tooth, unlike some people who are likely to kill for piece of cake, but I do get excited about a good cheesecake and also a well-executed pavlova, probably two of the world's sweetest creations.

The following two recipes here are of this second type of cheesecake. Yum!

Chocolate Cheesecake (Australia)

Ingredients

250gm packet sweet biscuits (Anzac, ginger nut, chocolate, or shortbread are good)
80gm butter, softened to room temperature
500gm block cream cheese, softened to room temperature
1/3 cup caster sugar
3tsp powdered gelatine dissolved in ½ cup hot water
200gm quality milk chocolate, melted
1½ cups cream, whipped with 1tsp natural vanilla essence and 3tsp caster sugar

Method

Break up the biscuits roughly, put them in a food processor, and mix together the biscuit crumbs and butter.

Press the biscuit mixture into the base of a pie dish or greased 20cm springform pan. You could carefully use the base of a heavy glass for this. Chill the base in the freezer until firm for about 10 minutes.

Meanwhile, beat the cream cheese and sugar together with an electric mixer until smooth. Now mix in the gelatine.

Fold in the chocolate and mix until smooth. Now fold through the whipped cream.

Pour the mixture into the prepared base, and chill for 3 hours or until it is set.

Grate a little extra chocolate over the top for decoration and serve.

Options

You could layer the cake by using ½ each of dark (70% cocoa) chocolate and white chocolate by dividing the mixture in half at the point where the chocolate is added. Freeze it for 10 minutes between layers.

You could decorate the top with fresh strawberries, raspberries, or blueberries.

Chocolate curls can also be made for decoration by melting some chocolate, spreading it on a tray, refrigerating it for half an hour, and then scraping up curls of chocolate from the tray with a knife.

Orange Liqueur Cheesecake (England)

Ingredients

250gm packet of your favourite sweet biscuits
125gm butter, softened
375gm packet cream cheese, softened
½ cup orange juice, and a little of the orange zest
2tsp natural vanilla essence
1Tbsp gelatine dissolved in 1Tbsp Cointreau orange liqueur
400gm tin of sweetened condensed milk

Method

Process the biscuits in a food processor and add the butter to the food processor to mix it in well.

Press the biscuit mixture into the base and sides of a 20cm pie dish (you can use the base of a heavy glass very carefully to do this).

Refrigerate the base for about 20 minutes or so to set it a little while preparing the rest of the mixture.

Beat the cream cheese in the food processor until smooth (this saves you washing up another beater).

Then add the orange juice and zest, the vanilla essence, and the gelatine mixture, and mix it in.

Slowly pour in the condensed milk and mix this a little till the mixture is smooth.

Pour the mixture into the biscuit base and allow it to set overnight in the refrigerator.

As an option you could decorate the top with some passionfruit pulp or some other type of fresh fruit (get a little creative with this).

This is an exceptional dessert.

Strawberry Cheesecake

Follow the recipe above, but with the following exceptions:

Substitute some lemon juice and zest for the orange juice and zest.

Dissolve the gelatine in ½ cup warm water.

Decorate the top with whole fresh strawberries.

Sieve a little icing sugar across the top of the cake.

As my wife would say, 'That's very decadent'.

PIES

Apple Pie (England)

Americans are big on pies of any sort, and apple pie has become a cultural icon. However, English and Dutch apple pie recipes go back for centuries. And they have travelled the world. Apple pie has to be near the top of the list for best-ever dessert dishes.

Ingredients

1½ cups plain flour
1½ cups self raising flour
2 Tbsp castor sugar
a pinch of salt
200gm butter
1 egg
10 sliced Granny Smith apples
1/3 cup lemon juice
40gm butter
½ cup castor sugar
1 tsp ground cinnamon

Method

Make some pastry by mixing together the flour, castor sugar and salt.

Rub in the butter to get a mixture with a texture like breadcrumbs.

Add an egg yolk and 1/3 cup iced water and stir to a soft mixture (keep the white of the egg aside).

Put the pastry in the fridge in cling wrap for a half an hour to rest.

Put about 2/3 of the mixture into a greased 22cm pie dish as a base after rolling it out flat between two sheets of baking paper, and brush a little of the whisked egg white around the edges to join the pastry. Put the filling in the pie (see below).

Roll the rest of the pastry out to make a top and join it on. Crimp the edges of the pastry together decoratively.

Brush the rest of the egg white on top of the pastry, and sprinkle a little caster sugar over the top. Put a couple of small slits in the top of the pastry to vent the hot air.

Bake it for about 45 minutes at $180^{0}C$ or until cooked. You can cover it with foil if it is browning too quickly.

Method for the filling

Sprinkle the lemon juice over the apples to prevent them discolouring.

Put the butter and sugar in a saucepan to melt. Add the apples and cinnamon and cook them for about 10 minutes until softened.

Bannoffee Pie (England)

This is my version of what is now served as Bannoffee Pie, the name being derived from the words 'banana' and 'toffee'. It commonly uses a biscuit base, something that the inventor himself detested. It was apparently developed in 1972 by Ian Dowding, chef of the Hungry Monk restaurant in Essex, England.

Ingredients for Pie Crust

250gm pkt sweet biscuits of your choice

100gm butter

Ingredients for Caramel Filling

400gm tin sweetened condensed milk

1/3 cup brown sugar

50gm butter

Other Ingredients

3 bananas, sliced

300ml carton whipping cream, whipped with 1tsp vanilla essence and 3tsp caster sugar

grated chocolate as a garnish

Method

Process the biscuits in a food processor till crumbly and fine. Add the butter to the processor and mix till well combined.

Press the biscuits into the base and sides of a pie dish with the bottom of a glass.

Refrigerate this until it is needed.

In a saucepan, heat the filling ingredients on low heat for about 10 minutes until it starts to caramelise.

Pour the mixture into the base and refrigerate for about an hour till set.

Arrange the banana slices over the top of the pie.

Top with the whipped cream, garnish with a sprinkle of chocolate, and serve.

Banana Cream Pie (United States)

These are the ones that you see in the movies when people throw pies at one another.

Bake a base of shortcrust pastry as for the Lemon Curd Tart, and allow it to cool.

Then make a custard mixture as for the Custard Pots recipe, and allow it to cool.

Slice three bananas and place the slices all over the base of the pastry evenly.

Pour the custard mixture into the pastry case over the bananas and smooth it out.

Whip some cream with caster sugar and vanilla essence as above, and spread it evenly over the top of the pie.

Refrigerate the pie and serve it cold.

MOUSSE

Chocolate 'Mousse' (France) – Foam

Ingredients

250gm quality dark chocolate 60% cocoa
50gm butter
400ml cream, whipped with 1tspn vanilla essence and 2Tbsp caster sugar
4 eggs, separated, at room temperature
2Tbsp caster sugar

Method

Melt the chocolate and butter in a bowl over the top of a saucepan of simmering water.
Take it off when melted, stir it, and let it cool for a couple of minutes.
Whisk in the egg yolks one at a time. You could also add a teaspoon of Brandy, Cognac, or Grand Marnier liqueur at this stage if you wish.
Fold the chocolate mixture into the whipped cream mixture with a spatula.
Whisk the egg whites in a separate bowl using clean beaters, making sure there are no traces of yolk in the bowl (or it won't work), until soft peaks form.
Then add the sugar and beat a little more.
Fold the egg whites into the mixture in about three batches (the first batch lightens the thickness of the mixture and makes it easier to fold in).
Divide into about 6 serving glasses and refrigerate for about 3 hours to set.
Grate a little extra chocolate on top for decoration, and maybe add a dollop of whipped cream as well
Note: As explained previously, the use of raw eggs in a recipe can present a small risk of salmonella contamination from the eggs.

Options

You could use white chocolate for white chocolate mousse, or layer the mousse 50/50 with dark and white.

Note: Using half dark and half white chocolate does not constitute a balanced diet.

Homemade Vanilla Ice Cream

This is what it says, and it is a very simple recipe. Heather gave me this one.

Ingredients

600ml carton of cream
400gm can of sweetened condensed milk
2tsp vanilla essence

Method

Put all the ingredients in a large bowl.
Mix them together well using an electric hand mixer until peaks form.
Pour the mixture into a plastic container and freeze for several hours. Presto!

CRÊPES

Crêpes are a French idea with many variations in accompaniments. The famous Crêpes Suzette takes this idea to the ultimate using a flambéed sauce done with liqueurs at the table — you set it on fire! There is dispute about the origin and name of the recipe.

Anyway, I take a minimalist approach here, as I don't want any of you blokes or sheilas losing your hair and eyebrows over it; or worse still, burning your house down!

Crêpes with Orange Sauce (France)

Crêpes Ingredients

1 cup plain flour
2 cups milk
3 eggs
butter for cooking the crêpes

Method

Sift the flour into a bowl, and add the milk and eggs, whisking until well combined.

Heat a medium size, non-stick frying pan over medium heat. A 22cm crêpe pan is made for the job.

Put a knob of butter into the pan to melt, swirling it around.

Pour a ladle of batter into the pan, swirling it to cover the base. Cook for 2 minutes or until light golden, then turn the crêpe over and cook for 1 minute.

Transfer to a plate and cover to keep warm.

Repeat with the remaining batter.

Orange Sauce Ingredients

3 Navel oranges

the rind from one of the oranges (after thoroughly washing the wax off the skin)

the juice of 2 of the oranges

orange segments from one of the oranges (cut down between the membranes)

2 Tbsp of Cointreau orange liqueur

½ cup caster sugar

Method

In a small saucepan, heat the orange juice, rind, and sugar until the sugar is melted and the liquid is hot.

Add the orange segments to heat through.

Arrange the crêpes on plates by folding them into quarters, and pour over the sauce.

Serve with some good quality vanilla ice cream.

TRADITIONAL PUDDINGS

Sticky Date Pudding with Caramel Sauce

Ingredients (Serves 6)

1 cup pitted dates, chopped into pieces
1 cup boiling water
1tsp bicarbonate of soda (baking soda)
60gm butter
½ cup brown sugar
2tsp mixed spice
2 eggs
2 cups S. R. Flour
300ml thick (double) cream for serving

Ingredients Toffee Sauce

125gm butter
1 cup cream
1 cup brown sugar

Method

Put the dates, boiling water and bicarbonate of soda in a bowl for about 5 minutes.
When cooled a little, put this in the bowl of a food processor with the butter, sugar, and mixed spice, and process till smooth.
Add the eggs and process till smooth.
Add the flour and process till smooth.
Put the mixture into a greased oven-proof dish and bake it at 180^0C for about 35 minutes until cooked.
Meanwhile heat the sauce ingredients in a saucepan till hot and thickened a little.
Cut it into squares, pour over the sauce, and top with the thick cream to serve.

Spotted Dick (England, Traditional)

This was originally made with suet. I have made it a little easier to prepare.
This was my father-in-law Dave's favourite dessert.

In a mixing bowl, mix together 1½ cups S. R. Flour, ½ cup sugar, 2 cups breadcrumbs, 100gm sultanas, 100gm currants, 2tsp grated lemon zest, ½tsp minced ginger, ½tsp salt, 1tsp ground nutmeg, and 50ml olive oil.
Stir in a mixture of 1 cup of milk and 2 eggs.
Shape the mixture into a log; wrap it loosely in baking paper to allow for expansion, then in a tea towel. Put it in the top of a steamer to cook for 2 hours, making sure that you keep topping up the boiling water in the steamer.
Serve with some nice egg custard.

Castle Pudding (England, Traditional)

Traditionally, castle pudding is baked in a dariole mould, producing a tall cylinder of spongy dessert. The pudding itself is usually plain, with perhaps some vanilla or lemon flavouring. It is therefore typically topped with a large dollop of strawberry jam. When castle pudding is served warm, the jam will run down the sides of the dessert, making a strawberry sauce.

Ingredients (Makes 4)

50gm softened butter
50gm sugar
1 egg
50gm flour (about 1/3 cup)
a pinch of baking powder

Method

Cream the butter and sugar together in a mixing bowl. Add in the egg. Sieve the flour and baking powder into the bowl. Mix well.

Grease 4 pudding moulds with butter, and half fill each one with the mixture. Bake in the oven at 180^0C for about 20 minutes. Push a skewer into the middle of the pudding. If the skewer comes out clean they are cooked. Serve with jam or custard.

Grandma's Apple Roly-Poly Pudding

Ingredients

25gm butter
1½ cups S. R. Flour
½ cup milk, or a little more
3 apples, peeled, cored, and sliced
1/3 cup brown sugar
1tsp ground cinnamon

Syrup Ingredients

25gm butter
½ cup brown sugar
1 cup boiling water

Method

Rub the butter into the S. R. Flour until the mixture is crumbly.
Then add the milk to form stiff dough.
Roll this out flat and place the sliced apples on top.
Sprinkle it with the sugar and ground cinnamon.
Roll the mixture up into a log shape and place it in an oval baking dish.
Mix the syrup ingredients together and pour the syrup over the pastry.
Bake in the oven at 180^0C for about ¾ hour until cooked.
The syrup will become quite thick and beautiful. I like this with just a little bit of milk poured over the top.

Bazza's Famously Miraculous Fruit Sponge Pudding

This recipe is based on my Mum's apple sponge pudding. You can use apples, apricots, pears, or any other fruit, or even jam for this recipe and it will work! She used to do steamed puddings as well in a pudding steamer using a similar recipe, but the way described here involves much less fiddling about, and requires a lot less motivation.

Ingredients

125gm butter, softened
½ cup caster sugar
2 eggs
1 cup S. R. Flour
1/3 cup milk, or a little more
sliced apples, fruit or jam
cream, to serve

Method

Mix the sugar into the melted butter in a mixing bowl.

Add the eggs, one at a time, and mix together.

Mix in the flour and stir until smooth.

Then add the milk to make a fairly runny mixture.

Pour the mixture over the sliced apples, or other fruit or jam (apricot jam works well), that you have placed in the bottom of a pie dish and bake for 30 minutes or until it looks cooked.

Serve with some cream over the top.

Bread and Butter Pudding

My wife, Correen, grew up on this stuff and loves it.

Ingredients

10 slices of buttered bread, quartered
4 eggs
300ml carton of cream
300ml of milk (fill up the cream carton)
1tsp ground cinnamon
½ cup brown sugar
½ cup sultanas soaked in a little brandy or whisky

Method

Put the buttered bread, quartered, in a greased pie dish, arranged decoratively.

Mix the rest of the ingredients together and pour the mixture slowly over the bread so that it soaks in and around the bread.

Bake for 45 minutes in the oven at 180^0C. Serve with some cream.

Leftover fruit loaf is ideal for this recipe as well.

Impossible Pudding

Ingredients (Serves four)

4 eggs
2 cups milk
1tsp vanilla essence
½ cup sugar
½ cup softened butter
½ cup plain flour
1 cup desiccated coconut

> Impossibly, this pudding somehow forms a crusty base, with an egg custard in the middle, and a crunchy coconut topping.

Method

In a large bowl, mix together the eggs, milk and vanilla with a whisk.
Add the sugar, butter, and flour, and keep whisking.
Add the coconut, and whisk until mixed through.
Pour the mixture into four oven-proof ramekins.
Bake them in the oven at $180^{0}C$ for about 35 minutes until set and the top is golden.

Rice Custard Puddings

Cook as for the recipe above but with the following difference:
Substitute ½ cup rice that has been cooked in water for the coconut.
An easy way to cook the rice is to just cover it with water in a microwave bowl, and cook it on high for about 6 minutes. It will cook a bit more while the pudding is cooking.

'Ryzogalo' (Greece) - Rice Milk Pudding

In a heavy-based saucepan, stir ½tsp salt, ½tsp ground cinnamon, ½tsp ground nutmeg, and ½tsp ground cardamom into 60gm butter on low heat for about a minute.
When the butter is melted and flavoured, stir in 1 cup Arborio rice so that it is well coated. Add 4 cups milk and 1tsp vanilla essence and simmer for about 30 minutes, stirring often. Add ¾ cup caster sugar and simmer for a further 15 minutes, stirring often, until the rice is thick and creamy.
Note: It is important to keep stirring this mixture often, to prevent it from burning, and also to bring up the cooked mixture from the bottom, giving it a nice caramel flavour and colour.

Simple Rice Pudding

Cook 1 cup of rice in the microwave by just covering it in water in a microwave container, and cooking it for about 6 minutes. Then mix it with 2 cups of milk, 4tsp sugar, a little orange rind, 1tsp vanilla essence and a sprinkle of ground cinnamon. Cook this in the oven at $180^{0}C$ in a covered dish for about 45 minutes.

SELF-SAUCING PUDDING

Chocolate Self-Saucing Pudding

Ingredients

1 cup S. R. Flour
¾ cup raw sugar
2 Tbsp cocoa
a pinch of salt
1 egg
½ cup milk
25gm melted butter

Method

Mix the above ingredients together with a whisk in an ovenproof dish.
To make the sauce, mix the following in a jug and pour the mixture over the top:
¾ cup raw sugar
2 Tbsp cocoa
50gm butter
2 cups boiling water
It looks a bit of a mess but, believe it or not, the stuff at the top sinks to the bottom to make the sauce. Bake for about ¾ hour and serve with some cream or ice cream.

Caramel Self-Saucing Pudding

Ingredients

1 cup S. R. Flour
¾ cup raw sugar
pinch of salt
1 egg
½ cup milk
25gm melted butter
1 tsp vanilla extract

Method

Mix all of the above ingredients together with a whisk in an ovenproof dish.
To make the sauce, mix the following in a jug and pour the mixture over the top:
¾ cup raw sugar
50gm butter
2 cups boiling water
Bake for about ¾ hour and serve with cream or ice cream.

Lemon Self-Saucing Pudding

For a lemon-flavoured self-saucing pudding, add ¼ cup lemon juice and a little lemon zest to the sauce of the Caramel Self-Saucing Pudding.

Chocolate 'Soufflé' (France) – Puffed Up

A soufflé, roughly speaking, is a mixture of a French crème pâtissière and a meringue. It will usually fall in height after about five minutes; if it lasts that long.

Ingredients

50gm butter
2 Tbsp plain flour
½ cup milk
100gm dark chocolate (70% cocoa)
4 eggs, separated into yolks and whites, at room temperature
¼ cup caster sugar
a pinch of salt
1 tsp lemon juice

Method

Pre heat your oven to 180^0C.

Grease 6 ramekins with butter then swirl around a little caster sugar to coat.

Melt the butter in a saucepan over medium heat.

Then add the flour and stir to a smooth paste until it starts to bubble but not burn.

Slowly add the milk to the saucepan and whisk till the mixture is smooth and thickened.

Transfer the mixture to a bowl and add the chocolate, whisking till smooth.

Add the egg yolks and again whisk until smooth.

In a separate bowl, beat the egg whites with an electric mixer till soft peaks form.

Add the sugar, salt, and lemon juice and beat the eggs till stiff and glossy in appearance. Do not over beat or they will not combine properly.

Fold a third of the egg whites into the chocolate mixture till combined. Then fold in the rest of the egg whites carefully till just combined (you don't want to lose any air).

Transfer the mixture into the ramekins, put them on a baking tray, and cook for about 20 minutes or until well-risen. They should rise above the edge of the ramekins.

Serve with whipped cream.

Easy Individual Trifles (Australia)

Make an easy egg custard by mixing together in a saucepan, 2 Tbsp cornflour, 1 Tbsp sugar, 2 cups milk, 2 egg yolks and 1 Tbsp butter. Stir this over low heat until it has thickened.

Cool it immediately by putting the base of the saucepan in a sink of cold water.

Pour it over some cake pieces that have had a dash of port tipped over them, along with some assorted fruit pieces, in individual parfait glasses.

VEGETABLES

MIXED VEGETABLE DISHES

'Ratatouille' (France) – Tossed Vegetables

This recipe is originally from the Provence region of France. Not only are there many variations, some more like a soup or stew, but there are similar dishes from other regions and other countries, such as 'Ciambotta' from southern Italy, which means something like, 'big mess'.

This is my easy roasted version which has everything thrown in together in the oven; you can't really make it any easier than that.

This is best eaten hot, but leftovers are also delicious when spread cold on bread the next day as a snack.

It could be served with meat, or eaten as a stand-alone vegetarian meal.

Ingredients

¼ cup (60ml) good quality extra virgin olive oil
5 roma tomatoes, sliced lengthways into 4 pieces
3 zucchini, sliced lengthways into 4 pieces
2 red or brown onions, sliced lengthways into 4 pieces
2 long red chillies, de-seeded, sliced lengthways into 4 pieces
2 green capsicums (green bell pepper), de-seeded, sliced lengthways into 4 pieces
1 red capsicum, (red bell pepper), de-seeded, sliced lengthways into 4 pieces
3 garlic cloves, chopped into 4 pieces
2 long sprigs of fresh rosemary
2 sprigs of fresh thyme
2 bay leaves
2tsp sea salt and 1tsp freshly ground black pepper.
¼ cup chopped fresh flat leafed parsley to use as a garnish

Method

Heat the oil in a large baking dish in the oven for 5 minutes.
Stir in the vegetables and herbs to coat and leave the herbs lying on the top.
Grind the salt and pepper over the top.
Bake for about 40 minutes in the oven at 180°C until the vegetables are shiny, tender and quite dry. Give it a stir half way through. Garnish with the fresh parsley and serve.
Option: If you wish you could add some quartered potatoes, or some pitted black olives.

Char-grilled Vegetables

Slice up lengthwise carrots, parsnips, zucchini, asparagus, and eggplant. Marinate them for an hour in olive oil, garlic, lemon juice, minced ginger, Worcestershire sauce, salt and pepper. Char grill the vegies on the barbecue grill for best results.

BARBECUE FRIENDLY

Leek and Potato Tart

This is a simple hand-made vegetarian tart using a homemade shortcrust pastry.

Ingredients

2 cups plain flour
a pinch of salt
125gm butter, roughly chopped (or use 60gm butter and ¼ cup olive oil if you prefer)
1 egg
2Tbsp approximately of chilled water (to make the pastry easier to work)
2 leeks, trimmed and washed, and thinly sliced
1 red onion, chopped
1 clove garlic, finely chopped
1tsp of flaked sea salt and 1tsp of cracked black pepper
250gm potatoes, washed and finely sliced
1 bunch bok choy, or some spinach leaves, wilted under hot water and dried
2 eggs and ¼ cup cream, lightly whisked together
extra virgin olive oil
fresh rosemary leaves
150gm fetta cheese, cubed

Method

Make the pastry by working the butter into the flour and salt with your fingers until it resembles breadcrumbs. This ensures that the flour is coated with fat and is less likely to form gluten, making it tough. Everything should be cold to avoid melting the butter, and the pastry should not be overworked. This makes nice flaky, and yet strong, pastry.

Add the egg and water and stir it through till you have firm dough. Knead it with the heel (coolest part) of your hand (called 'fraisage', or milling). Place the pastry between two sheets of baking paper and roll it out to about 40cm across and 3mm thick. Put it on a tray and refrigerate it for 30 minutes, to relax the gluten and help prevent shrinkage.

For the filling, fry the leek, onion, garlic, salt and pepper in a little olive oil till soft.

Partially cook the potatoes in salted water, remove them, slice them, and allow them to cool a little.

Take the top layer of baking paper from the pastry and fill the tart.

First put down the leaves to protect the pastry, then the leek mixture, and then the overlapping potato slices.

Pour the egg mixture over the top to drizzle down into the vegetables.

Drizzle some olive oil over the top of the potatoes, and sprinkle them with salt, pepper and some rosemary leaves. Fold in the edges of the pastry about 5cm.

Bake the tart for about 40 minutes in a moderate 180^0C oven.

Dress with the feta cheese cubes and serve.

POTATOES AND SWEET POTATOES

'Gratin Dauphinoise' Potatoes (France) - pron. 'do-fin-wahs'

This is a classic cheesy potato dish that comes from the Dauphiné region of France.

Ingredients (Serves 6)

1 knob butter, for greasing the dish
150ml full-cream milk
150ml cream
1 garlic clove, crushed
a pinch of freshly-ground nutmeg
2 sprigs fresh thyme, and some fresh rosemary leaves
1Kg waxy potatoes, such as Desirée, sliced to 2mm. A Mandolin is perfect for this job.
sea salt and freshly-ground black pepper
25gm parmesan cheese, freshly grated

Method

Grease an oven dish with the butter and some of the garlic.
Heat the milk and cream in a saucepan with the garlic, nutmeg, and herbs to near boiling point, and strain it into a jug.
Layer the potatoes in the dish, sprinkling each layer with a little salt and pepper, and pouring over some of the liquid every so often while layering. Add any remaining liquid and sprinkle the cheese over the top.
Bake for 1 hr in the oven at 180^0C until the potatoes are tender and the top is golden.
You can also use Gruyere or tasty cheese as an option, or in addition to.

Hasselback Potatoes (Sweden) – aka Accordion Potatoes

These are delicious, and a little more upmarket than plain baked potatoes.
I call my Australian version 'Ayers Rock Potatoes' (due to the similarity in appearance).

Ingredients

6 large potatoes, peeled and halved longways
20gm butter
20ml olive oil
1tsp minced garlic
1tsp sea salt
¼ cup breadcrumbs and ¼ cup finely grated parmesan cheese

Method

Slice each piece of potato from the top while it is sitting flat on a board.
Slice at 5mm intervals, but do not cut all the way through to the bottom (a chopstick on each side helps). As they cook the cuts will open up a little. Place them in a baking tray.
Mix the butter, oil, garlic, and salt together and pour over the top of the potatoes.
Bake them in the oven at 180^0C for an hour.
Fifteen minutes before the end of cooking, sprinkle on the breadcrumbs and cheese.

'Latkes' (Israel) - Potato Pancakes

Potato pancakes also go by the name of boxty, draniki, and potato bread.
Swiss potato rosti and hash browns are similar, but usually contain no eggs or flour.
With other leftover vegies included, they are often called 'bubble and squeak'.
Mine is a family hand-me-down recipe, and to this day is one of my all-time-favourites.

Ingredients

4 potatoes, peeled, coarsely grated, and drained of juice (a very important secret step)
1 large brown (yellow) onion, peeled, and coarsely grated
2 eggs
1Tbsp plain flour
1tsp sea salt and 1tsp ground white pepper
extra virgin olive oil for frying

Method

Mix ingredients in a large bowl. Fry spoonfuls of the mixture both sides in olive oil in a frying pan until golden and place on absorbent paper. Basic food at its very best!

Baked Potatoes (England)

Peel and chop some taters into halves or quarters and put them in a baking tray (that's where the name of the tray comes from). Rub them all over with some extra virgin olive oil with your fingers. Sprinkle them with some sea salt. Bake them for 1 hour at $180^{\circ}C$, or until golden brown, turning them over once to recoat them in the residual oil.

'Lemonades Patates' (Greece) - Lemon and Garlic Potatoes

Slice some peeled potatoes thinly and put them in a roasting pan. Add some extra virgin olive oil, plenty of crushed garlic, and the juice of one lemon. Make sure the potatoes are coated in the mixture, and then sprinkle some sea salt over the top of them. Pour in about half a cup of white wine at the edge of the dish. Bake the potatoes until golden brown and crunchy, about 1 hour at $200^{\circ}C$. It's mouth-watering. Thank you Helen.

Whole Baked Lemon Potatoes (Greece)

Boil some small washed potatoes for about 15 minutes until almost cooked. Let them cool a little, and then score a cross in the top and squash them a little with the palm of your hand to open them up a bit. Drizzle over some lemon juice and olive oil, sprinkle with sea salt, and bake for about 20 minutes in the oven, or until golden brown. Smashing spuds!

Scalloped Potatoes (Everywhere) – aka Potato Bake

Layer sliced potatoes, grated cheese and onion rings in a greased dish. Pour over a mixture of cream, milk, salt and pepper. Sprinkle over a layer of breadcrumbs, then some parmesan cheese and paprika. Put a few knobs of butter on the top and bake it in the oven for an hour. Terrific tucker!

'Papas Arrugadas' (Canary Islands) - Wrinkled Potatoes

Boil some egg-sized unpeeled, washed new potatoes in water to just cover, with about ½ cup sea salt. Keep cooking them until the water has almost boiled away, turning them often near the end of cooking time, about 40 minutes. They will be wrinkled up, with a salty crust. These are traditionally served with a mojo, chilli garlic, or capsicum sauce.

Garlic Fried Potatoes (France)

Boil potatoes and chop into chunks when two-thirds cooked. Sauté chopped garlic in some oil and butter in a frying pan and stir in the potatoes. When golden brown stir in some chopped chives and a little light sour cream.

Potato and Cheese 'Croquettes' (France) – 'to crunch'

To some mashed potatoes add an egg, some finely diced cheese, some chopped chives and parsley, salt and pepper. Spread the mixture on a plate and refrigerate for half an hour. Form into fingers, coat in plain flour, beaten egg and breadcrumbs. Refrigerate for an hour before frying them all over in some extra virgin olive oil.

Potato Wedges with Sumac (Lebanon)

Cut potatoes into wedges, and coat them in a mixture of 1 lightly whipped egg white, a little ground chilli, a small amount of tomato puree, a dash of olive oil, and about 1tsp sumac. Bake in a hot oven about ½ hour or so until golden brown.

Cajun Potato Chips

Cut potatoes into 1cm chip size and microwave them for 5 minutes. Dip into a mixture of 1 egg white and ½ cup water, and then shake in a plastic bag with Cajun spices to coat. Place on a greased oven tray in a single layer and bake for ½ hour, turning several times.

Glazed Sweet Potato

Boil sweet potato slices in salted water and drain when cooked. Add a little butter, brown sugar, grated ginger, orange juice and grated rind. Cook a little bit longer until they are glazed. This method also works well for carrots.

Boiled Spuds (from the same word as 'spade')

Chop some unpeeled new potatoes into quarters and boil them in salted water until tender, about 20 minutes, and drain. Serve with just a little butter, or a lemon or other dressing. Plain yoghurt mixed with a little wholegrain mustard and honey works well.

Mashed Potatoes (Ireland) - aka Murphy Mash

Boil some peeled and chopped praties in salted water for 20 minutes or until soft. Add a dash of milk, a knob of butter, salt and pepper, and mash them until they are creamy. As an option, add chopped onion or green shallots.

ONIONS LEEKS AND GARLIC

Here are the more common types of readily-available onions and their various names.

Storage Onions

Brown (Yellow) Onions. Store well, versatile. Less mature are known as pickling onions.
White Onions. Usually stronger in flavour than brown onions.
Red Onions. Also called Spanish Onions. Mild in flavour and often used raw in salads.
French Shallots, Golden Shallots, or Eschalots. These are fairly mild bunching onions available in brown, grey, red and purple varieties.

Fresh onions

Green Shallots. Very thin stalks. Sometimes called eschalots, or scallions.
Spring Onions. Also called Green Onions in the USA. Fairly large white bulb with thin green stalks. These are the more mature green shallots.

Fried Onions

Cook finely sliced onions in some extra virgin olive oil on the barbecue hotplate or in a frying pan and add 1tsp of sugar half way through cooking, and maybe a splash of beer.

Fried Green Shallots

Wash and trim some green shallots. Make a batter by whisking together 1 cup S. R. Flour, 1/3 cup beer and ½ cup ice cold water. Then mix in a beaten egg white mixed with ¼tsp cream of tartar. Dip the spring onions in the batter and fry both sides in hot oil.

Braised Leeks

Fry some coriander seed, garlic and oregano in a little oil. Add some baby leeks or leeks sliced lengthwise to brown a little. Add some grated orange rind and a little red wine and simmer for a few minutes.

Leek and Potato Gratin

Slice a couple of leeks and cook them in a pan with butter until soft and browned a little, about 10 minutes. Add some chopped garlic, a sliced onion, chopped thyme, salt and pepper. When browned a little, add a little chicken stock. In an oven casserole, layer sliced potatoes with the mixture and some grated cheese until all the mixture is used. Bake in the oven about 1 hour until browned on top.

Leek and Mushroom Gratin

Fry a sliced leek, a sliced onion, salt and pepper in a little butter in a frying pan till fragrant and then put them in a pie dish. In the same pan fry sliced brown mushrooms with some thyme in a little more butter till cooked and browned nicely, and then put them on top of the leeks. Sprinkle over the top about 1 cup grated tasty cheese, ½ cup grated parmesan cheese, and then ½ cup breadcrumbs. Bake for about 15 minutes.

MUSHROOMS AND ASPARAGUS

Stuffed Mushroom Cups (France)

Scoop out the stems and some of the flesh of about 8 medium-sized brown mushrooms. Fry this in oil with some chopped onion, chopped garlic, chopped chilli, fresh thyme, sea salt and freshly ground black pepper. Fill the cups with the mixture, top with some Gruyere cheese, bake for about 10 minutes in the oven at 180°C, and serve.

Mushrooms with Garlic

Fry some finely chopped garlic and onion in a little olive oil and butter. Add about ½ cup water and your chopped mushrooms, and a little salt and pepper. Simmer covered for about 10 minutes.

Fried Champignons

Fry some champignons (button mushrooms) in oil, with a little grated ginger and some chopped spring onions. Add a dash of sweet chilli sauce before serving.

Fried Mushrooms

Fry some finely sliced brown or button mushrooms in olive oil in a frypan or on the barbecue hotplate, with a sprinkle of fresh thyme. Garnish with a little chopped parsley.

Asparagus with Parmesan

BARBECUE FRIENDLY

Char grill some fresh asparagus (long, thick dark green spears are the best quality), and sprinkle it with parmesan cheese, a little lemon zest, sea salt and freshly ground black pepper. Drizzle over a little good quality extra virgin olive oil.

Asparagus with Garlic

Combine some butter with a little sesame oil in a frying pan. Add some finely chopped garlic and onion and fry it until softened. Add the asparagus spears and fry until bright green and just tender. Sprinkle with some sea salt flakes.

Asparagus in Breadcrumbs

Dip some asparagus spears in seasoned egg and then breadcrumbs, and fry in extra virgin olive oil, turning them to cook both sides.

Asparagus with Caesar Dressing

Boil the asparagus spears for 2 minutes only, and then rinse them in cold water to stop the cooking process. Combine in a cup some lemon juice, Dijon mustard, a chopped anchovy fillet, a dash of Worcestershire sauce, an egg yolk, salt and pepper, and a little extra virgin olive oil. Stir it together and pour over the asparagus.

CARROTS AND PARSNIPS

Carrots have long been recognised as a very healthful vegetable, but the related parsnips also contain many vitamins and minerals. They are both of the parsley family, as is fennel, dill, coriander, cumin, caraway, and celery. Choose smaller parsnips for tenderness. They are naturally sweet and can be eaten raw or cooked.

Devilled Carrots

Boil some sliced carrots in a saucepan until cooked, about 20 minutes, and drain. Add a finely diced onion with a little olive oil to fry for a couple of minutes. Then add 1Tbsp honey, 2tsp curry powder, ½tsp minced chilli, and a pinch of salt, stirring until heated through. This gives them a spicy but sweet twist.
You can also cook parsnips using this method.

Orange Glazed Carrots

Boil some sliced carrots in a saucepan until cooked, about 20 minutes, and drain. Add ¼ cup orange juice, a slice of butter, 2tsp raw sugar, and a pinch of white pepper. Serve when the liquid has reduced a little.

Buttered Carrots with Dill

Boil some sliced carrots in a saucepan until cooked, about 20 minutes, and drain. Add some butter, lemon juice, white pepper, and fresh chopped dill. Let them cook in the butter for a few minutes until well glazed and aromatic.

Parsnip Chips

Peel and slice some parsnips fairly thinly. Drizzle over some extra virgin olive oil, sprinkle over some salt and some ground dried chilli, and cook them in the oven in the same way that you would cook potato chips, for about 30 minutes.

Parsnip Mash

Boil three peeled and chopped parsnips in water for about 20 minutes. Drain well. Add 200ml cream, sea salt and white pepper, and stir over low heat until the mash becomes creamy.
Or, you can mash them with some milk, butter, salt and pepper in the same way that you would mash potatoes.

Roasted Parsnips

Bake parsnips in the same way that you would bake potatoes, pumpkin, carrots, and onions. Bake for about an hour in the oven at $180^{\circ}C$. Roasting them all together in a baking tray with olive oil makes a very nice dish. Include a few zucchinis and some cloves of garlic half way through cooking time.

PUMPKIN ZUCCHINI AND SQUASH

The zucchini or courgette is an immature marrow of the same family as melons, squash, cucumbers, and pumpkin. Although treated as a vegetable, it is really a fruit; the ovary of the zucchini flower. Male and female flowers are also edible.

Char-grilled Zucchini

This is the simplest and tastiest way to cook these. Simply slice them lengthways, rub them with olive oil and put them on a barbecue grill.

BARBECUE FRIENDLY

Zucchini Fritters (Turkey)

Grate about 3 or 4 zucchinis, and mix in 2 eggs, 1tsp crushed garlic, a pinch of salt and pepper, some grated parmesan cheese, a little finely chopped parsley, 1 finely chopped green shallot, and about ½ cup S. R. Flour. Fry small portions of the mixture both sides in good quality extra virgin olive oil until cooked and nicely browned.
Or, to make a slice, you can pour the mixture into a pan, and bake it for about ½ hour. When it is cooled a little, slice it into squares.

Fried Zucchini Flowers (Italy)

Snap the pistils or stamens out of the centre of the flowers and stuff them with ricotta cheese, anchovies, a little lemon zest, chives and parsley, and dip them into a beer batter. Fry them both sides in some extra virgin olive oil. Drain them on some kitchen paper and serve. These are great as an entrée.

Stuffed Zucchini

Cut large zucchinis lengthwise and scoop out most of the flesh. Fry the shells in a little oil until browned and remove from the pan. Fry chopped onion, garlic, shallots, celery, mushrooms, chilli, and red capsicum. Add the chopped flesh of the zucchini, mixed herbs, salt and pepper. Fill the shells with this mixture, sprinkle them with parmesan cheese and grill (broil) lightly.

Yellow Squash with Garlic

Boil these small, bright yellow squash with the scalloped edges in water for 4 minutes. Then, transfer them to a frying pan and cook for a few minutes in a little olive oil along with some freshly sliced garlic and a chopped green shallot.

Baked Pumpkin

Pumpkin was made to be baked, I reckon. Cut the pumpkin into large pieces, place them in a baking tray, and drizzle over them plenty of extra virgin olive oil. Bake for about 45 minutes in a moderate oven, turning them to brown on all sides.

BEANS AND PEAS

Beans with Almonds (Greece)

Cook some green beans in water for 3 minutes and drain. Sauté some slivered almonds in butter in a pan until golden, then stir in some lemon juice, grated lemon rind, the cooked beans, salt and pepper. Heat through and serve.

Beans in Balsamic Vinegar (Italy)

Cook some green beans in water for 3 minutes and drain. Pour over the top a mixture of 1Tbsp balsamic vinegar, 1Tbsp finely chopped flat-leafed parsley, 1tsp minced garlic, and 1tsp minced chilli in $\frac{1}{4}$ cup hot water

Green Beans with Pine Nuts

Steam some fresh green beans. Toast some pine nuts in a dry frying pan and blend these together with some olive oil, lemon juice, black pepper and parmesan cheese, and serve over the top of the beans.

Broad beans with Peas (Greece)

Cook some broad beans along with some peas for about 2 minutes. Remove the skins from the beans and mix in some fresh torn mint leaves. Add a drizzle of olive oil and some cubes of feta cheese on top.

Red Kidney Beans with Chilli (Italy)

Fry in some olive oil a chopped onion, a chopped clove of garlic, a chopped red chilli, and a chopped anchovy fillet until the onion is translucent. Add to this a drained, large can of red kidney beans, and a little salt and pepper if needed.
Kidney and cannellini beans require special preparation to remove compounds that can cause gastric distress, so it is simpler to just buy the canned ones.

Cannellini Beans with Chilli (Italy)

Fry in some olive oil a chopped onion, a chopped clove of garlic, and a chopped green chilli until the onion is translucent. Add to this a drained, large can of white cannellini beans (related to kidney beans), and a little salt and pepper if needed.
In Italy, the Tuscans are sometimes referred to as 'mangiafagioli', or 'bean eaters'.

Peas and Onions

Fry up a small chopped onion in a little olive oil till translucent. Add some frozen peas, a splash of white wine, and a couple of fresh torn mint leaves if you have them.
Frozen peas are of much better quality than canned ones, and easier than fresh ones.

SPINACH AND SILVER BEET

Spinach and silver beet (chard) are related members of the same family of vegetables. The recipes are pretty much interchangeable, depending on what you can buy at the market at the time.

Spinach with Chilli (Italy)

Fry a chopped hot chilli with a chopped clove of garlic in olive oil. Add chopped spinach until wilted, add a squeeze of lemon juice and serve. This is the way to eat spinach! You could also add some fried prosciutto slices on the top if you wish.

Spinach and Sesame Seeds (China)

Cook some spinach leaves lightly in water and drain. Add some lightly toasted sesame seeds, a dash of sesame oil, a splash of soy sauce and a teaspoonful of honey, and stir them through the spinach.

Sautéed Spinach with Mushrooms (France)

Slice some brown mushrooms and fry them in a little olive oil in a frying pan along with some garlic, a pinch of sugar, sea salt and black pepper until they are cooked. Add some spinach and cook until it is wilted. If you have it, 1tsp truffle oil at the start would also be a nice addition.

Spinach with Feta and Pine Nuts (Greece)

Fry a chopped onion and a chopped clove of garlic in some extra virgin olive oil in a frying pan until the onion is translucent. Then add your spinach to cook until it is wilted. Top with some cubes of feta cheese and some pine nuts that have been lightly toasted in a dry frying pan (with no oil).

Silver Beet with Chorizo (Spain)

Fry a chopped onion and a chopped clove of garlic in some olive oil in a frying pan until the onion is translucent. Add a chopped Chorizo sausage to fry until lightly browned. Then add your silver beet leaves to cook until they are wilted.

Creamed Silver Beet (England)

Add 1tsp minced garlic to some olive oil in a frying pan and then add the silver beet. Cook it gently until it is wilted. Add some salt and pepper, $\frac{1}{4}$tsp ground nutmeg, and $\frac{1}{4}$ cup cream. Stir until it thickens a little and serve.

CABBAGE TURNIP AND SWEDE

Here is a short list of Chinese green vegetables that provides some explanation.

Bok choy	Chinese chard	All year. All edible. Steam or fry.
Won bok	Chinese cabbage	Steam. Pickle.
Enn choy	Chinese spinach	Use like spinach. Purplish
Gai choy	Mustard cabbage	Mustard-like taste.
Choy sum	Chinese flowering cabbage	Stir fries or steam.
Gai lum	Chinese broccoli	Use leaves and florets.
On choy	Water spinach	Use within 2 days.
Gow choy	Chinese chives	Stir fries.

Braised Cabbage with Bacon (England)

In a large frying pan, fry together in some butter a chopped onion and 3 chopped rashers of bacon till almost cooked. Add ¼ Savoy cabbage, shredded, some chicken stock, sea salt and freshly ground black pepper, and allow it to simmer for a few minutes until cooked down a little and the liquid is reduced.

Braised Cabbage Continental (Europe)

Shred and fry a ¼ Savoy cabbage in some extra virgin olive oil.
Add some apple juice (or dry white wine), caraway seeds, sea salt and white pepper, and cook it for about 8 minutes in the pan. Thicken it with a cornflour, water and mustard mixture.

Colcannon (Ireland)

Boil up some finely sliced cabbage in salted water until tender, and drain. Mix this with some finely chopped green shallots, and plenty of mashed potato, and some cream, sea salt and white pepper. Top with a nob of butter to serve.

'Kim Chee' (Korea) - Pickled Cabbage

Chop a large Won Bok Chinese cabbage into 4cm squares and leave it overnight in water with plenty of rock salt. Rinse well and drain. Add 2 very finely chopped spring onions, a chopped onion, a small grated carrot, 3tsp sugar, 3tsp fish sauce, 2tsp minced garlic, 2tsp minced red chilli, 1tsp minced ginger root, 1tsp sea salt, 1tsp white pepper and mix it well. Put it in a large sterilised jar and cover it for three days before serving.

Braised Turnips (Israel)

Peel, and finely slice to about 5mm some small turnips or swedes. Cook them in salted water in a saucepan for about 20 minutes. Drain, and transfer them to a frying pan to fry in some extra virgin olive oil till browned a little. Add some chicken stock, salt and pepper, and let them simmer till the liquid is reduced and has glazed the turnips.

BROCCOLI CAULIFLOWER AND BRUSSELS SPROUTS

Boiled Broccoli with Almond dressing

Boil broccoli florets in water till tender. Serve with an Almond dressing made by lightly frying some slivered almonds in some butter and then adding some lemon juice, freshly ground black pepper, and Dijon mustard.

Boiled Broccoli with Honey and Soy dressing

Boil broccoli florets in water till tender and drain. Pour over the florets a dressing made by mixing together 1Tbsp dark soy sauce and 1Tbsp honey. As an option you could sprinkle over the top some toasted sesame seeds.

Broccolini with Lemon Dressing

This is a cross between broccoli and Gai Lum, and the whole thing can be eaten including stalks and flowers. Boil it and top it with a dressing made by mixing melted butter, lemon juice, grated lemon rind, freshly ground black pepper and seeded mustard.

Cauliflower au Gratin (France)

Make a Mornay sauce (see Sauces), and pour it over some lightly boiled cauliflower florets in a baking dish. Top this with some breadcrumbs, grated Parmesan cheese, salt and pepper, and bake it for about 20 minutes at $180^{\circ}C$.
Alternatively, simmer the florets in $2\frac{1}{2}$ cups milk along with a chopped brown onion, a little nutmeg, salt and pepper for 10 minutes, and remove the vegies to a baking dish. Then make the Mornay sauce using the same milk, pour it over the cauliflower, top it with the breadcrumbs and cheese, and bake it for about 20 minutes. Correen loves this.

Individual Cauliflower Soufflés

Make a quantity of white onion sauce (see Sauces). Add 4 egg yolks, a carton of sour cream and some horseradish (prepared horseradish or horseradish cream will do). Stir and cook for a few minutes. Then add the beaten egg whites that should be fluffy, and stir in gently. Add small boiled cauliflower florets to the mixture. Put this into some individual oven-proof ramekins and bake it in the oven for about $\frac{1}{2}$ hour.

Breaded Cauliflower

Dip partially cooked cauliflower florets in beaten egg and then breadcrumbs.
Fry them in extra virgin olive oil on both sides till golden.

Brussels Sprouts with Chives

Boil some Brussels sprouts in water until tender. Then drain and add some butter, chopped chives, chopped dill, grated lemon zest, salt and black pepper.

EGGPLANT AND ARTICHOKE

Eggplant is a member of the nightshade family and contains an enzyme that can leave an unpleasant taste in your mouth. A way to remove this flavour is to 'sweat' the eggplant first before cooking it to improve its flavour. Cut it in slices, sprinkle it liberally with salt and weight it down with something for an hour. Rinse it well, dry it off, and it is ready to use. It is related to the potato and tomato. The Italian word is 'melanzane', meaning 'noxious apple', the French is 'aubergine', and the Indian is 'brinjal'.

Breaded Eggplant

Salt some eggplant slices, leave weighted for an hour and rinse and dry them. Dip the slices in an egg that has been whisked with a little milk, and then some breadcrumbs, and fry them both sides in a little olive oil.

Eggplant rolls (Greece)

Salt eggplant slices, leave for an hour, rinse, and dry. Pan-fry the slices in some extra virgin olive oil until golden brown on both sides. Lay the eggplant slices on a board, add some cubed feta cheese, with a little chopped parsley, and roll them up.

'Melanzane' Pickle (Italy) - Pickled Eggplant

Slice finely 2 peeled eggplants. Salt, rinse and drain them as above. Put them in a stainless steel saucepan with $\frac{1}{2}$ cup white wine vinegar and 1 cup water to boil for about 4 minutes and drain them again. Put them back in the saucepan with $\frac{1}{2}$ cup high quality extra virgin olive oil, 1Tbsp white wine vinegar, 2 very finely sliced cloves garlic, 1 finely sliced red chilli, 1tsp dried red chilli flakes, 1tsp freshly chopped basil, 1tsp freshly chopped oregano, 1tsp freshly chopped parsley, 1tsp sea salt and 1tsp white pepper., and mix well. Place in a sealed container in the refrigerator for 3 days before use. It should then keep for a few more days after that. Really good pickle and a delicasy! Bene!

'Brinjal' Pickle (India) - Eggplant Pickle

Slice finely 2 or 3 peeled eggplants. Salt, rinse and drain them as above. Grill the slices with a light coating of extra virgin olive oil till slightly browned and then dice them up. In a dry frying pan toast some mustard seeds, cumin seeds, coriander seeds, fenugreek seeds, ground turmeric, cracked black pepper and a little ground cinnamon. Add a little olive oil, and some finely chopped onion, garlic, ginger and chilli to fry a little. Then add the diced eggplant, a little cider vinegar (or white wine vinegar), some sugar and salt. Simmer for 20 minutes. Serve with some fresh bread. Unbelievably good!

Boiled Artichokes

Artichokes contain cynarin; very good for bile production. Cut off the stems, peel off the outer leaves, chop off the tops, and scoop out the furry chokes. Pour the juice of half a lemon over the top to prevent browning. Boil in salted water for 20 minutes.

TOMATOES CAPSICUMS AND CHILLIES

Tomatoes, capsicums, chillies, eggplants and potatoes are all of the same family. Chilli is an Aztec word for the fruit of the genus Capsicum. Christopher Columbus brought them to Spain in 1493. The most common available are:

Capsicum annuum - bell peppers, cayenne, jalapeños, poblano, serrano, chiltepin
Capsicum frutescens - chiles de árbol, malagueta, Tabasco, Thai, birdseye
Capsicum chinense - (very hot) naga, habanero, Datil, Scotch Bonnet
Capsicum pubescens - South American rocoto, manzano
Capsicum baccatum - South American aji

Chipotles (pron. 'chi-poht-lays') date from Aztec times and are basically leftover, over-ripe, smoke-dried, red jalapeño chillies. There is large market for ripe red jalapeños in Mexico and the United States. After the season for green and ripe red jalapeños has ended, the remaining ones are kept on the vine till deep red and shrivelled, and then processed. 'Adobo' sauce is made from these chillies, and chipotle salt is also popular.

Smoked paprika of the La Vera DO (regulated) region of Spain 'pimentón ahumado', has a smoky flavour and aroma, is dried by smoking using oak wood, and can be obtained in sweet and mild 'dulce', medium hot 'agridulce', or very hot and spicy 'picante'.

Grilled Red Capsicum in Olive Oil and Garlic (Italy)

Grill (broil) halved red capsicums (red bell peppers) skin side up until the skin blisters. Put them in a plastic bag for 10 minutes to loosen the skin, and peel them. Slice them finely lengthways and add some chopped garlic lightly fried in some good quality extra virgin olive oil. Serve this in a bowl to eat with fresh crusty bread. This authentic Calabrian smoky-tasting recipe was shown to me by my old mate, Vince.

Roasted Stuffed Red Capsicums with Tomatoes

Chop the tops off some large red capsicums (bell peppers), reserving any flesh and removing the seeds. Mix the chopped reserved flesh with some lightly sautéed onions and garlic, some chopped anchovies, some chopped ripe tomatoes, some pitted and chopped black olives, chopped basil and thyme, sea salt and black pepper. Add some breadcrumbs to the mixture if it is too thin. Fill the bases with the mixture, drizzle over a little extra virgin olive oil, top the capsicums with some grated Parmesan cheese and bake them in the oven for about 30 minutes.

Slow-Roasted Tomatoes

Halve some fresh vine-ripened tomatoes and place them on a baking tray, cut side up. You will need to use good quality tomatoes for this dish. Sprinkle over some finely chopped garlic, some torn basil leaves, a little sumac powder, and a little bit of raw sugar. Drizzle with some balsamic vinegar and olive oil over the top, sprinkle them with sea salt flakes and cracked black pepper, and bake them for about an hour in the oven until they are a little charred and slightly shrivelled.

Bazza's Red Tomato Relish (Australia)

I have fond memories of my childhood favourites, such as this Red Tomato Relish and also the Green Tomato Pickles, made by my grandmother when the tomatoes came in, and preserved in sterilised jars. This is my attempt to re-create both of them in small quantities for immediate use. It is a fairly successful attempt I think.

Ingredients (makes 4 cups)

1.5Kg ripe tomatoes, chopped
2 large brown onions, chopped
¾ cup dry red wine (shiraz or similar)
¾ cup water
1 cup brown sugar
1Tbsp red balsamic vinegar
1Tbsp brown mustard seeds
1Tbsp sea salt and 1tsp ground black pepper
1tsp minced red chilli
1tsp minced ginger root
1tsp minced garlic
1tsp ground allspice (pimento)
1tsp ground cloves
1tsp ground cardamom
1tsp ground nutmeg
1tsp fenugreek seeds

> **Versatility**
> You can use either of these two recipes on sandwiches, savoury dry biscuits, or as a sauce for a variety of different meat dishes. Be creative!

Method

Put everything in a large stainless steel saucepan and cook for about 1 hour or a little more, uncovered, till the liquid is reduced a little.

Bazza's Green Tomato Pickles (Australia)

Ingredients (makes 4 cups) Use the same method as the above recipe

1Kg green tomatoes, chopped
½Kg cauliflower, chopped into small florets
2 large brown onions, chopped
¾ cup dry white wine (chardonnay or similar)
¾ cup water
1 cup raw sugar
2Tbsp yellow mustard seeds (or yellow mustard)
1Tbsp green jalapeño chillies, chopped
1Tbsp sea salt and 1tsp ground white pepper
1tsp minced ginger root
1tsp minced garlic
1tsp fenugreek seeds
1tsp turmeric

Bazza's You-Beaut Chilli Jam

Ingredients

1Tbsp olive oil
1 large brown onion, chopped
1 stick celery, finely chopped
2 green shallots, finely chopped
3 cloves garlic, finely chopped
10 hot red chillies, finely chopped
1Kg ripe tomatoes, chopped (preferably vine ripened)
3cm piece fresh ginger, finely sliced (or use bottled crushed ginger)
3 anchovy fillets, chopped
1 cup brown sugar
½ cup red wine vinegar
1Tbsp balsamic vinegar
1Tbsp dark soy sauce
1Tbsp brown mustard seeds
1tsp sea salt
1tsp cracked black pepper

> **Safety Tip**
> Make sure that you don't get vinegar in your ear – you could end up with pickled hearing.

Method

Fry the onions, celery, green shallots, and garlic in the oil in a large saucepan until lightly cooked.

Add the chillies to cook for a few minutes.

Add the tomatoes, ginger, anchovies, sugar, vinegar, balsamic vinegar, soy sauce, mustard seeds, salt and pepper.

Simmer uncovered on the stove top for about 1½ hours, stirring regularly, until it reduces and thickens.

Towards the end take care to stir it often so that it does not burn and stick to the bottom of the saucepan.

You can serve this with a great variety of dishes, including steak, chicken, or fish.

Oven-Dried Tomatoes

When you have an abundance of tomatoes, you may want to try oven-drying your own.

They develop a concentrated flavour, shrink a little in size, and are very useful as a garnish, as a side dish, to top pizzas, to use in pasta dishes, and to use in salads.

Just cut your tomatoes in half and place them cut side up and close together on a lined baking tray. Sprinkle them liberally with some good quality sea salt flakes and cracked black pepper, and a little finely chopped fresh oregano or thyme.

Bake them for about 3 hours at 180°C. They should be shrivelled, and fairly dry, but not brittle. Use them straight away, or they will keep in the fridge for a few days.

APPENDIX 1 – MEASURES AND CONVERSIONS

LIQUID

		APP
30ml		1 fl oz
60ml	1/4 cup	2 fl oz
80ml	1/3 cup	3 fl oz
100ml		3 1/2 fl oz
125ml	1/2 cup	4 fl oz
150ml		5 fl oz
180ml	3/4 cup	6 fl oz
200ml		7 fl oz
250ml	1 cup	8 3/4 fl oz
1 litre	4 cup	35 fl oz

WEIGHT

	APP	APP
	7gm	1/4 oz
	10gm	1/3 oz
	15gm	1/2 oz
	30gm	1oz
	60gm	2oz
1 cup grated cheese	80gm	2 1/2 oz
1 cup desiccated coconut	85gm	2 3/4 oz
1 cup breadcrumbs	90gm	3 oz
1 cup cocoa	125gm	4 oz (1/4 lb)
1 cup flour	150gm	4 ¾ oz
1 cup sugar	160gm	5 oz
1 cup sultanas	170gm	5 1/2 oz
1 cup choc bits	185gm	6 oz
1 cup rice	200gm	6 1/2 oz
1 cup olive oil	225gm	7 oz
1 cup cream	235gm	7 1/2 oz
1 cup butter	250gm	8 oz (1/2 lb)
1 cup yoghurt	260gm	8 1/4 oz

SPOON

			METRIC
teaspoon	(1tsp)	equals	5ml
dessertspoon	(1dsp)	equals	10ml
tablespoon	(1Tbsp)	equals 4tsp	20ml (Aus)
tablespoon	(1Tbsp)	equals 3tsp	15ml (USA, UK, NZ)

LENGTH

LENGTH	METRIC APP	OVEN TEMP CELSIUS	OVEN TEMP FAHRENHEIT
1 inch	2.5cm (25mm)	130°C	270°F
2 inches	5cm	140°C	280°F
6 inches	15cm	150°C	300°F
8 inches	20cm	160°C	320°F
9 inches	23cm	170°C	340°F
10 inches	25cm	180°C	360°F
12 inches (1 foot)	30cm	190°C	380°F
		200°C	400°F
		210°C	410°F
		220°C	430°F
		230°C	450°F

APPENDIX 2 – GUIDE TO HERBS AND SPICES

Home-grown or freshly-purchased herbs are best, but dried herbs are usually quite satisfactory.
With spices, some are best bought whole, such as cumin, coriander, fenugreek, nutmeg and cloves, but the ground spices are fine to use also. I buy dried spices in small quantities so that they are always fresh.
Cooking them along with a little oil somewhere in the preparation stage of a dish helps to release the beneficial constituents, or in some recipes they can be dry fried in a dry frying pan till fragrant to refresh their flavour.
There are many claimed health benefits for herbs and spices, and because they are naturally occurring plant products, many of these claims may well be true. Companies are unwilling to invest a lot of money to research these claims, due to the fact that it is very difficult to patent naturally-occurring plant substances. So, much of the value of these substances is still unknown. The same applies to the vitamins present in food.
Here are some of the known, and claimed, health benefits of some of these natural products, along with a little additional explanation, and some suggestions on how you can use them with maximum benefit.

Allspice
The only major spice still grown almost entirely on the Caribbean islands. Also called Jamaican pepper, or pimento. Used in sauces, pickles, baking, and in 'jerk' dishes. A key ingredient in 'mixed spice'. It tastes like a combination of cloves, cinnamon, and nutmeg, which is where it gets its common name.

Aniseed
From the anise plant, and native to the Middle East, it tastes like liquorice. The seeds are used to flavour everything from sweets to liquors, baked goods, and heavy meat dishes. The Greek beverage Ouzo is flavoured with anise. It is a different thing to star anise.

Basil
A member of the mint family, it was known as the herb of kings in ancient times. Good for digestion, as are many herbs. It goes well with many other herbs and spices, including thyme, garlic, oregano, and lemon. It also teams especially well with tomatoes. Fresh is best for this herb.

Bay leaves
These come from the bay laurel tree. Champions of ancient times wore wreaths of bay leaves on their heads. They are great used in slow-cooked beef or chicken dishes, adding a subtle earthy flavour.

Capers
These are the pickled, unopened flower buds of the caper plant, native to the Mediterranean area. The buds are picked by hand every day and the smaller the bud, the higher the quality. Used in small quantities, they can really add some depth to a recipe.

Caraway seeds
These taste similar to anise, with a hint of dill. The main use for caraway seeds is in rye bread and other breads, but they are also used in curries and in cheeses.

Cardamom
Available in ground form or in seed pods, and used in sweet and savoury dishes, especially curries. The pods are taken out of the dish before eating. Cardamom has anti-inflammatory and antiseptic properties and helps with digestive disorders. It reputedly breaks up kidney and gall stones.

Cayenne pepper
The dried and ground pods of the chilli pepper.

Chervil
This is used fresh in egg dishes, or with fish or chicken. Looks a bit like maidenhair fern and tastes like anise.

Chilli
Chilli is used widely to flavour meat dishes and curries especially. Chillies and capsicums (including cayenne and paprika) contain capsaicin which stimulates digestion, increases metabolism and fat burning, and reduces cholesterol and triglycerides. It has been shown to kill some cancer cells, and has cardiovascular benefits. Chillies also contain vitamins A and C, helping to prevent inflammatory conditions, and are a natural expectorant.

Chinese five spice
This is a blend of cloves, cinnamon, fennel, star anise, and Szechwan pepper. Often used in marinades and in barbecuing. Use it sparingly.

Chives
Tastes like onions or garlic and is used in similar ways. It can be used raw and finely chopped or used in cooked dishes.

Cinnamon
Native to Sri Lanka, it comes from the bark of the tropical evergreen laurel tree, is rolled into sticks, quills, or ground to powder. Different to the Indian 'cassia', which is stronger and hotter, and commonly used as cinnamon in the United States. Used in many curries and meat stews, especially those made with lamb. It is also used in cakes, puddings, breads, and stewed fruits. Cinnamon's essential oil has powerful anti-inflammatory, anti-oxidant, and anti-microbial properties, increases metabolism, and also improves the blood circulation.

Cloves
Cloves are dried flower buds native to Indonesia, and are used widely in many cuisines. From the Latin word 'clavus', for nail. An essential ingredient of garam masala, which is a blend of many spices, and Chinese five spice. Cloves have pronounced antiseptic and anaesthetic properties.

Coriander
The ground seed or fruit is used in many dishes including curries, and the leaves are used in Asian dishes. The leaves, seeds and roots combine especially well with chicken. Another name for it is cilantro. It is a member of the parsley family. Coriander has antioxidant and anti-bacterial properties, lowers LDL cholesterol and triglycerides, and increases HDL cholesterol by stimulating bile production. It also has beneficial effects on insulin activity.

Cumin
Native to the Mediterranean area, it has, like many other spices, been used for thousands of years. Used in curry blends, and many meat dishes, it really gives a kick to a recipe. It is great in pumpkin soup. It is a member of the parsley family. Cumin aids digestion, boosts the metabolism, helps to detoxify the liver, and contains antioxidants, as well as providing iron. This spice is useful for almost all meat dishes.

Curry Leaves
Their name comes from the fact that they go so well with curries. From the tree murraya koenigii of the family Rutaceae. It is usually fried in oil at the beginning of cooking. The fresh leaves are definitely the best.

Dill
Dill goes great in cheese, egg and seafood dishes. It is also used in salads. The seeds are also used as a spice.

Fennel
Fennel seeds are ground and used as a spice in savoury dishes. The bulb is used as a vegetable. It has an aniseed-like flavour.

Fenugreek
Used in many curry blends, and vegetable dishes. It is best fried in oil at the start to remove bitterness. Fenugreek has antioxidant and antimicrobial properties and aids digestive disorders and blood sugar levels.

Galangal
This is native to south-east Asia, and closely related to ginger. It is used very well in Thai cooking in particular.

Garlic
Garlic reputedly has anti-cancer properties, also antibacterial, antiviral, and antifungal properties. It also has cardiovascular, digestive, and insulin activity benefits, and is also high in vitamin C. Indispensable for many dishes.

Ginger
Used in many Indian and Asian recipes, curries, drinks, and sweets. It can be frozen and grated as needed. Ginger contains anti-inflammatory properties and has been shown to kill some cancer cells. It also boosts metabolism and inhibits nausea.

Horseradish
The root is used to flavour meat dishes, and is great with smoked salmon. The heat is created when the root is cut or scraped, forming an oil from two ingredients.

Kaffir Lime Leaves
Used commonly in Asian dishes, it is a member of the lemon family. Fresh leaves are best. Grow your own tree for convenience, as they are not difficult to maintain. They can be dried, or frozen and used as needed.

Lemon Grass
Used in Asian soups and stir-fries. This makes a good curry base when pounded with garlic and chilli. The green bit when frayed on the end makes a great barbecue basting brush. Pickled lemon grass is available in jars, a very convenient way to use it.

Methi Leaves
The leaves of the fenugreek plant, used as a herb in potato dishes, and also as a vegetable.

Mint
Mint is very versatile with many varieties available. Used in salads, desserts, and also in drinks.

Mixed spice
This is usually a blend of coriander, cinnamon, allspice, nutmeg, and caraway seed.
Mustard
Seeds that develop different amounts of heat when brought into contact with liquids and when cooked. Mustard seeds have anti-inflammatory properties, and contain magnesium, selenium, iron, zinc, calcium, manganese, niacin, and Omega-3 fatty acids.
Nigella
A seed used especially in roasted vegetable dishes, curries and chutneys. It is also used to make naan bread.
Nutmeg
A fruit kernel, it is considered to be the strongest of the sweet spices, and is native to Indonesia. Used in baking, desserts, and meat dishes, it goes very well with pumpkin. Nutmeg's essential oil contains anti-bacterial properties and assists in digestion.
Oregano
Used in many types of meat dishes. Closely related to marjoram, which is not quite as pungent in flavour.
Paprika
Paprika is a mild member of the capsicum family, and used in similar ways to chilli.
Parsley
Widely used in savoury food and as a garnish. Parsley is cleansing and rich in vitamin C.
Pepper
Grown on a tropical vine native to southern India, black pepper is a universal seasoning. An enzyme creates a volatile oil when the green peppercorns are dried and turn black. White pepper has had the skin removed. Green peppercorns and the fully ripe red peppercorns are also available in brine, or frozen. Black pepper contains antioxidants, has antibacterial properties, stimulates stomach acid secretion, stimulates fat cell breakdown, and is a diuretic.
Poppy seed
These are from the opium poppy, native to the Middle East, and used in curries and baking. They have a nutty flavour.
Rosemary
This is ideal with roast lamb and meat dishes. The stalks can also be used to assemble flavoursome kebabs.
Saffron
Dried crocus stamens used to flavour and colour food, and usually ground to a powder.
Sage
Often used with pork and duck dishes. It is commonly blended with the herbs rosemary, oregano and thyme.
Star anise
From a Chinese tree related to the magnolia, and used in Chinese five spice blends.
Sumac
A sun-dried fruit from the berries of a Lebanese shrub, used in many different types of dishes.
Tarragon
Often used with chicken, fish, and eggs. It is also used in soups, sauces, and in tarragon vinegar.
Thyme
This is a member of the mint family, closely related to basil, oregano and marjoram. It is a staple of modern European cuisine. There are over 100 different varieties. It can be used in Bouquet Garni along with parsley and bay. Thyme works well in almost any dish. It is used in stews, soups, meats and poultry stuffing, and is particularly amazing in fish recipes.
Turmeric
Turmeric is a stimulant and works as a tonic to aid digestion and metabolism. Used in curry blends, relishes, and Middle-Eastern recipes. It is a cheap alternative to saffron. Turmeric contains circumin, and has antioxidant, anti-inflammatory, antibacterial, antiviral, and antifungal properties, which means that it helps to guard against cancer, cardiovascular disease, and a variety of other chronic and contagious illnesses. Turmeric also boosts metabolism, lowers cholesterol, and aids bowel disorders. It contains potassium and vitamin B6.
Vanilla
Vanilla is from an orchid bean native to Central America. It is used in baking and desserts. Use the whole pod, or scrape out and use the seeds. It is also available in bottles as an essence.
Wasabi
This is often referred to as Japanese Horseradish, and as a spice is very similar to horseradish. Both are made from grated root bark, with a hot peppery taste.

APPENDIX 3 – AN AUSSIE SLANG REFERENCE

A bit dodgy	to be treated with suspicion
A bit lairy	it is outlandishly colourful
A bit of a dag	an eccentric person
A bit of a dork	someone that behaves strangely
A bit of alright	it is very good
A bit rich	it is in poor taste or excessive
A bit thick	not very quick witted
A boot stuck in the mud	not making very much progress
A brummy job	a cheap and shoddy job
A can of worms	to be potentially very problematic
A crummy job	of poor quality, shoddy
A cushy job	easy and comfortable job
A lick and a promise	to give it a hasty clean
A shoddy job	very little attention to quality
All beer and skittles	it is fairly easy going
Any tick of the clock	it will be sometime soon
Argy-bargy	to be argumentative and tedious
Around the traps	visit the usual haunts
As rough as bags	coarse and uncouth
Back of Beyond	past an unknown remote place
Back of Bourke	a very long way away
Backside out of his strides	he is very poor
Bag him out	put him down
Bag of tricks	tools of the trade
Bag your head	a command to be quiet
Bail out	to leave quickly
Bail up	to corner somebody physically
Bangers and mash	sausages and mashed potato
Beat around the bush	to not get to the point quickly
Belt doesn't go through all the loops	mentally not quite right
Belt up will you	please be quiet
Bend the elbow	a drinking session
Better than a poke in the eye…	much better than the alternative
Bewdy, mate	I am really happy about this
Beyond the Black Stump	a very great distance from here
Big-note yourself	to brag about your abilities
Black and tan	drink of a beer and stout mix
Bloody hell	expression of frustration and anger
Bloody oath	I am serious about this matter
Blowed if I know	an expression of total ignorance
Bob's your uncle	it is now solved
Bodgy job	project of inferior quality
Bog in	to get started on the food
Boil the billy	brew a cup of tea
Bonzer tucker, mate	this is really good food, friend
Break it down	a request for moderation
Browned off	to be annoyed
Buggered if I know	an admission of total ignorance
Built like a brick dunny	constructed like an outdoor toilet
Bullamakanka	a proverbial remote spot
Bung on side	to put on pompous airs
Bust a gut	work hard at something
Buy the farm	to die
Carry on like a pork chop	to behave outlandishly
Carry the can	to do the dirty work
Catch yourself on the way back	you are very slow
Chew out	to reprimand
Chock a block	to be very full
Clagged out	very tired, exhausted, worn out
Come a gutser	have an accident, serious mistake
Come off the grass	stop talking rubbish
Don't come the raw prawn	please stop being disagreeable
Cop an ear bashing	to receive a reprimand
Cop it sweet	to take what's coming to you
Crack a coldie	to open a beer
Crack onto a sheila	to chat up a girl
Cruel his act	to spoil his best efforts
Deadset, cobber	it is true, friend
Different kettle of fish	it is a different story
Dinky-di	the real thing, genuine
Do the trick	achieve the desired effect
Do your block	to lose your temper
Do your lolly	to get very angry
Done like a dinner	it's all over, or defeated
Don't get off your bike	please keep your cool
Don't know him from a bar of soap	he is not known to me
Don't talk gibberish	speaking incoherent chatter
Down the gurgler	it has failed, or totally wasted
Drive the porcelain bus	to vomit in the toilet
Drop a clanger	it didn't go down very well
Drop your bundle	get very depressed, or give up
Dry as a dead dingo's donger	to need a drink, or some rain
Every man and his dog	absolutely everybody
Fair crack of the whip	give reasonable consideration
Fair suck of the sav'	give reasonable consideration
Fair dinkum	true, honest, genuine, ridgy-didge
Fair enough	that is reasonable
Fancy clobber	nice clothes
Fandangled thing	an elaborate gadget
Feel like a gig	to feel foolish
Fiddle about	waste time on useless activity
Fit as a mallee bull	very strong and able
Full as a boot	to have overeaten, or intoxicated
Full as a butcher's dog	to have overeaten
Full as a goog	to have overeaten
Full as an esky	intoxicated, needing to be carried
Gave him a hammering	a verbal or physical beating
G'day cobber	hello, my friend
Get a knock back	a refusal or rejection
Get a knuckle sandwich	receive a punch in the mouth
Get a wriggle on	to hurry up
Get diddled	to be swindled
Get down to tin tacks	to get to the essentials
Get in a flap	to get unreasonably agitated
Get in for your chop	to get your rightful share
Get into strife	to get into trouble
Get knocked back	a refusal
Get lost	command to make yourself scarce
Get off my back	please stop harassing me
Get outside of that	invitation to eat your food
Get stuck into it	begin with great enthusiasm
Get stuck into the tucker	start eating with enthusiasm
Get the bullet	to be dismissed or sacked
Get your gear off	to get undressed
Get your nickers in a knot	to get very upset about something
Get your own back	to get revenge
Give a bit of lip	to give uninvited verbal abuse
Give a bloke a fair go	give me a chance
Give him a lift under the lug	to give him a hit under the ear
Give him the nod	give permission to go ahead
Give him what for	exact punishment or revenge
Give it a burl	to give it a fair try
Give it the flick	to get rid of it
Give us a hoy	let us know when you are ready
Gives me the pip	causes me great irritation
Go at it hammer and tongs	speak or act at maximum speed
Go bush	to leave for somewhere remote
Go for a burn	to go for a fast ride in a car
Go to billy-o	please go somewhere far away
Go troppo	suffer effects of tropical humidity
Go walkabout	to wander off
Going twenty to the dozen	doing something in a big hurry
Gone to buggery	departed for an unknown place
Good lurk	a clever enterprise
Good oil	useful information, the plain truth
Good on ya', mate	well done, may it go well with you
Good-oh then	alright then
Got his ginger up	he has been stirred to anger
Got his head screwed on straight	he is a sensible fellow
Green around the gills	you look very ill
Hack the pace	able to keep up
Had a skinful	had too much to drink, or, pickled
Had me in	I have been tricked, hoodwinked
Half a mo'	please wait for a moment
Happy as a pig in mud	he is in his element
Hare along	to travel very quickly
Have a barney	have an argument
Have a bash	to have a good try
Have a Captain Cook	have a look (rhyming slang)
Have a chinwag	have a discussion
Have a gander at	take a look
Have a go y' mug	fight me then, or try harder
Have a lend of	make fun of someone
Have a tub	to get cleaned up

He has got his back up	he is very angry	Put the kybosh on it	it will never go ahead now
He's a misery guts	he's an unhappy complainer	Put the skids under him	to cause to fail
He's a cockie	he's a farmer	Put the wind up you	to frighten you
He's a wally	he's hopeless	Really cranky	he is in a very bad mood, angry
He's a yobbo	he's a dim-witted layabout	Runs on the smell of an oily rag	car or person runs economically
He's as mad as a cut snake	he is really out of control	Sandwich short of a picnic	lacking in intelligence
He's gone a million	he is in deep trouble now	Sausage short of a barbie	a little lacking mentally
He's hard-done-by	has experienced great misfortune	Scrub up well	look good after a clean up
He hasn't got a brass razoo	he is very poor	She'll be apples	everything will be alright
He's ropeable	he is very angry	She'll be jake	everything will be alright
Higgledy piggledy	mixed up and disorderly	She'll be right, mate	everything will be alright
Hoity toity	to be pretentious and snobbish	Shonky business	it is a questionable venture
Holus bolus	completely	Shoot through	leave quickly for unknown parts
Hooroo, mate	goodbye, friend	Sitting on his clacker	he is not doing anything at all
Hot under the collar	very angry	Slug it out	to work or fight hard
How yer goin' mate; a'right?	a standard greeting	Smack in the moosh	a hit in the mouth
How yer goin', cobber	good day, friend	Spill your guts	confess to everything
I can pull it off	to be sure of success	Spin a yarn	to tell a story
I feel crook	I do not feel well	Spit the dummy	to get very angry
I'm all hot and bothered	I am upset and anxious	Stir the possum	to cause trouble
In the bad books	to be out of favour	Suck it and see	try it and find out
It gives me the heebie-jeebies	inspires worry and trepidation	Suits me down to the ground	I am completely satisfied
It gives me the willies	incites anxiety and annoyance	Take a running jump at yourself	an expression of contempt
It'll all come out in the wash	everything will be alright	Take a squiz at this	to have a look
It's a humdinger	it is exceptionally good	Talking to me or chewing a brick?	please repeat that
It's a worry	I am concerned	Tee it up	to set something up
It's cactus	it is no longer functional	That didn't even touch the sides	not enough to quench the thirst
It's carked it	It has died	That's a lot of malarkey	that is senseless and foolish talk
It's got whiskers on it	this thing is fundamentally wrong	That's torn it	it is now ruined
It's jiggered	it is no longer functional	The Aussie battler	working hard at making a living
It's not on	it is totally unacceptable	The back blocks	obscure place of lower importance
It's ridgy didge	it is genuine	The backside out of his strides	he is very poor
It's your shout	you buy the next round of drinks	The big smoke	the big city
I've been had	I have been tricked	The elevator doesn't go to the top	to be mentally challenged
I've got enough on my plate	I have a full schedule already	The full treatment	to receive the best service
Jump on your head	an expression of dismissal	The tide has gone out	my glass is now empty
Kangaroos in the top paddock	something is not right in the head	There is no wind in the windmill	to be mentally deficient
Keep your hair on	command to stay calm	Things are crook in Tallarook	something is very wrong here
Keep your hand in	to stay in practice	Throw a wobbly	to get very excited
Kick an idea around	consider the possibilities	Till the cows come home	it will be a long wait
Kicked from pillar to post	to have been treated badly	To have a crack at it	to try enthusiastically
Knock back a coldie	enjoy a quick cold beer	To play solitaire for money	to be totally self-absorbed
Like a bull at a gate	to be impulsive and aggressive	Too close to the bone	too near the truth for comfort
Like a dog's breakfast	all over the place	Too right, mate	I agree, friend
Like a headless chook	to be aimlessly rushing about	Trap for young players	a danger for the inexperienced
Like a lizard drinking	to be very busy	True blue	genuine Australian
Like a shag on a rock	to be very alone	Turn it up	you are not correct
Like a stocking on a chicken's lip	an amazing achievement	Up a gum tree	in a little bit of trouble
Like seagulls on a sausage roll	to be very busy at something	Use a bit of elbow grease	apply yourself vigorously
Like teats on a bull	totally unnecessary	Whack on the conk	a hit on the head
Load of bull dust	a lot of information without merit	Whadda you know?	expression of surprise, or greeting
Lob in on you	to arrive unexpectedly	What a goer	expression of personal admiration
Make a blue	to make a mistake	What a hodge podge	it is in a very big mess
Making big bikkies	making lots of money	What a yahoo	a loud and mischievous person
Mate's rates	a discount for a friend	Who opened their lunch?	someone has passed wind
More than you can poke a stick at	quite a lot	Would kill a brown dog	someone's cooking is very bad
Mucking around	playing silly games	Wouldn't be dead for quids	I'm doing very well thank you
My belly thinks my throat is cut	I am very hungry	Wouldn't it rot your socks	an expression of disgust
Mystery bag	a sausage	Wouldn't shout if a shark bit him	tight with the buying of drinks
No worries, mate	everything is fine	Wrap your laughing gear around it	to eat something
Not carrying a full set of clubs	he is not very bright	Yabber on a bit	to talk quite a lot
Not the done thing	it is socially unacceptable	Yanking his chain	to deliberately provoke him
Not within cooee	beyond calling distance	You are a drongo	you are not acting sensibly
Off his face	he is very drunk	You are a legend	you have done very well
Off like a bucket of prawns in the sun	to be spoiled, or to leave quickly	You are a stupid galah	you are being very irrational
On the nose	it is very smelly	You are a woos	you are lacking internal fortitude
One short of a six-pack	he is mentally deficient	You old bastard	term of endearment
Pain in the binge	a stomach ache	You lazy bludger	you are a lazy person
Pull up stumps	to give up and go home	You little beauty	I am very pleased with you
Pull y' head in	a command to be quiet	You little bottler	I am really impressed
Pull y' socks up	you really need to improve	You little ripper	I am totally delighted
Put him in his box	to bring someone down to size	You mongrel	you despicable person; or in jest
Put in the boot	to take unfair advantage of	You wouldn't read about it	an expression of surprise
Put the bite on	ask for money	You've got Buckley's and none	you have no chance of success

Barry Bakes © 2013

www.ingramcontent.com/pod-product-compliance
Lightning Source LLC
Chambersburg PA
CBHW080910230426
43666CB00013B/2659